D0143364

KRISTEVA AND THE POLITICAL

Julia Kristeva is one of the most influential French thinkers of the twentieth century and is best known for her work in linguistics, feminist theory and psychoanalysis. *Kristeva & the Political* is the first book to explore and assess the relation of Kristeva's work to politics and the political.

Kristeva & the Political casts new light on her work, connecting her to recent developments in literary theory, political theory and cultural studies. In particular it shows how Kristeva's account of art and psychoanalysis widens the notion of the political.

Each chapter introduces a fundamental theme in Kristeva's work, highlighting a specific period of development in her thought and drawing on texts from the 1960s through to the 2000s. The book shows the continuity of her work on the political, as well as its scope. *Kristeva & the Political* demonstrates that her theory of revolt draws on specific notions of maternity and alterity, love and recognition, embodiment and temporality, illuminating the radical potential of intimate spaces that are not traditionally regarded as politically relevant.

Cecilia Sjöholm is Senior Lecturer in Comparative Literature at Södertörn University College, Sweden. She is the author of *The Antigone Complex: Ethics and the Invention of Feminine Desire*.

THINKING THE POLITICAL
General editors:
Keith Ansell Pearson
University of Warwick
Simon Critchley
University of Essex

Recent decades have seen the emergence of a distinct and challenging body of work by a number of Continental thinkers that has fundamentally altered the way in which philosophical questions are conceived and discussed. This work poses a major challenge to anyone wishing to define the essentially contestable concept of 'the political' and to think anew the political import and application of philosophy. How does recent thinking on time, history, language, humanity, alterity, desire, sexuality, gender and culture open up the possibility of thinking the political anew? What are the implications of such thinking for our understanding of and relation to the leading ideologies of the modern world, such as liberation, socialism and Marxism? What are the political responsibilities of philosophy in the face of the new world (dis)order?

This new series is designed to present the work of the major Continental thinkers of our time, and the political debates their work has generated, to a wider audience in philosophy and in political, social and cultural theory. The aim is neither to dissolve the specificity of the 'philosophical' into the 'political' nor to evade the challenge that the 'political' poses the 'philosophical'; rather, each volume in the series will try to show it is only in the relation between the two that the new possibilities of thought and politics can be activated.

Volumes already published in this series are:

Foucault & the Political by Jon Simons
Derrida & the Political by Richard Beardsworth
Nietzsche & the Political by Daniel W. Conway
Heidegger & the Political by Miguel de Beistegui
Lacan & the Political by Yannis Stavrakakis
Lyotard & the Political by James Williams
Deleuze & the Political by Paul Patton
Levinas & the Political by Howard Caygill

KRISTEVA AND THE POLITICAL

Cecilia Sjöholm

DISCARDED

BOWLING GREEN STATE
UNIVERSITY LIBRARY

Routledge
Taylor & Francis Group

LONDON AND NEW YORK

First published 2005
by Routledge
2 Park Square, Milton Park, Abingdon, Oxon OX14 4RN

Simultaneously published in the USA and Canada
by Routledge
270 Madison Ave, New York, NY 10016

Routledge is an imprint of the Taylor & Francis Group

© 2005 Cecilia Sjöholm

Typeset in Sabon by Taylor & Francis Books
Printed and bound in Great Britain by MPG Books Ltd, Bodmin

All rights reserved. No part of this book may be reprinted or
reproduced or utilised in any form or by any electronic,
mechanical, or other means, now known or hereafter
invented, including photocopying and recording, or in any
information storage or retrieval system, without permission in
writing from the publishers.

British Library Cataloguing in Publication Data
A catalogue record for this book is available from the British Library

Library of Congress Cataloging in Publication Data
A catalog record for this title has been requested

ISBN 0–415–21365–7 (hbk)
ISBN 0-415-21366-5 (pbk)

BOWLING GREEN STATE
UNIVERSITY LIBRARY

CONTENTS

v

CONTENTS

PREFACE

As always many individuals have been present in the studies and inves-
tigations leading up to this book, although only a handful will receive a
mention in this limited space. I must, however, begin with Julia Kristeva
herself, with whom I studied in the late 1980s and early 1990s and who
not only taught me an extraordinary amount of things on psychoanalysis
and literature, but also whose engagement in intellectual issues never
ceased to function as an inspiration to my own teaching and writing. The
chosen theme of my writing, Kristeva and the political, only reflects a frac-
tion of the issues I would have liked to raise in her vast authorship.

I would like to thank the Swedish Research Council, who financed the
possibility of finding the material in France and for spending time to work
on it at the University of Essex in England, and the Baltic Sea Foundation,
who financed the research conducting up to this book, and my colleagues
Hans Ruin and Marcia Cavalcante who conducted separate studies in the
same project. Along the way, the material has been presented in various
contexts that deserve to be mentioned: the International Association of
Women in Philosophy, the Association for the Studies of Culture and
Psychoanalysis, the University of Middlesex, the University of Nijmegen,
the Perugia meeting for research in phenomenology, Södertörn University
College, the University of Essex and the Spindel conference held at the
University of Memphis. Most importantly, however, I was kindly invited
to spend a semester at the University of Minnesota where I taught the
material of the book as a graduate course for students at the Department
of Comparative Literature and Cultural Studies and the Department of
German, Scandinavian and Dutch. The discussions with the students
present on the course were of crucial importance for the development of
the text. I have also had the opportunity to publish studies leading up to
the book: in *Knowledge Power Gender*, published by the International
Association of Women in Philosophy, *Agora*, *Radical Philosophy*,
Thinking in History at Södertörn University College and *The Southern
Journal of Philosophy*. Among the colleagues who have taken part of the

material and given invaluable feedback some deserve special mention: Simon Critchley, Philippe van Haute, Peter Osborne, Stella Sandford, Sara Beardsworth, Tina Chanter, Kelly Oliver, Ewa Ziarek, Fredrika Spindler and Courtney Helgoe. I am grateful for their help in making the writing of this book a great pleasure.

INTRODUCTION

In what way may we consider a theory of art to be politically radical? Political theory has yet to acknowledge and accommodate theories of art and aesthetics. Kristeva's project is unique in that it consists of a systematic displacement of the political from the universal (or public) domain to the singular and intimate spaces of signification. Such displacement has been figured in a variety of ways throughout her work: from the symbolic to the semiotic, from Oedipus to the object, from the socio-symbolic contract to the body, from the public sphere to the intimate domain. This book will inquire into the issue of the radical potential of such a systematic displacement. The first chapter considers the radical potential of pleasure in subjectivity, the second that of 'theorism' as a politically challenging textual practice, the third the insistence on a heterogeneous identity, the fourth the aspect of embodiment and its relevance to politics, whereas the fifth chapter shows how a psychoanalytic notion of temporality will undermine the fixation on goal-oriented projects in politics.

The link between psychoanalysis and emancipation has been explored in different waves. In the 1930s and 1940s Freud was taken up in the service of the schools of leftist criticism, such as surrealism and the Frankfurt School. Here, psychoanalysis was primarily considered as a challenge to bourgeois ways of life and to the repression of sexuality, which was necessary for bourgeois society to persist. Second, psychoanalysis was being reconsidered in the 1960s and 1970s, and explored again in various leftist traditions, ranging from Habermas to the *Tel Quel* group, from feminist groups to Fanon's insights into the function of racial identification. Again, the agenda was set by a need to question the norms sustaining bourgeois society, but it was done so from a more sophisticated point of view than that of the surrealists, for instance. The fact that feminists such as Juliet Mitchell and Julia Kristeva were able to read Freud from a sympathetic point of view helped develop a new kind of Freudianism, one that was not to take theories of penis envy and so on too seriously, but rather pay attention to the facets of Freud showing sexuality to be a function of fantasy and identification. Moreover, Lacan theorised the Freudian

1

unconscious in ways that developed its scope of interest in decisive ways. The contribution of Kristeva was to recognise practices such as psychoanalysis, literature and art to be multilayered processes of condensation and displacement. In the surrealist version, the unconscious is an unlimited source of liberating and creative potentialities that must be freed in order to create a more just society, based on an authentic notion of the self. The unconscious, as source of authenticity, was repressed in bourgeois society, creating individuals with distorted desires. Kristeva, however, does not subscribe to the idea that the unconscious has an emancipatory potential of authenticity. The political dimension is its undermining of given categories of social identity and goal-oriented projects, through a radical negativity at the core of the subject, resisting adaptation to linguistic and symbolic norms. The subject of negativity is irreducible to social and culturally determined identities. Its corporeal aspect allows for a notion of universality based on fragility and vulnerability rather than laws and rights. That these features be present in Kristeva's thought, and that they are all of interest to political thought, is something I hope to show simply in discussing her work.

Kristeva has been criticised for not providing an adequate political theory, and for not providing a direction for emancipation. But her project, I believe, must be assessed on other grounds. Its ambition is to formulate a politics conveying dimensions that tend to be overlooked in political philosophy and theory. The political domain must be displaced from the public to the intimate, and radicality is a negativity of movement and change, a heterogeneity of drive, body, language and meaning. Such a form of negativity is produced not between subjects but in each and every subject. It gains its meaning through a metaphorical principle of love replacing the recognition of a traditional emancipatory politics.

Kristeva the psychoanalyst is no less radical than the young writer of the avant-garde revolution. Starting out in the 1960s as a radical intellectual with Marxist, Maoist and feminist inclinations, she makes the literary subject of psychoanalysis her focus in the 1980s and 1990s. The radical Kristeva of the 1960s deconstructs metaphysical pretensions of meaning, whereas the psychoanalyst Kristeva reinstalls the necessity to create meaning. The feminist of the 1970s challenges the primacy of the phallus, whereas the psychoanalyst reinvents the imaginary father. However, it is one of the claims of this book that there is an observable continuity between early, revolutionary Kristeva and her 'terroristic' aesthetics and the psychoanalyst of melancholy and love. Placed in focus is the general question of how the intimate sphere of psychoanalysis, literature and art may have a political function. Domains that are commonly not regarded as political are held as privileged spaces of political transformation. Still Kristeva's ideas, while having been so important to the critics and scholars of art and literature in the last couple of decades, have not really been considered in a context in which they equally belong, that of the intellectual left, of politics and philosophy. Over the last few years, however, a new body of work has emerged in philosophy and politics by scholars such as Iris Marion Young, Kelly Oliver, Drucilla Cornell, Ewa Ziarek, Sara Beardsworth and Tina Chanter. The comments offered by critics such as Judith Butler and Nancy Fraser, for instance, have also contributed to re-establish the status of the work.

The writings of Kristeva were, already from the start, politically motivated. Rather than wanting to formulate a theory of aesthetics and situating it in a political context, the project has consisted of a systematic displacement of politics from the public to the intimate domain of signification. A revolutionary theory of the political is primary to a theory of modern aesthetics. The attempt to recreate meaning through literary processes and psychoanalysis departs from the radical heterogeneity and splitting of the subject. One may indeed speak of another kind of meaning than the one relying on imaginaries of homogeneity and identity, and a kind of meaning that would resist the submission under any symbolic authority. Only practices that manage to affirm the flexible and open character of the subject are capable of creating such a meaning.

Chapter 1 of this study describes early Kristeva's development in and contribution to the revolutionary scene of the 1960s. She emerges as an ideologue with a very defined project: she wants to theorise the revolutionary potential of literary discourse. In other words, Kristeva is not primarily interested in a theory of literature, but in developing a theory of the revolution that includes literature. In her early writings we find a notion of the political emerging, insisting that politics had to be removed from the central stage of political decision onto the margins of avant-garde practices. Political forces cannot be explained by economic or historic currents alone; they can only be explained through the negative forces operating in the subject. This basic idea of Kristeva – which is to form the core of this book – is clearly laid out in her early work.

In my second chapter, I will discuss the theory of literature offered by Kristeva as a terrorist aesthetics: avant-garde language and thought reflects a stance of absolute negativity that does not only present an alternative to traditional political discourse, but also rejects it altogether. Such kind of rejection carries with it a nihilist streak, which could be translated as a terroristic aesthetics. In *The Revolution of Poetic Language*, her famous dissertation of 1974, Kristeva emphasises the relation between the political and marginal forms of discourse, claiming that the unconscious and the political are intertwined categories. The questions we have to concern ourselves with are of course: subversive of what, the rules of who? What is 'subversive' literature and who writes it? What is 'subversive' philosophy and who thinks it? How could psychoanalysis, which sometimes, not least in Kristeva's own discourse, tends to be reductive and 'scientist', be considered a challenge to repressive norms? Is the unconscious really a space on the 'outside' of the norms and rules of social conventions and of language, a space from which we would be able to challenge and transform repressive tendencies of norms and values?

In my third chapter, I will discuss the challenge to identity politics. Some of these themes have been well commented and remarked upon, and have found their way into the feminist political discussion above all: the notion of a flexible and open subject, for instance, defying attempts to found a politics on a stable definition of identity. As many feminist theorists have observed, Kristeva's notion of subjectivity could be considered as a corrective to modern identity politics, undermining the notion of a stable self. While few consider Kristeva to be a political feminist, many do consider her 'subject-in-process' to be an important contribution to the elaboration of a feminist politics. But feminists disagree on the actual usefulness of this insight. Some, such as Iris Marion Young, Noëlle McAfee, Drucilla Cornell and Ewa Ziarek, have used the notion of an unstable, flexible and split subject-in-process to elaborate an alternative to identity politics. Others, such as Nancy Fraser and Allison Weir, have appreciated Kristeva's theory of the subject as open and thought provoking, but have argued that it implies a retreat from identity as a valid ground for political strategies, which in turn implies a sacrificial logic of subjectivity. Many commentators have complained about Kristeva's unwillingness to give much of a theoretical foundation for political agency, or much of a response to pressing issues on identity, difference and multiculturalism. In my opinion, however, it would be wrong to judge the political dimension on these grounds. The negotiations of political issues are less important than the political dimension of the subject. This theoretical strategy consists of finding a hollow and indefinite kind of universalism, which will serve to liberate the political dimension of the subject, unbound by social and cultural definition. One may certainly argue, as Seyla Benhabib does, that Kristeva's political concerns are middle-class, first-world and heterosexual. On the other hand, it appears that the 'terrorist' streak is underestimated. Although the work may identify with all those interests mentioned above, the politics is difficult to situate within such categories.

The fourth chapter discusses the notion of the body as a central concept. Clearly identifying the enlightenment heritage of the body-politic as an all too restrictive notion of the political, one of Kristeva's most important contributions to contemporary theory has been her involvement of the body in practices that have rarely been considered as corporeal: practices such as language, art and politics. Rather than consider the affects involved in the acquisition of language as marginal sidetracks, she highlights their continuous involvement in all uses of language and other symbolic activities related to language. Throughout her work, Kristeva is careful to situate the subject not just in language, but also in the corporeal affects related to language. The body in itself, however, is situated in a pre-discursive domain. Corporeal affects are intertwined with language, but emerge from a domain of impulses more archaic than language. Moreover, the interest in the body is directed towards the pre-Oedipal sphere, where sexual identity is not yet formed. The model of the body – defined as the *chora* by Kristeva – could also be considered a model of the political where the modern differentiation of public and intimate have not yet been formed.

The final chapter argues that the psychoanalytic notion of temporality present throughout the work of Kristeva could be regarded as a key to the political. Insisting on a Freudian view of the unconscious as timeless, Kristeva argues that Freud has in fact discovered a negativity that must be regarded as the condition for all forms of questioning. Freud shows that philosophical issues, as well as art, must be regarded as dependent on an experience of nihilation that can only be explained through a psychoanalytic notion of a timeless unconscious. Thus psychoanalysis hands us the tools not only for an interpretation of the unconscious but also for a better understanding of thought as such, showing that the modern revolt in art and philosophy is dominated by a movement of negativity. Rather than progress, modernity is a time of productive repetition and nihilation.

In this book, I hope to have been able to convey at least some of the extraordinary depth and richness that Kristeva has offered us in rethinking the relations between psychoanalysis, aesthetics and politics. I have come to regard her work not only as original and important for a better understanding of the function of art, but also as a key to the importance of Freudian thought and its relevance for domains that tend to leave out psychoanalysis altogether. I can only hope that the work will remain important for those who have already discovered her writings, and be discovered in due time by those who have yet to go there.

1

A REVOLUTION BETWEEN PLEASURE AND SACRIFICE

Materialism and Marxism

The often told story of Kristeva's arrival in Paris as a *boursier de l'état français* from Bulgaria is associated with precocious brilliance and intellectual stardom: she becomes the favourite of Roland Barthes, gets involved with the *Tel Quel* circle and Philippe Sollers, introduces Bakhtin and the concept of intertextuality.[1] Named *L'Étrangère* by Roland Barthes she becomes a main influence in *Tel Quel*, publishes a Maoist manifesto, goes on a scandalous journey to China, becomes a professor, a psychoanalyst, a writer, etc. In her writings from the 1960s, Kristeva emerges as a radical with a very defined goal: she wants to theorise the revolutionary potential of literary discourse. In other words, the primary aim is not to formulate a theory of literature, but a new form of materialist critique. The work on literature is motivated by a desire to fill in a blank in Marxist theory, not the understanding of literature. This project goes hand in hand with a consistent emphasis on the radical value of aesthetic work. Removing the political from the central stage of decision-making onto the margins of avant-garde practices, literary discourse is made a weapon for political change. The writings from the 1960s give evidence of an aesthetic militancy that later books to some extent have served to cover. But there is an obvious continuity between the youthful, militant Kristeva, and the mature psychoanalyst. The early political engagement would not have been so interesting had it not been for the fact that much of her work on psychoanalysis and literature could be seen as an elaboration of the political. Set at the crossroads between psychoanalysis and materialist cultural criticism, Kristeva challenges the traditional emancipatory politics of the left. Rather than be prone to reflective and critical discourses, her political subject is rooted in a body of drives and desires, taking pleasure not only in the challenge to repressive institutions but also in corporeal affectivity itself. The replacement of critical analysis for affectivity, regression and pleasure seems to belie the idea that the work is done in the name of 'the political'. The theory has been accused of being stuck at an impossible crossroads between an affirmation of the pleasures of a singular subject and a critical assessment of the totalising forces of modernity. But although a definition of the political as avant-gardism, subjectivity and intimacy may be debatable, her writings not only make it impossible to dismiss these spheres as apolitical, but they also clearly demonstrate the way in which the subjective discourses of art and psychoanalysis are tied in with modern political thought. Proceeding in three moves, this chapter will begin to uncover the intellectual engagements that have led Kristeva to replace the analysis of capitalism and class struggle with an affirmation of the workings of the unconscious. It is necessary here to tell the story of Paris in the early 1960s and Kristeva's place in that context. Second, I will discuss the definition of pleasure as being based on the Freudian notion of polymorphous sexuality. Third, I will argue that Kristeva's affirmation of pleasure is conceived as a logic of pleasure and sacrifice. This means that enjoyment is the ultimate motivator of the formations of subjectivity, and that sacrifice, or the giving up of enjoyment, is only the momentary giving up of a pleasure that is to be retrieved in a new form.

Kristeva's notion of the political emerged at a scene were art, philosophy, politics and ways of living just in general were subject to experimentation. Politics, philosophy, film and literature were rejuvenating themselves, and the intellectual scene was becoming increasingly radical. In his extensive history of the journal *Tel Quel* Philippe Forest has shown that its politicisation took off in the summer of 1966, when Philippe Sollers became chief editor. A political committee of the review was formed in 1967, and a first article announcing the liaison with the Communist Party was published the same year. In the year to come, *Tel Quel* presented itself as revolutionary and avant-garde. In other words, the group wanted to create a new kind of environment for the political left, where aesthetic practices were considered as revolutionary in themselves. The project at that point was to create a theoretical superstructure for the practices of the avant-garde, similar to the manifestos of early avant-gardisms such as, for instance, Russian and Italian futurists or French surrealists. But the interest of *Tel Quel* was almost exclusively dedicated to literature and language, leaving out art, photography, film and music, although these art forms were more innovative and experimental in the 1960s than literature. Certain authors, such as Georges Bataille and Céline, were considered to be avant-garde, whereas the original French surrealist movement was left outside, never mind the international scene of other modernists. In such a context, the influence of Julia Kristeva must have been like a breath of fresh air. She knew only of two French avant-garde authors before she came to France (Céline and Blanchot),[2] but this in turn seems to have propelled her curiosity. Cultivating a particular interest in modernism she inspired a new perspective on authors such as Rimbaud, Bataille and Mallarmé. Moreover, she was familiar with

Russian, German and English-speaking literature, and served to introduce authors and theorists from other contexts, opening the door towards a wider notion of avant-gardism than the French one. Although at times she would appear infuriatingly syncretistic, even superficial to some, she was always a daring and inspirational thinker.[3]

The insistence that the political be defined as a revolution of the subject must be considered within a context where a radical politics was an object of incessant disputes. It would be easy to presume that the 1960s were a time of solidarity, where the radical thought of the avant-garde merged with the quest for social and political change of the political parties. This was, however, not the case. To many of the intellectual left the discourses of deliberation and decision-making were considered hostage to a certain notion of power that was dismissed, and towards the end of the 1960s there was little common ground between the *Tel Quel* group and the communist party to which they originally had adhered, the PCF. The actual details of the dissensus are, however, not as interesting as the discourse that was cultivated in its wake, and in this Kristeva was not the only contributor. As the autobiographic novel *Les Samuraïs* implies, the group was not particularly dedicated to activism. Originally conceived as a publication promoting a new kind of aesthetic, *Tel Quel* gradually came to aspire towards subversion of those areas of life that tended not to be considered as political by the mainstream: art, culture and psychoanalysis. Even more importantly, these areas of life were not thought of as alien to the theoretical apparatus of the intellectual elite. In fact, one must underscore that the real originality of the *Tel Quel* group lies in its promotion of marginal areas of life such as intellectualism and avant-gardism as the actual motor of the revolution. Increasingly, the aim became to make theory subversive in itself.

In the manifesto of the *Tel Quel* group from 1968, *Théorie d'ensemble*, Marxism and grammatology are pronounced to be the same thing, whereas capitalism and logocentrism are made equivalent with one another. The revolution is made into a question of text, not of political manœuvres, and the goal of the volume is as advocated in the preface: 'to articulate a politics logically linked to a non-representative dynamic of writing'.[4] Such a 'non-representable dynamic' consisted in a theorisation of textual processes, irreducible to critique or analysis, which relied on the productive force of the theoretical machinery that was set in motion. One could describe Kristeva's early work in three stages, although these stages intercept and overlap. The articles appearing before the publication of her seminal thesis *Revolution in Poetic Language* as well as that book itself could all be described as early work. All of these stages could be described as dynamic but raw attempts to formulate a materialist theory of literature, infusing literature into the concerns of the radical left. All these stages could also be regarded as allied to the idea of a non-representative dynamic of theorisation, underscoring not its analytic but rather productive power.

The first stage is the sémanalyse, as presented in the *Semeiotiké* (1969), where literary texts are brought into a kind of discursive laboratory and examined with 'scientific' precision. The second stage comes with the introduction of Maoism and the *Tel Quel* manifesto published in 1971, declaring the need for a cultural revolution in the intellectual movement of the left. This stage signals a turn towards experience and interiority. The third stage comes with feminism and a more systematic integration of psychoanalysis so that corporeal and affective aspects of the subject are underscored.

Referring to Althusser in *Théorie d'ensemble* Philippe Sollers establishes that theory is a practice, and that the study of the text in particular is a site of the practice of dialectical materialism.[5] The field through which such theoretico-political challenges are to be made is, according to Kristeva, semiotics (or the study of science), or, as she calls it in *Théorie d'ensemble*, semiology. Semiology (named by Saussure) emphasises the privileged place of language and argues that any study of signification would have to be referred to language. What is so specific about Kristeva's version of semiology (or semiotics, as she calls it in other texts) is the emphasis of theory. Semiology, in fact, is nothing but theory: it constructs its objects, and reflects its own theorisation in that very construction. In this, it poses a threat to the belief in the viability of scientific discourses lacking this form of self-reflection. In relation to traditional discourses of science, semiology is aggressive and subversive, showing that all discourses are ideologically permeated, even discourses pretending to a high level of scientific value such as logic and mathematics.[6] Signalling a new materialist theory of literature, the sémanalyse is more radical than critical analysis, more concerned with Marxism than literary theory.[7] The interest in the text is a new, materialist science where one has to

> analyse the particularities of the poetic or 'literary' text in the general sense and specify the specific rules for the function of meaning in these texts as well as the exact place which the subject will occupy — this could become an essential and pure contribution to the constitution of a Marxist science which Lenin showed us that we need but which is currently lacking, a science of signifying practices.[8]

Literary analysis must focus on the production of meaning, not on meaning as an object. But the history of signifying practices is relatively independent in relation to materialist history, and so one cannot simply translate the history of Marxism into literary terms.[9] The literary text is never simply a mirror of social life. Its subversive status derives from the fact that it is produced through a relation of negativity to the social fabric. A radical theory of literature must therefore elucidate those mechanisms of negativity, and take the subversive status of the text into account without translating it in terms of the values and norms of a system of exchange in the form of a meaning made object to the text itself. Making meaning into an object, something which may be discovered as a given truth of the text rather than realising the heterogeneity and polyphony of the text, literary historians implicitly resort to metaphysics. Moreover, they tend to rely on the values and assumptions originating in a given class system. A new science of literature must therefore circumvent both of these problems, avoiding the reproduction of a given social system and the objectification of a content. However, the leftist contention that literature could be made into a scholarly discipline of analysis – read formalism – is ridden with problems. The ideology of linguistic scientism implies that literature be reduced to the object of language, a fixation on representation, making the text itself vanish under a formalist construction.[10] Art and literature are transformational signifying practices and therefore irreducible to metaphysical conceptions of meaning. The text itself, and the dialectics implied in the production of the text, must be the only meaningful object of study for a materialist science of literature.

Any notion of meaning is intertwined with a set of values constructed in a given social structure, such as a class system. A new Marxist science of literature would therefore have to start with the notion of literature as a signifying practice, obeying certain rules of production. But these rules of production cannot be identified as entities outside of the text, and so cannot be reduced to sociology. As it is, literature does nothing but support a given class system. The upper classes have made it into an ideological support for their hegemony, whereas the working classes have made it into a substitute for religion. In order to challenge such metaphysical presuppositions, Kristeva, unlike Lucien Goldmann, does not look into the sociological structures of the reception of literature. She goes straight to the question of how literature signifies. This is a question that cannot, however, be reduced to linguistic presumptions. The text neither names nor determines an outside: it can only be described as a Heraclitean mobility with a double orientation – on the one hand it is produced in a specific signifying system, and on the other in a social context. Given that the text is produced between these systems, it overshoots both of them and overcomes a reduction to representation in either terms. The text never has one meaning (*un sens*), the textual practice 'decentres the subject of a discourse (of one meaning, of one structure) and is structured like the operation of its pulverisation in one undifferentiated infinity'.[11] Rather than considering artistic practices as spaces of alienation, illustration and expression, Marxism must take their productive processes into consideration.[12] This means that the new materialist science of signifying practices must focus on the *text*.[13] The focus on the text is in itself not a particularly original claim, given the context: Sollers, Derrida, Barthes and others all made the text the focus of their study. Kristeva's own motivation for doing so, however, must be set apart from the rest. Already from the start, the political was focused on the subject being produced through textual processes. The text is the becoming of the subject. In order to understand how such a subject appears, one has to challenge a discourse on literature that has made use of certain metaphysical and ideological presuppositions.

However, the project of attempting to found a theory of literature as a Marxist science, focusing on a textual subject studied through a linguistic-semiotic theoretical apparatus, falls short of its goals. Her texts were accused by fellow Marxists of being too scientistic and too abstract.[14] An intervention against *Sémeiotiké* by Mitsou Ronat at the big colloquium on literature and ideology in 1971 is illuminating in this regard. Ronat, critical of Kristeva's claim to have surpassed the Indo-Eurocentric problems of Chomskyan linguistics, accuses her of scientism. The claim to be subverting the logical and scientific concepts of discourses such as Chomsky's in reverting to a notion of a textual subject rather than linguistic system, guides her attention towards processes through which signification is produced rather than the given system of its production. But Ronat shows that the argument of Kristeva is circular. Her ambition is to move beyond the science of linguistic signs towards an analysis of how the sign is produced. This happens through a turn from linguistics to semiotics, which distances itself from the scientific discourse of linguistics. At the same time, semiotics is declared as the founding science of the dialectics of materialism. The question is, however, what motivates the practices that are to be explained by semiotic models. The semiotic model is replacing a theory of materialism, without qualifications. However, she insists that semiotics is a more fundamental science than a material dialectics in the traditional sense. Moreover, her assurances that semiotics is superior to linguistics as a materialist science fall short of its examples; Kristeva keeps assuming an unconscious subtext (or *génotexte*) to be present in the text she is analysing. But she fails to prove the existence of that 'other' text. The very modes of production that she wants to explain are presumed in her semiotic theory.[15] Ronat's criticism of Kristeva's claim that semiotics is to be regarded as the founding science of dialectical materialism is legitimate. Nevertheless, Kristeva is right to insist that her work cannot be reduced to erroneous scientism. Investigating some fundamental terms of linguistics, such as sign, sense, subject, her intention is to apply these to a new notion of text. The semiotic work is thus involved in an investigation of the premises of linguistics, rather than a variety of it.[16] It wants to observe and respect the plurality of signifying practices, rather than aim towards the fixation of one, given kind of discourse. Already from the beginning of her work, Kristeva's use of the term materialism is interchangeable with that of negativity; accounting for the resistance of an exteriority that makes it impossible for the discourse to close. A traditional materialist notion of literature would aim to reduce the importance of the subject. Negativity, however, is a notion close to the Freudian drives, striving to occupy a place in Marxist theory. This is done in the article 'Matière, sens, dialectique' (1971a), which declares the incorporation of Freud into a radical Marxist position. 'Matière, sens, dialectique' presents a model of dialectical materialism where matter, negativity and drives are interchangeable forms of resistance to the construction of meaning as unified and historically independent. Rather than resorting to the dynamics of social structures, Kristeva refers the term of negativity to the Freudian body, thereby indicating its proximity to a theory of the drives that takes the human body of pleasure and displeasure as its model.[17] It appears that the human body itself is the form of matter that harbours the Kristevan term of negativity. Unlike the hard matter of classical materialism, the soft, human body is an unreliable focus that in turn will produce the processes of displacement and condensation that create signification. Her theory cannot, in other words, be reduced either to Marxist or Freudian formalism. Textual processes include the presence of many voices, and many other texts. The notions of dialogicity and polyphony were brought over from Bakhtin, who used them in order to describe the presence of multiple voices in a literary work, thereby undermining the notion that a literary work would be a closed universe and opening for a view of it where a social and political reality is present through these voices.[18]

The sémanalyse is aiming to distil levels of signification informed by, but not reducible to, social and historical reality. These levels are the most potent political weapons of the transformation in that they infuse our perception of things, and therefore our social habits and everyday lives. No revolution can come about without such a profound impact being made on our perceptions. The revolution is not, and can never be, a matter of political decisions made at the top-end of a hierarchical structure of decision-makers. The political cannot be reduced to anything like actions undertaken on the basis of mutual decisions. It has to be involved in the study of a contemporary as well as in a systematic study of the undercurrents that structure the layers of modern subjectivity. In the text these undercurrents manifest themselves through the *génotexte*, and the task of the critique is to unravel the processes of the *génotexte* producing the result. Literature, or at least modern literature, originates in a position of radical negativity that makes it challenging to begin with. The dissolution of art has its beginning in romanticism and German Idealism, when the unity between form and content is ruptured. Art and literature are transformational signifying practices against metaphysics and absolute knowledge. Kristeva's method of literary studies then proposes to pursue aims that would all be truthful to the kind of radical challenge inherent in literary discourse. First of all, literature can never be reduced to the object of language. Second, it would have to transcend the fixation on representation.

Third, it would have to withstand all formalist attempts.[19] The kind of dialectics Kristeva is positing, then, does not simply posit negativity as a force of differentiation similar to that of negation, which is focused on the concept or, in modern psychoanalysis, the signifier. Negativity, a reoccurring term in early Kristeva, shows that signification is a process taking place in a subject that is never reducible to a signifier, but must be considered through its investments in the drive. The term of negativity indicates that all processes of signification are traversed by the unconscious, a traversal that can only be produced in and through an embodied subject of desire and drives.[20] Such a radical negativity escapes the dialectics caught in the paternal axis of symbolic laws. As Kristeva makes clear in her writings from the 1970s. negativity is another name for presence of the maternal body in the life of the subject. A new science of signification would therefore be a field of contradiction and struggles, taking place in the void left from a lost father.[21] With the introduction of the maternal sphere in later writings, the meaning of the term negativity will be elucidated.

From Marxism to Maoism to Freud; the fourth term of the dialectic

In the autumn of 1971, Sollers and Kristeva published a manifesto together, the 'POSITIONS DU MOUVEMENT DE JUIN 71'.[22] The manifesto was the outcome of a long process of fracturing of the intellectual left, the *Tel Quel* group being more or less at war with the Communist Party, the PCF. The 1960s were not just a time of transformation, but also of splits and conflicts. Small fractions arose between leftist intellectuals unable to agree on a common agenda. Signifying a turn away from the conservative Communist Party and the Soviet Union, the *Tel Quel* group declare themselves as 'real' revolutionaries in the manifesto. The turn towards Maoism is motivated by the Cultural Revolution, and the ongoing upheavals in China. The group expresses regrets for not having protested against the Soviet invasion of Czechoslovakia in 1968, and in not having known enough about the Cultural Revolution to have supported it already from the start. It dreams of a merger between the Soviet Union and China. And it promotes, above all, 'the great revolution of the Chinese cultural proletariat'.[23] Unsurprisingly, there is not much social and historical reality in *Tel Quel*'s China. It is nothing less than the utopia of their dreams as European intellectuals, and they were rightly criticised already in their own time for their political *naïveté*.[24] The China described in Kristeva's *Tel Quel* articles and her book *On Chinese Women* is an imaginary one, and her writings contain little or no analysis of actual events. This may also account for the fact that she never repented or questioned her naïve support for the Cultural Revolution, a bloody and repressive movement causing personal disasters for millions.[25] Given the *naïveté*

13

demonstrated by the manifesto, it is all the more astonishing that the blind belief in the Cultural Revolution could turn out to be so fruitful. In the end, the lack of political realism became a great theoretical asset. In fact, later on Kristeva will explain her travel to China through *a lack* of interest in politics. This can be explained by the harshness of the political climate in which she lived. The turn towards Maoism went hand in hand with a deep scepticism against a growing political extremism. Rather than denigrate the fascination of Maoism of the group, Kristeva later explained it as a healthy reaction to the perverted attachment to communism, which was a regrettable outlet for personal passions. Although Kristeva was certainly part of the political culture of her time, her pledge was that of a discourse avoiding dogmatism. Extremism is, for Kristeva the psychoanalyst, not a question of political standpoints, but an investment of the drive. Scrutinising the political afflictions of Céline, she will come back to this viewpoint.[26] The fascination that attaches an individual to a political idea is produced through the same logic of the drive that attaches an individual to a perverse fixation. In that regard, there is in fact not much difference between the fascism of Céline and the compromised communism of the *Tel Quel* group. Political perversions are all commanded by an ideal that refuses reality in favour of non-sublimated forms of gratification. Maoism, somewhat paradoxically perhaps, was less of a political solution for Kristeva and more of a dissolution of the symptom of extremism itself.[27] Signifying a 'pure utopia' without visions of implementation or final purpose, Maoism offers a remedy against sectarianism and a way out of dogmatism, opening for scientific and cultural experimentation, presenting a whole new form of revolutionary subjectivity and disabling all kinds of 'empiricism, dogmatism and revisionism'.[28] Whereas Marxism theorises a practice without subjects, rather than an active subject of practices (a subject-in-process), the Maoist subject emphasises personal experience. Maoism and the Cultural Revolution are not merely aiming to change economic and social structures, but the inner life of the subject. Maoism involves finding 'another social and historical origin, an "inner experience"'. Not only was Chinese religion and political culture revolutionary forces in process, but also Chinese writing and 'a poetry subtle as jade'.[29] Chinese culture provides access to an inner experience where the Western ego and its pathologies are overcome. Ancient China is foreign in the same way that Greece is foreign for Heidegger. Its language may not point to the elusive origin of being but to the elusive origin of inner experience. Chinese poetry unravels and transcends the symbolically and metaphysically saturated language of Western cultures, revealing that which is suppressed in the modern culture. A retrieval of inner experience would therefore have to pass through the linguistic, ideological and subjective sensations of Ancient China.[30] Kristeva's eyes were brought to these phenomena by a review of a translation of Ancient Chinese poetry by

Michelle Loi. Rather than enveloping some kind of lack of interiority or inner liberty, as claimed by Hegel, Ancient Chinese poetry incarnates an excess, traversing the Western notion of subjectivity.[31] Ancient Chinese poetry, just like contemporary modernist poetry, is interwoven with music, repetitions, alliterations, silences; signifiers are played with. Effectively, such a kind of writing announces the birth of a new kind of subject. Such a subject is not comparable to the metaphysical subject of the ego, but is a subject of the people, traversing Western notions of egocentrism.

The inability to focus on the subject, rather than the mechanisms that determine the object, makes Kristeva leave Marxism behind. Maoism, on the other hand, goes beyond a limited conception of practice as an exchange of surplus value, accentuating personal experience instead.[32] The idea of 'personal', here, however, must not be understood as individual, but in its connection with the immediate – a term that lends an almost mystical dignity to the Maoist project as a pleasurable transgression of the self. In Kristeva's reading, Mao insists on two aspects of practice: first of all, it is personal. Second, it is intertwined with the immediacy of experience. In order to transform reality, a personal engagement is necessarily needed. Only the personal offers a way to engage with appearances and phenomena at a level that can be authentic. All authentic knowledge comes from immediate experience. This does not mean, however, that Mao describes a subjectivity tied to individuality. It is, rather, a vehicle for a new kind of knowledge. The subjectivity of inner experience is the very motor of social transformation and revolution: 'One of Mao's most important contributions to the theory and practice of dialectical materialism consists in the rediscovery ... of such a subjectivity.'[33] Moreover, such a form of subjectivity is uninterested in questions of consciousness. Its experiences have more to do with the unconscious, such as it has been theorised by psychoanalysis. Psychoanalysis, therefore, is an excellent supplement to Maoism, and can if necessary intervene in order for it not to end in another form of dogmatism.[34] What psychoanalysis has shown is that the important conflicts do not take place in the social sphere, but rather in the subject itself, which will interiorise these conflicts. The subject will present itself as a bundle of conflicts, of desires and drives, and social relations as well as personal ones will create an ecstatic form of subjectivity where conflicts of class as well as conflicts in relation to more intimate objects of desire will play themselves out.[35] The focus on inner experience is, as recovered through Chinese thought, supplanted by a reading of Bataille. The desire of Bataille must be looked at differently from that of the way desire is depicted in the Hegelian tradition, and in materialist philosophy. Hegel's notion of desire is directed towards the constitution of unity, whereas Bataille's notion of desire is the experience of transgression as performed by a highly rational mind, who has already formed a unified self and whose desire can only be directed towards the sensation of having that unity come to pieces, in the splitting vertigo of transgression.[36] Whereas the philosophy of desire is fixated on the object, the desire of Bataille produces an experience, not an object. The realisation of what Bataille calls inner experience puts the object in question, producing *a lack* of objects rather than objects.[37] This lack throws the subject back on its own pulverisation in the moment of transgression. One sees here, in its origins, the theory of the abject take form – a term borrowed from Bataille and later developed in the analysis of culture. A theorisation of experience cannot be constituted out of a simple subject–object dichotomy. It has to be thought from another point of view, a subject-in-process *produces the lack through a pulverisation of the self.* Such a subject is determined not by the lack of desire, which marks the phallic, Eurocentric and Lacanian subject, but by the enjoying experience of the pulverisation of desire for unity.

The semiotic and the symbolic

Revolution in Poetic Language introduces the two main concepts that will become operative in her analysis from that point on. These concepts are the symbolic and the semiotic. Known from Lacanian theory, the notion of the symbolic takes on a new meaning in Kristeva, primarily because it cannot be considered without the semiotic as its auxiliary. The two concepts are primarily presented as a critique of traditional linguistics, which assumes the existence of a transcendental ego. Two dimensions of language are dissociated: one preoccupied with 'meaning' and another with 'signification'. The study of meaning is concerned with signs and their correlate in propositions. It defines the subject through the sign, and its use of signs. The study of signification, however, works with prelinguistic processes that constitute the predisposition for meaning.

In introducing these two concepts, Kristeva does not merely resort to Lacanian theory. Although Lacan established the symbolic as part of the psychoanalytic vocabulary, the term is used in a different sense.[38] Kristeva makes clear that subjectivity lies beyond even the signifiers referred to by Lacan, and must be found precisely in the work of negativity.[39] Lacan makes the symbolic into an effect of the law, which in itself is a form of prohibition that renders the very function of the symbolic possible. As such, the symbolic is made timeless and absolute, a purely formal construction whose different articulations are less interesting than the condition for its being: a primary prohibition and restraint that makes the social order possible but which is irreducible to it. The symbolic is an unconditional law. Its effects can be seen in and through the operations of language on the subject. And although it would be misleading to claim that language *is* the symbolic for Lacan, at least not in his later work, it is quite clear that the law of the symbolic order is effectuated in and by language, whether

16

that law concerns the prohibition against incest, family relations, sexual difference or other basic structures of human society. As such, however, the symbolic does not have a content of signification.[40]

Kristeva moves away from Lacan on several counts. First, sexual difference is a complex of biological facts and social determinations, whereas Lacan considers it to be the product of a phallic logic of exchange. Although Kristeva emphasises the role played by the symbolic in establishing the subject position as male or female, the biological factor is hidden but not removed (see the discussion of femininity as dissidence in Chapter 2). Second, Kristeva, unlike most Lacanians, is persistent in her claim that the father can only be a metaphorical one, a space of transference rather than a site of law.[41] The symbolic is theorised through the relation to the other as object, as introduced by Melanie Klein. The symbolic is mediated through the effects and affects of a relation to a primary object, and the law is continuously challenged and transgressed through drives and desires produced with the establishing of that object. In Lacanian theory, object relations are referred to the domain of the imaginary, which must be traversed for analysis to come to the point of its truths. Kristeva is interested in precisely those aspects of its formation that Lacan would consider imaginary: the symptoms and narratives of melancholia, narcissism, abjection and so on.[42]

Finally, and most importantly, the symbolic is not a foundation of culture, a law *ex nihilo* as in Lacan. It is intertwined with the semiotic, and cannot be understood as its opposite. While the symbolic refers to the underlying structures and laws of language and society, the semiotic refers to the layers of signification that are irreducible to those laws: phenomena such as rhythm and sound-patterns. The most important aspect of this model is that it shows that the unconscious is organised by language, but language in turn is invested with aspects of the unconscious overshooting the laws of signification.[43] The two modalities are inseparable within the signifying process: 'Because the subject is always both semiotic and symbolic, no signifying system he produces can be either "exclusively" semiotic or "exclusively" symbolic and is instead necessarily marked by an indebtedness to both.'[44] As dialectical constructs they represent two systems that can both be transposed into the other in the process of signification.

Establishing a sphere that precedes the inscription of the symbolic, if not in a temporal than at least in a logical sense, the subject of the semiotic challenges Lacanian theory. Rather than placing itself under the constraints of the law and the Oedipal structure of social life, the subject-in-process of the semiotic is always up and against such a law and such a structure. The dominance of the pre-Oedipal does not exclude the Lacanian notion that the symbolic is effective in all psychic functions, including the drives. But the pre-Oedipal sphere introduces another aspect of subjectivity, which from a Lacanian point of view would be impossible. In Lacan, there is no aspect of the subject preceding the establishment of the symbolic: everything that appears as a pre-history is in fact predetermined by Oedipalisation. What appears to precede is in fact a retroactive construction. The pre-symbolic and pre-Oedipal sphere does not so much, however, assume the existence of another sphere in time even if there sometimes appears to be a factor of evolution in Kristeva's presentation. The pre-Oedipal is typically represented by the infant, but rather than referring to a stage in human development it assumes another layer of subjectivity dominating or at least supplementing the symbolic structure. In Kristeva's dialectics, the linguistic order is dominated by a prelinguistic order, the symbolic by a pre-symbolic order, the Oedipal by a pre-Oedipal order. This institutes another kind of retroactive logic where the symbolic becomes instituted *après coup*, rather than as a function always already there. Such a retroactive construction of the subject aims to identify the subject as corporeal in its linguistic being, as irreducible to language in the complexity of its many layers of significa-tion. The aim of Kristeva's deviation from Lacan's more rigid terminology is to emphasise the place of the body in the process of signification. The subject-in-process has a flesh of sensitivities and a memory of affects that cannot be transposed into language. The subject is not reducible to the logic of signifiers, but is constituted through several layers that are all part of that process of signification.

The *chora* and the resistance of matter

The introduction of the *chora* in Kristeva's theory underlines, above all, the undermining of a metaphysics of representation, as she calls it. Already *Sémeiotiké* makes it clear that the text does not represent society, but transforms it. The text incorporates a resistance against representation and a homogenous definition of meaning. The resistance is that of matter itself, a function of negativity that disallows for a straightforward relation of designation between language and thing. A metaphysics of representation would presume the relation between word and thing becoming one without passing through the processes of signification dominated by nega-tivity. In Kristeva's early dialectics, material resistance and negativity are interchangeable concepts, introducing a function of transposition rather than point of conflict. The resistance of matter can never fully account for the transformative powers of signification.

The *chora* is not cast under the symbolic law, but it is nevertheless cast under a regulating process. What the *chora* produces, however, is not a subject of the law, but a subject in process/on trial [*sujet en procès*]:

> Our discourse – all discourse – moves with and against the *chora*
> in the sense that it simultaneously depends upon and refuses it.
> Although the *chora* can be designated and regulated, it can never

be definitively posited: as a result one can situate the *chora* and, if necessary, lend it a topology, but one can never give it axiomatic form.[45]

All signification consists of the positing of an object through a linguistic proposition. This means that the constitution of an object will somehow always be present in the proposition. The *chora* refers to a stage in the process of signification in which the linguistic sign is not yet articulated as the absence of an object. It will actually be present in the metaphysical sense, as criticized in post-Husserlian philosophy. It means, rather, that it will constitute itself as object simultaneously with the constitution of the subject. The subject properly speaking is always absent in the process of signification. Signification itself is the boundary rather than the origin of the process. All language will simultaneously involve the coming into being of subject and object. The positing of the object always involves an economy of drives such that the process of signification is continuously traversed by extra-linguistic layers of signification. The moment of the thetic phase, as Kristeva calls it, is that in which the object of the proposition is bracketed and separated from the subject. In her model, however, such Husserlian bracketing of meaning and scission of the object–subject relation is never fully accomplished, in that every proposition always encompasses the relation to an object in the sense of a human other.[46] The alterity of the other will make itself known through the excesses of signification known as the semiotic.

In the *Timaeus*, Plato introduces the *chora* as a third principle between matter and the idea: a space or room in which a thing is.[47] It could also be used in the sense of place or space. In Plato's own text, the term for space, *chora*, is paralleled with the word for receptacle, *hypokeimenon*, and is approximated to a maternal sphere. The *chora* is a receptacle that nourishes everything that is created, in the space between the original, available only for thought, and the visible, worldly representation. This third principle is necessitated by the argument of the *Timaeus* in order to explain that the four elements can be transformed into different substances, disappear or mix together in an eternal kind of circulation. Plato then needs a principle to explain the movement and transformation outside of the form of the original and the copy, the changes gone through by the elements. The original is compared to the father, the copy to the son, while the maternal principle is the nourishing receptacle. In order to fill her function the mother must be situated outside of the speculative relation original–copy. She is invisible, without forms, lacking idea:

Wherefore, let us not speak of her that is the Mother and Receptacle of this generated world, which is perceptible by sight and all the senses, by the name of earth or air or fire or water, or

19

any aggregates or constituents thereof: rather, if we describe her as a Kind invisible and unshaped, all-receptive, and in some most perplexing and most baffling way partaking of the intelligible, we shall describe her truly.[48]

The mention of a maternal function as being's outside, excluded from Plato's ontology of the real, has often been commented upon and has been looked on as a puzzling kind of leftover in his ontology.[49] In Kristeva, the *chora* is an element outside of any metaphysical principle. Outside of time, outside of matter, it stands for that which is radically heterogeneous in relation to any principle used in dialectical materialism. The *chora* is the space outside of being because it engenders transformation, mobility, motility, novelty, not a psychic site but a site of investments. Although it may be a container of affects and memories, it is not immediately translatable as the body, but rather the quasi-transcendental condition that makes corporeal mediation possible. The *chora* is a term of mediation irreducible to the terms of negativity and signification, not governed by law, but by a kind of organisation for which Kristeva tells us that the maternal body is the model.[50] This *chora* is the maternal as a principle of motility, as that which cannot be named but shown in the form of rhythm, form, excess. The *chora* is a principle of production and motility, rather than stasis: the very engendering of representation that cannot itself be represented, the space preceding the actual space of representation. Not simply a shape but a space of energies, investments and drives, the *chora* allows the fragmented body to find its correlative in the different words and sounds, colours and shapes that belong to the sphere of representation. The *chora* corresponds to Freud's primary process, or the model Freud uses in order to explain the energies moving between the sphere of symbolisation and the sphere of the drive. In *Psychology of the Dream-Processes*, Freud supplements *The Interpretation of Dreams* through underlining the role of the primary process: the 'thought' of the preconscious in which the processes of condensation and displacement make sure that no forbidden content is allowed into the sphere of consciousness. The primary process is a form of 'irrational thought', in which repression causes psychic investments to pass from one element to another; it is dominated by affect. Intellectual activity, however, will aim to free itself from that domination. The primary process, therefore, is at odds with rational thought: 'thinking must concern itself with the connecting paths between ideas, without being led astray by the *intensities* of those ideas'.[51] Dominated by affect, the primary process presents a threat to the functioning of the secondary process.

In other words, the *chora* does not produce a variety of representation, or a version of language. It traverses representation and language, investing it with pleasure and displeasure, *jouissance* and abjection. The elements of the semiotic are voices, gestures and colours. Also, various phonic entities are the mark of libidinal investments, as are metaphor and metonymy. All these elements are aspects of the semiotic, traversing and adding to signification. Language is not simply communication and representation.

In this respect, Nancy Fraser's criticisms deserve attention. Fraser has identified the main problems in Kristeva's theory as the result of ambiguity: Kristeva is well aware of the fact that subjectivity must be considered a historically and socially specific kind of agency. But she does not draw the consequences from these insights. Instead, she keeps referring to the ahistorical and apolitical abstraction of Lacanian theory: the symbolic. Thereby she loses the pragmatic stress on contingency and historicity. There is no place for interaction and social conflict in Kristeva's all too structuralist notion of subjectivity.[52] The insistence that marginal discourses are revolutionary in themselves and the invention of 'the semiotic' compensates little for this fact. According to Fraser, the tendency to valorise transgression simply in itself, and her belief in a hidden repressed undercurrent of society – the semiotic – are dead ends in an otherwise fruitful discursive analysis; the transgressive tendency runs the danger of becoming nothing but a fruitless challenge if it does not translate into the social sphere. Arguing that Kristeva's dialectics is constructed around polarised dichotomies, Fraser is concerned that the notion of a subversive semiotic still forces us to validate the symbolic. The semiotic subject, says Fraser, is located beneath rather than within culture and society. Thus, 'it is unclear how its practice could be a political practice'.[53] Arguing in a similar vein of criticism, Jacqueline Rose thinks that the concept of the *chora* is the least useful in Kristeva's terminology since it implies a primitive underside of culture that is repressed and hidden but also privileged and thus attaining a mythical status.[54] On a similar note, Judith Butler contests that the privileging of the semiotic is the dead end of a self-defeating strategy. On the one hand the semiotic is constant upheaval and a source of subversion, while on the other it cannot sustain itself but needs the symbolic as a source of negative support for its powers to emerge. In the end, the resistance of the semiotic only serves to reinforce the rule of the symbolic, since the semiotic is a territory beneath the law:

> By relegating the source of subversion to a site outside of culture itself, Kristeva appears to foreclose the possibility of subversion as an effective or realizable cultural practice. Pleasure beyond the paternal law can be imagined only with its inevitable impossibility.[55]

In other words, Fraser, Rose and Butler all designate the semiotic as a transgressive form of discourse and the symbolic as a conservative form of constraint. Consequently, the semiotic is described as the subversive undercurrent of the symbolic, as an untamed and asocial 'outside'. The weak link in Kristeva's dialectics, then, is her attempt to postulate the existence of a realm that the symbolic is attempting to repress, and to consider that realm to be loaded with a meaning that is hidden for and threatening to culture. The fact that this hidden aspect of culture is associated with the maternal realm makes it even more suspicious, since it implies that the maternal is associated with subversion as such, given that it is defined as a pre-Oedipal site, preceding symbolisation.

The question, however, is whether or not the semiotic is situated underneath, beyond or above the symbolic, as these critics tend to argue. It would appear that the tendency to blend in developmental language confuses the theoretical issues at stake. But if one considers that the semiotic is a term born out of Kristeva's materialism, rather than a concept describing a developmental stage of subjectivity, its role may well seem more challenging. The semiotic is not a transgressive, aggressive discourse, hidden underneath the symbolic. It is a dialectical construction, or theoretical supposition, neither preceding the symbolic nor holding a privileged place in relation to it: '[the semiotic] exists in practice only within the symbolic and requires the symbolic break to obtain the complex articulation we associate with it in musical and poetical practices'.[56] The fact that the semiotic and the *chora* belong to a pre-Oedipal dimension does not mean that they are to be considered developmental stages preceding the Oedipal construction of the symbolic. The semiotic, rather, indicates a resistance at work in the signifying process. It is not a murky undercurrent of language, but an aspect of it. It is best considered as that which demands a return to subjectivity and the axes of negativity dominating the subject, traversing the fields of representation in which the subject is buried. The semiotic, in other words, is a theoretical concept insisting a return to issues of subjectivity. Whereas a Marxist approach to dialectical materialism has been avoiding subjectivity, and structural linguistics has avoided affectivity and embodiment, Freud has shown that these are powerful aspects of human practices. Representing subjectivity, affectivity and embodiment, the semiotic is not presymbolic or presocial, it is *already an aspect of society and culture*. It is to be considered the resistance through which subjectivity makes itself known, irreducible to those social constructions of identity, gender and class through which individuals are being designated in the symbolic.

Considerations of non-representability

Developing the Freudian theory of the *dreamwork* and his notion of the primary process in particular, Kristeva shows that the production of signification is irreducible to meaning. In *The Interpretation of Dreams* Freud explains how the dream is created through what he calls its 'work'. This is not unimportant. The Freudian notion of work refers to a process that can never be reduced to a Marxist theory of values: the elements of the dream have no meaning (or value), but are constituted through a free play of associations. It is thus the theoretical model of the dreamwork that Freud brings into focus, and not the meaning (or value) of the dream. In this, Freudian theory offers an important correlative to Marx's version of dialectical materialism. Not only is the dream a semiotic system, but also more importantly the work behind it.[57] That work, is moreover, the definition of the unconscious itself, a transformative process rather than a repressed content in Freudian thought.

The elements of the dreamwork can be counted as four: condensation, displacement, considerations of representability and secondary elaboration. Condensation puts together several thoughts into one element, image or word. Displacement lets the manifest dream move its emotional weight, without letting the signs necessarily change. This allows for less important elements to get a prominent place in the dream, which would otherwise be difficult to explain. Central to Freud's theory is that the dream is a transcription of a latent content, transposing the dream thought into a manifest content or visual imagery. The dream thought is a kind of original text transposed onto what Freud calls the 'other stage'. The element of visualisation is crucial for the formation of the dream. The dream is like a picture, rather than a narrative, indicating the timelessness of the unconscious itself. It has to show everything, and there is a limit as to what can be shown. The dream cannot negate, or say no, says Freud. It cannot show contraries and contradictions. Lacking logical means, the dream still disposes of a kind of syntax of its own, which is ours to interpret if we hold the key to its workings. The element of the dreamwork striving towards visualisation is in German *Rücksicht auf Darstellbarkeit*, in English *considerations of representability*, in French *la figurabilité du rêve*. An active process behind the imagery of the dream, the third element is in fact a process of displacement. The words of the dream thought are being processed and displaced in order for a more visually gratifying language to serve as a blueprint. This displacement has one aim: to make the dream visual. But the images of the dream are not representations of the dream thought, or symbols with a given referent or a given meaning. All images are the result of a continuous process of condensation and displacement. And it is to that very process, the dreamwork itself, which the interpretation must refer. This second kind of displacement that occurs in the dream is not only of great theoretical interest but is also specially well calculated to explain the appearance of fantastic absurdity in which dreams are disguised. The direction taken by the displacement usually results in a colourless and abstract expression in the dream – thought being exchanged for a pictorial and concrete one.[58] The images of the dream are colourful displacements of the dream thought or the inscription, always striving towards the rich and visually saturated. Jean-Francois Lyotard has suggested that such striving for saturated, visual images equals the discursive desire incarnated by art; a desire carrying a weight and a density that is irreducible to the linguistic terms of representation. Freud's *The Interpretation of Dreams* is dominated by a desire for the figural; the *Darstellung* dominating the dream process begins and ends in the same opacity in which we find the creation of images in a work of art; these images work, produce, hide and reveal, all at the same time.[59] For that reason, it appears reductive to define the elements of the dreamwork as language, as has been done by Roman Jakobson. For Jakobson, one of the most prominent linguists to be used in literary theory, the connection between the unconscious and poetry can be named according to certain rhetorical figures, which Jakobson defines wholly linguistically. Jacques Lacan uses Jakobson's findings in his description of the structure of the unconscious in 'L'Instance de la lèttre dans l'inconscient' (1966). Metaphor is the figure of condensation. Lacan sees in the word *Verdichtung* the hidden word *Dichtung* as a crucial part of Freud's use of the term. Condensation is the truly creative element of the dream. Metonymy is the figure of desire and lack that can never stand on its own, be saturated on its own; it is a place in a chain. Metonymy is always a sign for the desire for something else.[60] The model of Jacobson is reducing the dreamwork to linguistics, whereas Lacan shows the displacing function of the dream to be a function of desire. The dream is always a form of transference.

Kristeva's own understanding of transferential displacement places the light on the transpositions of signs: *Darstellbarkeit*, the consideration of representability through which the relation between words and images becomes mobile and versatile. The imagery of the dream, says Freud, recreates the dream–thought into something visual. The words in the dream–thought are displaced so that they can be put up on the second stage: the stage of dream–imagery. The unconscious process displaces and condenses, creates new and absurd words, put together like riddles, or rebuses, secret signs that point towards a meaning that we can only understand if we hold the key to the transformation of discourse. Freud indicates a mobile relation between word and image where the dimension of textual productivity overshoots the actual images of the dream.[61] In *Revolution in Poetic Language* Kristeva is also particularly interested in the fact that the language of the dream arises from an infantile world, a remainder that has never been expressed in words. When Freud says that the dream is the fulfilment of an infantile wish, we have all reason to take this hypothesis seriously. The dream is trying to show what cannot be said, because the psychic layers it is representing originates at an age where the subject did not fully possess articulate language. The displacement is working towards the creation of images, but these images mean something only in the context of infantile desire, and have been visualised through the motility of the primary process.

Kristeva transposes Freud's analysis of the dreamwork to her analysis of poetic language, which is only partly linguistic: the most important feature of the dream is its impressive imagery. The visual quality of the dream constitutes a layer of representation, but it is not language as such, or language seen as symbolic order. It is a kind of surplus, which Kristeva calls the semiotic. The dreamwork thereby becomes the very model of poetic language, created through semiotic layers such as rhythm, prosody, figurability, saturating language with affects and transposes the question of signification to layers beyond the linguistic chains of metaphors and metonymies: a process of transposition between signs. Freud's description of consideration of representability, *Rücksicht auf Darstellbarkeit* is used by Kristeva to describe how poetic language creates meaning. Metaphor and metonymy create a kind of meaning that cannot be referred either to a transcendental or a symbolic subject. The third element in the dreamwork, the consideration of representability or figurability, is a form of transposition specifying 'the passage from one signifying system to another'. Through such a transposition, the subject position changes without becoming fixed: the two systems are permutable and flexed into one another.[62] The theory of language as transposition is particularly relevant in the kind of language Kristeva calls mimetic: the language in which an object is constructed without being represented or reproduced. Such a mimetic construction activates the dream–thought, a displaced version of something that has never been put into words, the navel of the dream, as Freud himself called it. In the motility of the primary process, the free circulation between words and images allows for those infantile affects and impressions to find representability, although not representations. The important thing is not the signs themselves, but rather the way in which they are processed, condensed, displaced in the transposition of one sign system to another and, above all, the way in which these processes mimic the positing of an object that Klein has told us is itself that of drives. Semiotic transpositions take place constantly and are determined by energies that Kristeva refers to as a specific, psychic site: the *chora*.

A revolution between pleasure and sacrifice

In Kristeva's model of transposition, the processes of displacement are unthinkable without the psychic investments of a corporeal subject. Whereas the Freudian theory of the interpretation of dreams may be a tool for the understanding of the subversion of representation as such – as we have seen in Jakobson and Lacan – Kristeva adds affectation and corporeal sensation to that subversion. Language, in Kristeva's model of mimetic transposition, is always tainted by an alterity infusing enjoyment. Mimetic transposition is resisting representation without offering any possibility of hegemonising such a resistance. In Kristeva's understanding, the mimetic object of the maternal body, or the *chora*, is reproduced in all signification. Her focus of analysis is directed precisely towards that object, making the relation between signifier and signified, word and thing, a less relevant and less poignant focus of analysis. The semiotic has been widely regarded as a challenging and potentially subversive aspect of language. What has been less commented upon, however, is that the *pleasure* taken in the semiotic revolution has a subversive significance in itself.

Correlative to experiences of pleasure and enjoyment are two kinds of sacrifice in Kristeva's thought. The first one, which will be considered in this section, relates to the process of signification. The second one, which will be considered in Chapters 3 and 4, relates to the social sphere and its creation of fixed identities through what Kristeva calls the socio-symbolic contract. The concept of pleasure has never been pre-eminent in the Marxist tradition and has also been made useless in the service of the left. Naturalised conceptions of pain and pleasure have, in Adorno's own critique, become transformed into cultural products. The cultural industry, in fact, lives off the overcoming of pain: after work, the entropy of pleasure slowly kills the distinction between leisure and work, and thereby the motivation for struggles: pleasure 'hardens' into boredom, as he puts it[63] – 'pleasure always means not to think about anything, to forget suffering even where it is shown. Basically it is helplessness. It is flight; not, as is asserted, flight from a wretched reality, but from the last remaining thoughts of resistance.'[64] The strategy of the pleasure industry, therefore, consists not in sublimating, but in repressing, and 'stimulating the unsublimated forepleasure which habitual deprivation has long since reduced to a masochistic semblance'.[65] This pleasure production of the culture industry, however, has its counterpart in the creation of the works of fine art where, as Fredric Jameson has pointed out, the distinction between pain and pleasure has been eradicated. Neither popular culture nor fine arts fulfil the promise of fullness, but whereas one is true to the suffering whereby the faith of happiness is upheld, the other is busy providing substitutes.[66] Slavoj Zizek, for his part, has argued that the production of pleasure has long since been overtaken by the unmistakable production of enjoyment, or the collapse of distinctions between suffering and pleasure, which the hypertrophied submission under strong, symbolic systems has produced both in post-communist Europe and the capitalist West.[67]

In order to reclaim pleasure in the service of a politics for the left one must therefore begin by quoting Barthes in his attempt to demythologise pleasure as a simple and rightist concept: the left has all too often been led to believe that pleasure is a 'simplist residue, at best the price to be gained at the end of a rationalist and concerned emancipatory project'.[68] Pleasure is always a contradiction, a contradiction inherent in the ambiguity of the word itself: the subject taking pleasure in the text, which *is* the subject of pleasure, is nothing but a 'living contradiction' – 'a split subject, who simultaneously enjoys, through the text, the consistency of his selfhood and its collapse, its fall'.[69] In Kristeva's work, pleasure has the same ambiguous status. The very concept of pleasure is, in Kristeva's early discourse, commensurable with enjoyment or *jouissance*; it is the enjoyment of the sons after the killing of the father – imbued with guilt but sexually loaded. This means that it is not used in the Lacanian sense, where enjoyment is opposed to pleasure. Kristeva's sexualised, embodied, semiotic and enjoying subject posits the Freudian notion of infantile, polymorphous sexuality as its motivator; such a subject is never dominated by a symbolic other to which the subject of Lacanian *jouissance* is given. Her use of the term *jouissance* or enjoyment is not the same as Lacan's. For Lacan, *jouissance* is a form of annihilation, a submission and sacrifice to the *jouissance* of the other. Lacan's enjoyment is the repetitive act of subjuga-tion under the enjoyment of the other and experienced as pain, not pleasure. Not confined within the logic of the pleasure principle, enjoy-ment is the going beyond of the pleasure principle, which constitutes the death-drive. Although there are elements of Lacanian *jouissance* as submis-sion in Kristeva's texts, the pre-Oedipal aspect of the subject tends to enjoy rather than suffer, and tends thus to have a nihilistic relation to the law rather than a submissive or masochistic one.

The pleasurable aspect of Kristeva's revolution has been almost forgotten. But it is crucial for her argument that the poetical language of the *chora* and the free motility of signs in the primary process is propelled by the pleasure principle. The little child enjoys its first wording, and takes pleasure in the oral formation of sounds. Infantile language, just like poetic language, is playful and affective. In aesthetic practices, signification is independent of a normative sociality. Driven primarily by pleasure, signification overcomes the repression instituted through the symbolic function. In other words, the subject is not determined by the foreclosure demanded by a normative social sphere, where the 'other' of the maternal body of enjoyment is simply lost and barred. When the sign is instituted in the place of the body, it produces not only repression but also a 'jubilant loss' mixed with aggression, turned against the object of mimetic transpo-sition (the maternal body). The subject thus comes to live with rejection and jubilant loss as part of the process of all signification. The primacy of the Oedipus complex as it has been upheld as the paradigm of psycho-analytical theorisation must be seen in this light: in the Greek myth, the bifurcation where the physical meeting between father and son takes place is also a metaphorical one – signification is instituted between desire and murder. Kristeva's own interpretation of the Oedipus complex and its dissolution through castration must be seen in this light; the process of symbolisation itself is eroticised. There is, therefore, a direct equivalence between phallic pleasure and the acquisition of language.[70] In the language of everyday communication, it is of course impossible to make use of such a pleasure. But there is one mode in which it can be reinvoked: in a language dominated by the semiotic, of tonality of music, of rhythm, a language in which the maternal body is no longer merely expelled, but reinvoked again as breasts, voice and skin. Language is not only meaning, It can also be an 'unlimited and unbounded generating process', neither anarchic, fragmented nor schizophrenic, but a structuring and destructuring passage to 'the outer *boundaries* of subject and society. Then – and only then – can it be jouissance and revolution'.[71] In fact, Kristeva's notion of the political is inseparable from her emphasis on the *pleasure* of semiosis. Her use of pleasure can be related to Freud's economic model of instincts, and above all to a Freudian concept of sexuality situated at a limit between the somatic and the psychic (rather than the libido).[72]

Kristeva's subject is always one of corporeal (sexual) pleasure and her use of the term pleasure never leaves the instinctual logic of the Freudian theory of sexuality: enjoyment is the corporeal experience of pleasure, the sensibilisation of erotic zones and of the whole body. In *Three Essays on the Theory of Sexuality* (1905), Freud shows that infantile sexuality, as experienced and obliterated in memory in the so-called prehistory of the individual, is awakened not through the genitals but through other zones satisfying the auto-erotic impulses of the individual. To these zones belong the mouth and the pleasure of thumb-sucking, which in Freud's view is a continuation of the gratification gained in the sucking of the mother's breast: 'No one who has seen a baby sinking back satiated from the breast and falling asleep with flushed cheeks and a blissful smile can escape the reflection that this picture persists as a prototype of the expression of sexual satisfaction in later life.'[73] However, sexual gratification is later separated from the needs of nourishment, in the process where the child begins to discover his own auto-erogenous zones. Any region of the body, says Freud, can serve this function. The child has a polymorphous-perverse disposition and can therefore be seduced into all kinds of transgression. Also, sexual difference is not yet explored in the pregenital phase, and sexuality is more to be characterised by passivity or activity, the latter of which may contain an aggressive and sadistic factor that Freud relates to anal impulses. More important for the sensibilisation of the body than the actual zone of the body is the kind of stimulus it receives. What is characteristic of auto-erotic stimulation, says Freud, and therefore of the production of pleasure, is that it is supported by some kind of rhythm. This goes for the oral, anal, muscular sensations that are being discussed in Freud's categorisations. Sucking, licking, stimulating, etc. always have a rhythmic character. The sensibilisation of the body, in other words, driven by what Freud calls partial impulses, is awakened through such a rhythmic stimulation. It is this rhythmic sensibilisation that Kristeva sees at work in the signifying process. Desire, says Kristeva, in contradistinction to Lacan, does not suffice to explain the signifying process. Desire, in fact, is superseded by a movement that surpasses the desiring structures: this movement is called 'rejection', or expenditure. All signifying practices, that is language, poetry, art, etc., find their precondition in the movement of rejection. This does not mean, however, that rejection is at the origin of language. Rejection, rather, is a movement of negativity, or return, and it designates the instinctual and repetitive act of return to a prelinguistic mode of signification.[74] This is, for Kristeva a corporeal act, involving the organs in the service of the pleasure principle: mouth, anus. In the article 'The Negation', Freud posits that expulsion is a first move towards symbolisation, where an object is constituted through negation: I am not this. In this logic, the pleasure principle seems to be in the service of repression, since it creates unification: there is indeed no difference between inside and outside in this logic, and there is no need for renunciation for pleasure. Expulsion, however, acts against the consequences of repression. Expulsion, and its symbolic correlative in the sign, releases man from the compulsive dominance of the pleasure principle. Judgement, the capacity of distancing oneself and of intellectual work, is put in place as the symbolic end of the economy of the drive. This means, according to Kristeva, that Freud, in the end dissociates the symbolic function from pleasure, and that

> the only way to react against the consequences of repression imposed by the compulsion of the pleasure principle is to renounce pleasure through symbolisation by setting up the sign through the absence of the object, which is expelled and forever lost.[75]

What Freud does, then, is to distinguish between expulsion and pleasure, a move that Kristeva is opposing. Expulsion, she argues, is itself motivated by pleasure. This pleasure may later be repressed. It can, however, return and combined with oral pleasure disturb and dismantle the symbolic function.[76] The pleasure derives from the anal drive, or anality, which is the sadistic component of sexuality, according to Freud. This sadism is harboured by *jouissance* in which repressed, sublimated repression is unburied. In Kristeva's archaeology of the process of symbolisation, and therefore of subjectivity in itself, the oral, urethral, anal and muscular pleasure that is taken in the sensational process of discharge is the precondition for language itself. In expulsion, the body is posited as an object in a moment of enjoyment, before the dialectic between body and sign is put in place under the hospice of the desexualised symbolic order. Expulsion, therefore, has an ambivalent function. On the one hand it is the first step towards the desexualised discourse of the Other, where sexuality is a question of identification with the Oedipal order. On the other, the moment of expulsion itself is one of pleasure, a pleasure that will always be retrievable in a language challenging a desensitised order of discourse.

The sensitising of language, argues Kristeva, happens precisely through rhythm, alliteration, repetition, all those infantile means that seem to bring children such pleasure in the acquisition of language. But also in the use of figurative language such as metaphoricity, for instance. And since language is always the transposition of one set of signs to another, undergoing the processes of displacement and condensation that Freud has told us belong to the primary process in the production of signification, one could argue that it is in fact the sensitised language or discourse, the language of pleasure, in which signification actually takes place, whereas as a desensitised of desexualised discourse does nothing to produce new forms of signification. Sexuality is radically heterogeneous, offering a language and thought that are never sublimated in the symbolic, but one aspect of sexual enjoyment as such.[77]

Such is poetic language of the revolution, propelled by the pleasure principle. The text of the avant-garde is the annihilation of the literary work, and the annihilation of one meaning (*un sens*). Inhabiting the text, the subject is enjoying the pulverisation and differentiation of the textual body. But it cannot be an uninterrupted flow of enjoyment. All revolutions must end with decapitation, or the sacrifice of pleasure. Kristeva's books all explore the movement between surge, challenge, revolt, subversion, and the necessary loss or sacrifice that any revolution will necessarily claim. Sacrifice, in this context, is a condition for symbolisation and signification. The negativity defining the subject is in fact the term of a dialectical process, which could be described as a pulsating movement, instituted by the death-drive and its correlative the pleasure principle. Symbolisation is made possible through the death-drive rather than the libido, the death-drive being the repetition motivating the symbol in place of the absent thing. This process also represents a moment in which the body itself becomes an absence in relation to the sign, and foreign to itself in this respect. The death-drive defines subjectivity as the result of a sacrificial logic, balancing the enjoyment of the semiotic:

> Sacrifice sets up the symbol and the symbolic order at the same time, and this 'first' symbol, the victim of a murder, merely represents the structural violence of language's irruption as the murder of soma, the transformation of the body, the captation of drives.[78]

Sacrifice is accompanied by a semiotisation of the drives, be that in the form of the cult of dance and music, as in the tragedies and the Dionysian festival they were part of, or other religious services. Sacrifice is proceeded by animality, which takes the form of the semiotic expressions such as song, dance, music. The animality and semiotisation miming the sacrifice is not the practice of violence, but the end of violence. Sacrifice is the institutionalisation of sacred representations, the theologisation of the rupture of the drives.[79] There are two sides to the sacred and the sacrifice: on the one hand installation of social norms and bonds through ritual, and on the other the sacred evokes those uncertain spaces where identity and norms are installed. Phallic culture is also a mystery culture: referring to the veil and the mystery of the plies of the veil.[80] Since sacrifice is the theologisation of the rupture of the drive, revolt and mystery belong to the same logic of recovery of the body which has proceeded the symbolic rupture.[81] This explains why, for Kristeva, there is one more social event that accompanies sacrifice at the institutionalisation of the symbol. This is the event that has lived on from ancient times up until now as art. Art represents the flowing of *jouissance* into language, transgressing the sacrifice of the body that has to take place in the social order: 'We thus find sacrifice and art, face to face, representing the two aspect of the thetic function: the prohibition of *jouissance* by language and the introduction of *jouissance* into and through language.'[82] In approaching ritualistic sacrifice to the working of poetry and art, Kristeva is attempting to show that there will always be practices of enjoyment present at the limits of the dominant social order, practices that will both threaten and challenge the origins of its own institution. This double face of the sacred and of art will create religious and artistic rituals of ambiguity. On the one hand they will ascertain the values of faith, while on the other they will assure the enjoyment of transgression. In practice, we can see this ambiguity not least in the rituals of defilement evoking the holy ritualistic abject. Secular filth becomes sacred defilement.[83] Naturally, the defiled, the object of sacrifice, holds an extraordinary position: it is the abject, both excluded and found again through the repetitive act of sacrifice. The movement between surge, challenge, revolt, subversion, and the necessary loss or sacrifice that any revolution will necessarily claim recuperates new possibilities into the life of the subject. A productive form of sacrifice is necessitated by symbol-formation and motivated by the drive itself.

The promotion of such a pleasurable revolution, through art and other forms of transgression, may well be considered irrelevant or frivolous. But the fact is: the political arena is already steeped in regression and affectation. Right-wing groups know very well how to make politics out of the economy of the drive: nationalism, authoritarianism, xenophobia, homophobia, etc. are all examples of political attitudes investing in the drive. Political fixations are often commanded by an ideal that refuses reality in favour of libidinal or sublimated form of gratification. There is a direct link between political dogmatism and the refusal to give up on that gratification, directed by the drive and shooting through the demarcation line between fascination and horror, heroic subversion and perverted disintegration. A revolution between pleasure and sacrifice may well, in fact, act against the economy of drives fuelling such investments. And the reason why the left may want to re-explore a politics that affirms the semiotic,

31

oscillating between pleasure and sacrifice, is that it may, in actual fact, be a safeguard against a politics of the drive, exploiting mechanisms of exaggerated identification and nationalism.[84] The upset of the semiotic is formulated not beyond the social framework, but within it. And the question is: do we respond to that upset with the erection of even more norms, or are we capable of accepting the ambiguity? The revolution-revolt is accompanied by pleasure that may act against the economy of drives fuelling political illusion. A politics of pleasure is, in actual fact, a safeguard against a politics of the drive. Returning to the question of the relation between pleasure and the left, we may perhaps conclude that the revolution of the semiotic does not challenge or change norms for any given reasons, or with any given goals in mind. It takes pleasure in challenging them, going through the motions of displacement and destabilisation. But it is precisely its unwillingness to simply replace one norm instead of another, or to erect a stronger law in the place of a weak one, which makes the semiotic into such a powerful political concept. It lives in ambiguity, rather than deteriorates into fixations.

2

A THEORIST AESTHETICS

From terrorism to theorism

In the beginning of the 1970s, the political question of terrorism was made acute in Europe through violent underground organisations such as the Baader-Meinhof, Brigado Rosso, IRA and ETA. But the politics of terrorism was placed on the agenda also by leftist organisations that were up and out in the open. The Maoist newspaper *La Cause du people*, sold in the streets of Paris by, among others, Jean-Paul Sartre and Simone de Beauvoir, argued for a so-called ethical terrorism. In order to be considered ethical, a terrorist attack must fulfil certain criteria: the target of violence must be hated by the people, innocent people must not get hurt, and the political explication of the act must be made clear both before and after the event. If these criteria are fulfilled the act would contribute to show who the real terrorists are, namely the police and the *patrons*, or capitalist exploiters.[1] Today, terrorism is connected with catastrophe and worship of death. In the 1970s, however, the support for 'ethical terrorism' was at least semi-accepted on the far left; given that such terrorism was supposed not to perform indiscriminate mass murders but rather violent demonstrations limited on casualties. Correspondingly, the threat of terrorism was also very real for those fearing social and political upheaval.

The *Tel Quel* group could certainly be branded as 'terroristic' in theory: the strategy they chose in relation to the cultural and academic establishment was inspired by the terrorist's total rejection of prevalent political discourses. Rather than debate with the establishment on its own terms, the *Tel Quel* group identified with society's 'outside', and the dissident's ambitions of upheaval. Their main goal was to create alternative discourses of political subversion, through theory for instance. For the *Tel Quel* group, subversive theorisation was not an alternative to revolutionary activities such as activism and demonstrations. It was another kind of revolution, aiming to transpose and translate political activity into discursive subversion. Theoretical activism could also prove to be violent and subversive, far from an impotent armchair activity. They succeeded in their aims. The cultural and academic establishment did in fact deeply fear, or at least resent, the *Tel Quel* group. Their highly abstract and scientistic theorisation of avant-garde literature was considered destructive and therefore as something that must be fought. Although it did perhaps not threaten society's fabric overall, the *Tel Quel* discourse was successfully challenging the language and social construction of cultural and academic institutions.[2]

Aiming to politicise theory and to theorise politics, the *Tel Quel* journal could be regarded as a training ground for textual activism. Originally conceived as a publication promoting a new kind of aesthetic, it gradually came to aspire towards subversion of those areas of life not usually considered political: aesthetics, culture and family life. Theory was the means to effect such all-encompassing subversion, not only substituting but also dismissing political discourse as a weapon for actual political change. The dismissal of political discourse and the search for other weapons for radical political change implies, of course, that the project of the *Tel Quel* group is argued in the same terms as the terroristic project: dismissing the scenes of political argumentation, another space of action was explored in a violent manner. As Kristeva's autobiographical novel *Les Samouraïs* implies, they were not particularly dedicated to activism. Instead, the aim was to make theory subversive. Theory was transposed into *theorism*, a kind of terrorism in writing.[3] Aiming to reveal the constrictions and restraints of normatively instituted discourse, and then to challenge those restraints, the *theorism* of the *Tel Quel* group made theoretical language into a kind of activism in itself.

Theorism appeals to an 'outside' of political discourse, a space of subversion more efficient and more 'true' to the political. Rather than promoting the cause of repressed identities and classes, rather than ideologically motivated statements, theorism works through subversion. The dismissal of political discourse is shown, rather than stated, demonstrated rather than phrased. The oppression it is revolting against is assumed, not provoked: theorism not as action *for* something but as rejection and revolt. Decision-making, deliberation, lawmaking and so forth are given little consideration. Any kind of goal-oriented politics is shown disdain, owing to experiences of disappointment: 'I belong to a generation that no longer believes in the miraculous political solution. We try not to be political.'[4] This is not weakness, since political commitment has little chance of offering the kinds of truth that are needed. Political commitment, rather, offers a kind of security blanket: 'it settles the subject within a socially justified illusion'.[5] In the nineteenth century, the political was no longer fused with freedom. Instead, politics has become one with a totalitarian vision, levelling and exhausting.[6]

Kristeva's own theorism is intrinsically intertwined with her feminism, formulated as a response to the desperate need for an alternative to the double-bind created by patriarchal powers, forcing the subject into a position of authoritarian mimicry. Either phallic power is allowed to act as a force of subjection, or it is mimicked and overthrown. In her essay on 'Women's Time' Kristeva examines the political potential of terroristic attitudes. When the essay was written, in 1977, the frustration of the European left had paved the way for such organisations as the Brigado Rosso in Italy, and the Baader-Meinhof league in Germany. Many of the terrorists were women, and Ulrike Meinhof in particular had become a mythical figure among radicals. Asking why so many women have become attracted to terrorism, the essay rejects the sacrificial logic implicated by the social contract. Through that logic, women are deemed to fall outside of the institutions through which symbolic representations of power are upheld. The various strategies of feminism have all been fraught with some kind of deficiency in relation to the symbolic. Feminine language is yet to take shape in the modern age, given that women have not gone past several stages in their struggle towards independence. The emancipatory movement of women can be divided into three waves, all of which may well exist at the same time. First comes the English wave of liberal feminism in which women demand access to the symbolic order in terms of equality and rights. Second comes radical feminism in which women reject the male symbolic order in the name of difference. A third era could offer possibilities representing Kristeva's own position, where women reject the dichotomy between masculine and feminine as metaphysical and as a constraint construed according to a given socio-symbolic contract. If feminism does not recognise that its political options are dependent on such contractual constructions of female identity, it will not come to terms with the shortcomings of the liberal and radical model on offer. Through the socio-symbolic contract currently dominating Western societies, women are deemed either to remain in a situation of symbolic deficiency in relation to men (the radical option) or to sacrifice part of their identity (the liberal option). The contract itself is fraught with a castrating violence offering little space for women to negotiate symbolic representations of empowerment: 'modern feminism has only been but a moment in the interminable process of coming to consciousness about the implacable violence (separation, castration, etc.) which constitutes any symbolic contract'.[7] So why do women join terrorist groups? Because they do not subscribe to either the socio-symbolic contract or its counter-investment represented by the feminist options available.[8] The representations of empowerment available – liberal and radical – are both implicated in the castrating violence of the symbolic. So what happens when women 'refuse power and create a parallel society, a counter-power which then takes on aspects ranging from a club of ideas to a group of terrorist commandoes?'[9] Such a counter-movement can only manage to create a simulacrum of the society of power. In choosing between 'the terror of power or the power of terrorism' women find themselves caught in an impossible situation. The power of terrorism is a response to the violence of a socio-symbolic contract, but not a way out of the deadlock. Terrorist groups do not oppose themselves to terrorist regimes but act against liberal systems. Although the stated accusation against the system may show that it is oppressive, the terroristic impulse indicates something else. The unconscious accusation against the system, hidden under the belief in a fight for liberation, is not that it is too oppressive but rather that it is too weak. The terroristic motivation is built on an unconscious desire for strength and authoritarian structures, rather than emancipatory demands. Such a desire brings us straight back to the arms of an archaic, phallic mother. The desire for power is a desire for a utopian, all-encompassing archaic mother, redeeming the frailty and anxiety of the kind of powerlessness that comes with the existential concerns of the subject. The unconscious motive of terrorism is the belief in and longing for a kind of supremacy that can only be found in the fantasy of the archaic mother. Women are forever separated from that mother, and can rejoin her only through childbirth or possibly homosexuality. Terrorism, on the other hand, is a fruitless symptom produced by anxiety and loss.[10]

However, it is precisely in offering an impossible political alternative that terrorism comes to reveal a truth inherent in the crisis of contemporary politics.[11] 'Truth' is then no longer a logical or ontological category, but bound up with the real or that which has been foreclosed – through symbolic decapitation – in the subject, and bound up with a traversal of those fantasies that psychoanalysis has taught us will always contain a grain of truth. If we are to develop a Freudian notion of truth we must always begin with *Moses and Monotheism*, in which Freud explains that we are prone to invest in an illusion we believe to be true. Such an idea of truth is intrinsically bound up with religious investments in an absolute law. From a psychoanalytic point of view, however, truth is something that can only be discovered. It is a mechanism of displacement, discoverable through the Freudian work that 'confronts it in its safest haven, religion, destroys it as *identity* (Being, correspondence to Being, etc.) and leaves behind only a system of passages, folds, thresholds, catastrophes – in short, negation'.[12] Freudian truth confronts those mechanisms that remain foreclosed and displaced onto the real in the production of the religious illusion of an absolute authority: that real revealing itself as alterity, strangeness, disavowal of identity, separation and murder.[13] If terrorism is the real of political discourse, then, it is because its operations of violence and its credo of disavowal forces us to confront all those illusions of dominating power structures as based in an absolute law. Through terrorism we are forced to traverse illusions about the law as an absolute, an illusion that has its origin in the Judeo-Christian tradition confronted by Freud. The religious illusion is based on a logic in which one can only grasp the absolute status of the law through the mechanisms of murder and disavowal. Terrorism sacrifices to the illusion of an absolute law, whose face continues to withdraw. The problem with terrorism is not that it finds the law too strong and oppressive but rather that it cannot face the weakness, instability and motility that marks a secular, modern society. Terrorism is the true-real of politics because it forces us to face our own desire to sacrifice to that fleeting, disappearing law, and live in a disavowal made all the stronger in the wake of its absence.

The unconscious and the question of emancipation

Jürgen Habermas, representing another aspect of the intellectual left of the 1960s, brings psychoanalysis into the service of emancipation through 'providing a rational basis for the precepts of civilization'.[14] Whereas Marx lacks it, Freud has a reflective knowledge of the origins of institutions that always carries a pathological component that calls for their overcoming, through traversing the function of illusions, power and ideology. There is a decisive tension between political engagement and psychoanalysis that corresponds to the division of modern society into a public sphere of communication and the distortions of the unconscious. A combination of hermeneutic understanding and causal explanation obtains explanatory power in psychoanalysis. Psychoanalysis can only become a force of emancipation in so far as it 'cures' language of these distortions, showing that meaning structure is threatened by internal conditions; what needs to be established, according to Habermas, are the biographical connections that make up the meaning structure of the self-understanding of an individual. When these fail, a memory or a connection between life events has become inaccessible to the subject. Psychoanalysis, therefore, is governed by a hermeneutic impulse in which the disturbed memory function is supplanted by an explanation that reinstalls a coherent meaning structure. If the meaning structure is ruptured, the subject has been unable to communicate with itself. Consequently, the subject deceives itself about itself in expressions that are not properly co-ordinated: parapraxes, forgetting, slips of the tongue, misreadings, bungled actions, chance actions. Neuroses distort symbolic structures in three dimensions: language, action, bodily experience. The analyst reads the dreamwork, the process of distortion, although a layer of symbolic content remains that resists interpretation that makes us relieve the pathological condition. Resistance, according to Habermas, is an intrapsychic social agency, excluded from public communication. The very construction of the unconscious, then, builds on distortions of that which withdraws from the sphere of communication. Freud's model of the dreamwork as the realisation of a desire superseded from infantile life is a model transferred onto all pathological forms of behaviour: 'wrong behaviour means every deviation from the model of the language game of communicative action, in which motives of action and linguistically expressed intentions coincide'.[15] Psychoanalysis therefore can be used where 'the text of our everyday language games are interrupted by incomprehensible symbols. These symbols cannot be understood because they do not obey the grammatical rules of ordinary language, norms of action, and culturally learned patterns of expression'.[16] The subject has a communication disturbance with itself that analysis serves to correct. The task of analysis, then, is to encourage self-reflection.

Of course Habermas's account of psychoanalysis brings us far from the ethos of Kristeva, in which the task of psychoanalysis is not to hinder the processes of displacement and transposition but rather to affirm and encourage such processes beyond the constraints of rationality. Symptoms are not deviations from the language game of communicative action, but transformations typical of language itself. The unconscious is not a hidden content, but the transformations taking place in the processes of transposition. In referring to psychoanalysis as an emancipatory project, Habermas notes with surprise that Freud does not include reconciliation into his metapsychological concepts: 'Strangely enough, the structural model denies the origins of its own categories in a process of enlightenment.'[17] There is no rational, reconciliatory ego, only an ego showing itself in pathological modes, through defences and displacements, split off from its other, the symptom. There is no way to reconcile the ego with its other in psychoanalytic terms. This is what Habermas regrets. This is, however, what Kristeva applauds, and makes her forward the subject of psychoanalysis at the cost of the self. The main dynamic of psychoanalysis is not to aid rationality, but to show a tension inherent in language itself that is deeply perturbing, and a dialectical mechanism produced within the splitting of the subject. In this way, psychoanalysis can never 'cure' pathologies, only recast them through a form of sublimation in which the processes of displacement continue. When Habermas argues that the goal for psychoanalysis is 'providing a rational basis for the precepts of civilization',[18] he misunderstands that psychoanalysis is overtly working towards, not against, the displacing processes set in motion by the unconscious. As such, its practice can never be detached from the transpositions of the primary process itself. The reason for this is, however, not that it promotes the irrational, but rather that it considers all forms of signification, all cultural forms and institutions, to be affected by these forms of transpositions, The unconscious is not underneath culture, but a presence in all cultural forms.

The political dimension of the unconscious does not merely lie in the subversive power of a repressed content, but in the fact that it creates a factor of instability that undermines linguistic norms, categories of social identity, and the desexualised discourse of politics. Kristeva herself calls this factor of instability the heterogeneous element of a symbolising logic that takes dialectical materialism as its point of departure. This means that all signifying practices may well take place in a social order, but are irreducible to their social dimensions, of class and gender for instance. The destabilising factor defined as heterogeneous to the social sphere is intertwined with affect and with corporeal memory: the semiotic. An excessive form of expenditure, the semiotic is: 'semantico-syntactic anomaly, erotic excess, social protest, jouissance'.[19] Many feminists, such as Toril Moi, Seyla Benhabib and Nancy Fraser, have commented upon the progressive potential of such a destabilising and displacing factor. At the same time, however, they are protesting against the lack of social and political definition: how are we to find new forms of solidarity in a theory celebrating destabilisation and transgression? The weakness of a theorist discourse would lie in its inability to help construct a feasible project for the left. The transposition of the political from the public sphere to subjective experiences remains a problem. According to Terry Eagleton, the political correlative of her thought of the semiotic is, he argues, some kind of anarchism. And anarchism, or simply the unending overthrow of fixed structures, is as inadequate in theory as it is in politics. The idea that a literary text undermining meaning should be revolutionary is simply wrong-headed: 'It is quite possible for a text to do this in the name of some right-wing irrationalism, or to do it in the name of nothing at all.'[20] Echoing a similar kind of criticism against the hidden reactionary trait in de(con)structivism, Dorothy Leland says that

> feminism needs to move beyond the rejection of existing social codes to the construction of new, more equitable social, economic, and political relations. Kristeva's view of revolutionary politics is thus inadequate for two reasons: it rejects too much and it hopes or aims for too little.[21]

Anthony Elliott is critical of Kristeva's incapacity to fully distance herself from the Lacanian model in which the law is omnipotent, lack made into an authentic foundation of the subject and the self in turn narcissistic and derivative. Undercutting possibilities of representation means undercutting visions of social bonds that become regarded as terroristic instead. Although her model is more open to transformations than the Lacanian one to transformations of the imaginary, her model is doomed since it does not leave the destructive folds of the Lacanian concept of the subject as lack, rather than investigating the Freudian belief in the ego's development out of primary narcissism.[22] What these criticisms all have in common is that they reject the emphasis on negativity and the lack of constructive phases of the imaginary: calling for a vision in which a social bond is manifested and realised. Such a criticism does not, however, correspond to the actual challenges of a theory of the political in which such emphasis on a constructive imaginary is radically undercut; the result being less of relativism and anarchism than a displacement of political processes from the construction of social and symbolic bonds to complex forms of subjectivity situated at the very limits of such bonds. Such a model does not entail a denial of the legitimacy of modern democracies, social contracts and dominating discourses of political negotiation, but it shows that the institution-

alisation of such contracts may result in exclusion and repression. The terrorist may be an extreme example, but the feminist is not; the problems discussed in feminism indicate that modern subjectivities – and not just 'women' – conceive of themselves as caught in a double-bind in relation to socio-economic institutions of power. As long as socio-symbolic and economic institutions continue to regulate political negotiations, thereby maintaining the double-bind in relation to the political subject, then the true possibilities of the political must be conceived of as a form of 'revolt', that is as a productive form of negativity harboured not in public discourses where the socio-symbolic contract is already accepted and naturalised, but in subjectivities in which that double-bind is bared and challenged.

The lack of an emancipatory project in Kristeva's writings is due to the fact that the practice of political negotiation and its correlative in social identities is considered less important than the revolutionary practices taking place in the space of signification: issues of empowerment and representation are being displaced onto issues of signification in order to avoid destructive forms of investment in power figures and ideologies. In order to safeguard the revolutionary potential of signifying practices, these areas of life must be kept apart. The task of revolutionary discourse is not to demand a new kind of politics, but to find a way out of the double-bind created by phallic constructions of power. Emancipatory demands of empowerment threaten to remain within the terms of the double-bind. Rather than pointing to what kind of projects that could possibly lend themselves to realisation in political and social life, and that threaten to become objects of fixation in a phallic structure of meaning and power, she is designating those areas as political that offer resistance against symbolic fixations and representations, and make new subjectivities emerge. Moi, Eagleton, Leland, Elliott and Fraser are all asking for ways of constructing political identities and solidarities out of Kristeva's theory. We have already seen, however, that Kristeva refuses the necessity of such a translation from theory to practice. Theorism being a practice in itself, it elevates the subversive potential of other signifying practices. Subversion is not *supposed* to be translated into a politics of emancipation, justice or recognition. The subject of the *chora* is not a social one, conscious and aware of its oppression and its rights. It is semiotic transposition, unconscious and unaware of the values to which any politics of emancipation must subscribe. This does not make it politically impotent. An apolitical subject is rather a social one, staked out through given forms of symbolic exchange. The other subject is political precisely because it offers a space unimpaired by socio-symbolic limitations. The apparent asociality of such a notion of the political is therefore what makes it subversive. A political subject does not emerge through its demands; only in signifying practices of transposition can subjectivity expand beyond its socio-symbolic limitations.[23] Therefore, there is decisive tension between the ethos of psychoanalysis and political emancipation. The most pressing issue is not if Kristeva has an adequate understanding of the politics of emancipation, but if the social and the political can be regarded as continuously conflicting terms in one and the same subject.

From negation to negativity

Diana Coole has rightly pointed out that Kristeva's theory can be defined as a politics of negativity. Suggesting that negativity is a dominating aspect of the politics of modernity, Coole wants to draw attention to philosophy's capacity of thinking about that which lies beyond the scope of political theory. In her discussion of negativity in such diverse philosophers as Kant, Nietzsche and Adorno, she has pointed to a highly diverse tradition of thought where social transformation is a continuous process of differentiation. It cannot be theorised in one form. Social thought must therefore take diverse forms of negativity into consideration. The political, although it must define the domain of collective life, ought also to negotiate all levels of intersubjective life that are an 'unstable, dynamic process' that can never fully be defined through political institutions and strategies that are 'themselves in process'.[24] If we are to define a politics of negativity, it would be deferring issues of relevance from rooms of negotiation to other spaces. Placing Kristeva in such a context is certainly useful, and Coole rightly includes the semiotic in such a politics of negativity. Like Moi and Fraser, Coole notes that the semiotic is a useful theoretical tool to account for the destabilisation of social and symbolic norms. Unlike the latter, however, Coole does not demand that a politics of negativity be transformed into strategic negotiations of symbolic representation; a politics of negativity is rather indicating that such representative forms remain inadequate in relation to transformation, change and differentiation.

The distinction between negation and negativity used by Kristeva is inspired by Hegel, who in *Phenomenology of Spirit* introduced the conception of negation in order to explain the historical movement of self-consciousness. Hegel, also, placed the concept of negation in the material realm or the realm of things, overcoming the distinction between consciousness and materiality. Things eventually affirm themselves as 'negation of negations', negation becoming a mode of affirmation in a movement that produces distinctions. It is this very movement or process of negation that is called negativity. Hegelian negativity is, in Kristeva's conception and following Lenin, the fourth term of the dialectic, but the very term that determines Hegel's own conception of Being. Negativity is the 'indissoluble relation between an "ineffable" mobility and its "particular determination"'.[25] It is the very motivation of the dialectic, overcoming negation and producing distinctions through a dissolving movement, which in the end becomes a mode of affirmation. In its highest form, negativity is freedom. In her critique of post-Hegelian materialist philosophy, Kristeva points to the fact that dialogical conceptions of the negative forget about negativity; that force which in Hegel creates the moment in which the movement of negation becomes differentiation. And yet it is through the force of negativity, she argues, that negation is brought into substance, into the world of culture and social distinctions.[26] Her own reading of Hegel, also, indicates a move away from ideologies advocating a notion of revolution that would appear as a sudden break. Any abstract imposition of freedom, Hegel has shown, is doomed to fail. There is no space for political terrorism; the introduction of the force of negativity makes any such actions not only vile but also intrusive. *Terror* is the face of death encountered in absolute freedom, a moment in which death has no significance 'for what is negated is the empty point of the absolutely free self'.[27] Thus, one cannot simply realise freedom in terms of an abstraction, or a form of self-consciousness that remains abstract in itself; such realisation of the absolute turns from the positive realisation of thought to the negative differentiation of substance. Absolute freedom, therefore, shudders at the terror provoked by its own realisation and turns to a production of differences that one may, perhaps, call a fear of death or self-annihilation, The movement of negation can never complete itself as absolute freedom. What happens is rather that culture and ethical life is transformed. Kristeva therefore draws two conclusions: first, that Hegelian negativity is the beginning of dialectical materialism, and, second, that it is the beginning of an understanding of the subject-in-process, and of subjectivity as revolutionary activity. But although Kristeva's conception of negativity is indebted to Hegel, it cannot be understood as a mere adaptation of his thought. Whereas the Hegelian subject is a conceptual one, Kristeva's is primarily corporeal; it can only be conceived of through what she herself insists to be a 'heterogeneous' dialectics.[28]

The thinker to open the question of a negativity beyond Hegel's disembodied spirit is Freud. In his short article 'Die Verneinung' (1925a), Freud links the function of negativity not only to thought and language, but also to repression. For a psychoanalyst, says Freud, a negation is always a form of denial; if a patient denies a certain trail of association this means that it has actually presented itself to him but he denies its relevance – 'negation is a way of taking cognisance of what is repressed; indeed it is already a lifting of the repression, though not, of course, an acceptance of what is repressed'.[29] In the process, affect and intellectual acceptance are separated, a process installing the capacity of judgement. The subject of judgement distinguishes between itself and the object, between inside and outside. He is capable of setting up limits and borders, and of separating fantasy and reality. Moreover, the agent of judgement is capable of representing through language: of naming objects and of differentiating between them. The function of symbolisation has its origin in the capacity to negate. Another dimension overshooting the order of negation is then added: negativity. Negation installs the ego at the cost of a loss: body and affectivity and symbolic language are separated. Negativity, however, *negates that loss* and reintroduces the body and affects associated with embodiment into the function of language. The symbolising movement of negation is intertwined with the pulsation of the drives. The subject suffused by negativity is opened onto and by objectivity; he is 'mobile, nonsubjected, free'.[30] The Hegelian conception of negativity is insufficient in that it proposes the subject of freedom to be a unit, capable of overcoming the contradictions inherent in the movement of negation where concept and reality are opposed and overcome. Kristeva, however, proposes that the movement is never overcome. Negativity prevents symbolisation from becoming hypostasised. It is an affirmative pulsation of the death-drive, or a productive dissolution. The semiotic, traversing the symbolic, is neither oppositional nor complementary. It is bound to forces of expenditure and rejection: 'the sole function of our use of the term "negativity" is to designate the process that exceeds the signifying subject, binding him to the laws of objective struggles in nature and society'.[31] A principle of mobility, negativity breaks through static structures and motivates new formations of subjectivity and social and economic relations.

The subject, then, is constituted through negation on the one hand and negativity on the other. Whereas negation is a function of symbolisation making identity possible, negativity is the 'mythical' force of the drives splitting and traversing the self. The function of symbolisation or the capacity to use language is closely intertwined with the function of identity or the capacity to constitute a self. The moment the subject is capable of judgement, he is also capable of separating himself from the object: 'I am not this.' The subject, therefore, can never have an identity determined in positive terms, and it will always be determined through negation; an aspect of the subject will set itself up against and in contradiction to social and linguistic norms. This phenomenon is, for Kristeva, the most important mark of subjectivity. The process of becoming can never be reduced to a secure identity. The formation of subjectivity is linked to a 'process of rejection which pulsates through the drives in a body that is caught within the network of nature and society'.[32] The body of negativity is rejection, a body that is, however, already social. Rejection is, in fact, a social function, although it may be articulated in the form that Freud would call drives; the kind of rejection that leads to the positing of an outside, of an object, through the repetitive formation of a symbol in the place of an absence. Negativity is a pulsating mode of rejection. Negation is a mode of control, a position in which the subject can be designated in the symbolic. Negativity, on the other hand, is that part of the subject-in-process which operates in and through the process of signification, through the processes of rejection. The pulsating movement of negativity undoes the unifying processes of social discourse As such, it produces new social and cultural forms. That which has been expulsed and rejected can never be fully intellectualised, or successfully repressed. Negation can never 'conquer' or undo the subversive forces of negativity.

The subject caught between negation and negativity is a paranoid one: trying to overcome the schizophrenia of the split inherent in self-consciousness. In other words: there is no 'neutral' ground on which these splits can be thought, they are always caught in the social game of becoming, always part of a continuous process of introjection and projection. In positing these terms as the pre-condition for sociality, Kristeva also forms a critique of the post-Hegelian notion of desire that posits a unitary subject as opposed to a split and paranoid one. It is a mistake to discuss the subject of the social world as a unified subject of desire, since, in that capacity,

> man remains an untouchable unity, in conflict with others but never in conflict with 'himself'; he remains, in a sense, neutral. He is either an oppressing or oppressed subject, a boss or an exploited worker or the boss of exploited workers, but never a subject in process/on trial who is related to the process – itself brought to light by dialectical materialism – in nature and society.[33]

When the subject is reduced to a product of family, state and of religion, the paranoid moment of projection and introjection is foreclosed. While nineteenth-century political movements have striven to work with that unity, the subjective urge is to reopen it. The space of transformation must be found in this porous and faulty relation between social order and subject.

The subject's capacity to negate, reject, abject is the most powerful expression of the *chora*: the death-drive, or the repetition compulsion. In the life of the subject, that compulsion is situated between the social and the psychic. It appears as a daemonic force, splitting, doubling, rejecting, acting against the social sphere rather than in coherence with it. Kristeva does not allow for any Heideggerian notion of *das Man*, living his life in blind habit without touching its very core, or any Sartreian notion of bad faith. In so far as there is subject, it can only exist as negativity, or not at all. Subjectivity emerges as a resistance against, rather than identification with, a dominating discourse. Although it will never leave its boundaries altogether, it exists at the limit of the symbolic.[34] The subject, for Kristeva, *is* this very symptom of the unconscious, breaking with the symbolic. Therefore, the social organisation we invest in is less interesting for the understanding of the symbolic system dominating our lives than the symptoms and the phenomena that appear in discourses of narcissism, melancholy, abjection and so forth. The question is, of course, if Kristeva's own notion of subjectivity as a function of radical negativity, as a continuous deconstruction and reconstruction of meaning and so on, can be brought up from the cellars of the unconscious, avant-garde poetry, perversion and psychosis and so on, and assessed in terms of contemporary political thought. As we have seen, she has been heavily criticised for not offering much of a suggestion of how political work could possibly function. The semiotic does not merely disturb social and symbolic discourses, it displaces the site of the political from practices of decision-making to other kinds of practices, such as those of art, poetry and psychoanalysis.

The fact that the site of the political is displaced onto aesthetic practices is regarded as a problem by Coole: Kristeva's politics runs the risk of being reduced to ethics or aesthetics.[35] Although Coole herself is favourable to Kristeva's aesthetic project in her conclusions, this is a common point of criticism and has been forwarded also by Fraser: Kristeva's idea that transgression is part of a poetic practice is an aestheticisation of politics.[36] Neither Coole nor Fraser discusses the difference between an aestheticisation of the political, and a politicisation of the aesthetic, which would be a more just description of Kristeva's project. A politics disregarding those processes of displacement of the political, made manifest in cultural forms, would lose the perspectives of singularity and dissent for the benefit of a politics of adaptation to collective goals. Concepts such as the semiotic, the subject-in-process, the abject and so on all gained their relevance through the deep conviction that the revolution had to align itself with these processes, best witnessed in contemporary art. Arguing that art is a practice that intervenes at the level of metaphysics and of ideas, Kristeva makes it a paradigm for political practices that serves as a remedy against totalising forms of the political.[37]

Modern poetry is produced by a heterogeneous subject, split between the semiotic and the symbolic, between language and a body of memories and affects and drives. Never a passive, suppressed or subsumed entity in Kristeva, the subject of poetry and art is not simply a challenge to the law. The subject of negativity, unlike the subject of negation, refuses the compelling power of the law. Traversing the symbolic order, the negativity produced in the subject itself is productive of many faces of productive differentiation, whether they express themselves in language, thought, pathology or politics.

Femininity as dissidence and geniality

In her writings on femininity and dissidence, Kristeva's theory of negativity takes on flesh and substance, showing how the feminine is irreducible to the gender identity of woman and defiant of any mode of 'cultural construction'. In an interview with a feminist group from 'Psychanalyse et politique', published in the *Tel Quel* issue on China in 1974, Kristeva formulates her resistance against feminism as a representational politics in the following way:

> Believing oneself 'a woman' is almost as absurd and obscurantist as believing oneself 'a man', I say almost because there are still things to be got for women: freedom of abortion and contraception, childcare facilities, recognition of work, etc. Therefore, 'we are women' should still be kept as a slogan for demands and publicity. But more fundamentally a woman cannot *be*: the category woman is even that which does not fit in to *being*. From there, women's practice can only be negative for in opposition to that which exists, to say that 'this is not it' and 'it is not yet'. What I mean by 'woman' is that which is not represented, that which is unspoken, that which is left out of namings and ideologies.[38]

In her work on feminism, Kristeva has consistently argued against the idea that the future of feminism could ever lie in a definition of 'woman' as social or biological identity. Femininity is a kind of 'third' term between essentialism and constructivism, implying a political project that is futural and productive of new subjectivities. Kristeva has consistently refuted dominating feminist traditions. The deadlock between 'essentialists' and 'constructivists' has stifled feminist thought for decades, leaving it in want of a political project. A feminist politics would first demand a radical politicisation of femininity. Toril Moi, although critical of Kristeva's politics, agrees with the idea that femininity could be identified as a form of political and cultural dissidence, and therefore as a futural project of possibilities rather than a given identity. Ewa Ziarek sees Kristeva's project as a way of opening for a notion of femininity that is neither encapsulated in the symbolic nor situated on the outside of the symbolic.[39] Judith Butler begins *Gender Trouble* by proposing that 'women' can no longer be the political subject of feminism; the mechanisms producing the category of women are in fact the same mechanisms that produce the idea of feminism as a unified project, representing women. Such an idea of unification ties the feminist project to a certain ontological conception of a female identity that is both politically restraining and philosophically suspicious.[40] Nevertheless, Butler distances herself from Kristeva: not only is Kristeva's project derivative of structuralism through its very conception of femininity, but also her reliance on the Lacanian conception of the symbolic as a contingent, transcendental law. In spite of the criticisms, however, the fundamental problem for both thinkers is not unrelated. The proposal of *Gender Trouble*, that feminism ought to undo the representational, ontological category of 'women', is present in Kristeva's own work.

The task of feminism can never be simply to formulate a project of emancipation for women as a group: any such project would run the risk of
enforcing the double-bind that all forms of politics constructed on representation must build on.

Two major articles on the fate of contemporary feminism offered by
Kristeva, 'A New Kind of Intellectual: the Dissident' (1977b) and 'Women's
Time' (1977), must be read as a sharp critique of *representation*, or the
belief that woman is a fixed identity, politically or sexually.[41] The article on
dissidence makes it quite clear that such an inauguration of a new feminist
era for the journal of *Tel Quel* does not signal an interest in women, but
rather a political project of which feminism is but one aspect: the task of
intellectuals is to defend the political value *of singularity*.[42] The cutting
edge of dissidence kills the humanist vision of human beings, producing an
excess of language and thought that cannot be solved by reason.[43]
Dissidents are the spectres of rationalist, universalist Europe. But only the
dissidence of the feminine can truly serve the site of another politics. The
rebel attacking political power is still sacrificing to the symbolic, ending up
in the old master–slave dialectic. The psychoanalyst is a reservoir of dissidence because he transforms the discourse of desire into a context between
death and sexuality. He still believes in the community, i.e. the imaginary,
and so does not fully affirm dissidence in its threatening form. Third,
the writer is a dissident, situated at the extreme limits of identity where
the law is polyvalent, and desire stripped to sounding and music of
language.[44] Fourth, the feminine is another dissidence. A woman is exiled
in relation to the law, and therefore always singular: a *daimon* anterior to
signification and conceptuality.[45] As such, the dissident woman leaves the
social and gendered category of women and becomes the polymorphous
process of the feminine. Thus, the potentiality of feminist revolt for
Kristeva concerns a philosophical category distinct from biological or
social women, 'an "other" without a name, which subjective experience
confronts when it does not stop at the appearance of its identity'.[46] The
feminine transgresses the symbolic construction of male or female, and
avoids succumbing to the sacrificial notion of identity dominating the
political cultures of the West. In claiming femininity as dissidence Kristeva
presents her extreme view of the political as *singularity*, rejecting all
formations of negotiated bonds as sacrificial and as alienating for political
subjectivity. However, it is at this point that the critique against her work
as individualist and apolitical began to find expression. In her history of
the *Tel Quel* group, Marx-Scouras argues that the depoliticisation of the
Tel Quel in the 1970s was linked precisely with the emergence of the dissident as a political alibi. The ideal of the dissident is, she argues, not a
political stance but a form of cultural ethics in which the elitist class of
intellectuals is effectively separated from the realities of a class-based
society.[47] Toril Moi comments that 'the specificity of the individual subject

is fore-grounded at the expense of a general theory of femininity and even of political engagement *tout court*'.[48] In forging the political motivations of the construction of the dissident as a political subject, however, the critique does not really find its target. As we have shown above, the Marxist analysis of material reality and class society were found inadequate by Kristeva, since it is caught in restraining and crude notions of identity. The dissident, however, offers the possibility of a more mobile and revolutionary form of subjectivity, indistinguishable from the feminine. The only possible voice of dissent must come from a position of the other of the symbolic.

Femininity is not a physical or psychical quality but a semiotic construction of marginality and alterity. Transcending the symbolic determinants of sexual difference, figures like Baudelaire, Proust and Céline were the dissident 'feminine' or androgynous voices of their age. Women writers too, however, can be found in a privileged relation to the semiotic, although on other grounds: for the feminine genius the symbolic positions of sexual difference do not offer productive possibilities of transgression. Instead, it is the possibility of maternity that will be transposed into discourses of female genius. Such discourse will deny the universality of the feminine condition (thus, once again, disqualifying the universalist claims of emancipatory feminism after Beauvoir) and, paradoxically, present singularity as the only possible platform for rethinking a feminist politics.[49] Female genius, such as it has been offered to us in the work of Hannah Arendt, Melanie Klein and Colette, has certain themes in common: the cult of maternity or natality, and the closeness to and respect of life. These common traits, however, only enforce the diversity and differentiation (negativity) at work in their thought. The celebration of birth and maternity in Kristeva's work has less to do with maternal care than with the temporal occultation of a futural perspective that lies beyond projection: a temporality of a displacing form of return, where the origin of an action will continue beyond the limited bounds of a mortal subject.[50] Women are not a species, but have the capacity to mother in common: in this they become the protectors of the value of singularity. A politics of singularity is at no point to be mistaken for individualism, as has been clearly shown in the trilogy on female genius (Arendt, Klein, Colette). The politics of negativity as argued in early articles rejecting orthodox Marxism is echoed in the reading of Hannah Arendt, where the temporality of natality is shown to be congruent with the emphasis on plurality. The temporality to be inferred from the concept of natality, or birth, corresponds to a politics of plurality. Such a politics makes possible the displacement of the political from universalist tendencies of the enlightenment towards an affirmation of the political animal as a speaking, thinking and embodied being, whose life can only be measured against the negative totality of future lives and generations. In this, the female genius is the true servant of a politics of singularity, dissident not so much in a transgressive manner through a challenge to cultural or social boundaries, as in her denial of universality. The female genius is the killer of a feminism which remains the fruit of ideologies that can only be contingent formations of beliefs, reflecting the incapacity to truly dissent from the double-bind of the subject in relation to power. The female genius, however, through her inherent dedication not only to life but also to *the life* (as narrated of the political person in Arendt, as belonging to the patient in Klein, as fictionalised with respect to an era of women by Colette), undermines the universalising tendencies of modernity as well as the liberalist tendencies mistakenly keeping feminism hostage. In this, the occultation of the maternal and of the feminine comes to correspond to a politics of singularity rather than a new brand of (essentialist) feminism.

The impossibility of feminine desire: the mother

The move to separate the feminine from the representation of 'women' has been significant for contemporary feminist theory. However, it raises theoretical issues that must be scrutinised; the vision of the feminine/dissident/androgynous/poetic subject as the future of the political is still cast in the mould of an Oedipal destiny. If the feminine is the most potentially subversive position that a subject can occupy, that subversion tends to be equated with maternity. The relation between women (as representation in the symbolic order) and femininity (as a dissenting position of negativity) is more complicated than that between masculinity and femininity. The definition of 'feminine' femininity is restrained in relation to radical dissidence through its formulation within an Oedipal grid.

Nancy Fraser has voiced the complaint that Kristeva has a tendency to manifest 'alternating essentialist gynocentric moments that consolidate as ahistorical, undifferentiated, maternal feminine gender identity with moments that repudiate women's identities altogether'.[51] The tendency to disessentialise femininity, Fraser argues, has gone hand in hand with a tendency to idealise maternity, a criticism that seems to apply not least in the trilogy on female genius, where the feminine is defined as closeness to life and birth. But what kind of maternity are we talking about? Maternity, in the language of Kristeva, has little to do with the care provided by a maternal figure. A disessentialised femininity corresponds to a disessentialised maternity. Any human subject would then be situated between a paternal and a maternal axes: the maternal striving towards the transgression of the paternal, but unable to complete such a movement. It is no good to identify with the maternal sphere or simply to identify with transgression; such a position would condemn us to 'remain in an eternal sulk before history, politics, society'.[52] A singular insistence on the maternal path must end in failure. A single-minded father-identification, on the other hand, entails a perverted rejection of the maternal side as a vile force of irrationality, corporeal drives and infantile needs. Kristeva argues, therefore, for an 'impossible dialectics', or an alteration between these two spheres. Such an impossible dialectics is situated between the maternal, singular body of corporeality and the paternal, symbolic body of limits and laws. The maternal grid challenges a simplist dualist conception of sexual difference in that it makes difference irrepresentable and irreducible to the other of the same: maternity is the epitome of feminine negativity that cannot be represented. Dissolving metaphysical pretensions of sexual difference, maternity, like dissidence, cannot but be negative; even *the* force of negativity undoing dominating norms and ideologies of our culture. A feminine/feminist ethics would therefore have to situate maternity between nature and culture, in a position of exile in relation to culture that will determine its singularity.[53]

At the same time, it is perhaps not such a radical view of maternity that Fraser had in mind when she observes the close connection to femininity as dissidence. After all, the mother is not always a radical figure in Kristeva's writings. The negativity of maternity is not a Nietzschean negativity, overturning and questioning. At best the maternal is protecting those aspects of life that appear as the negative to dominant discourses of Western society: the singular, the ethical, that which gives life, that which it is not possible to subsume under given, phallocentric notions of universality. Such a notion of the maternal is to be found in Arendt's concept of natality, or birth. At worst, however, maternity is mirrored as a phallic and punishing instance of the subject, or as that body of denial through which abjection is produced. This is the archaic mother to which Melanie Klein has given witness, thus producing a world of fantasy in which the maternal is an inhibiting other rather than a productive model of natality. In this sense, maternity comes to serve not as a model of empowerment but rather as a castrating object of identification for women, inhibiting their access to the symbolic rather than producing the challenges of negativity. Kristeva's view of the female relation to the mother and the maternal body is the most debated aspect of her writings; there is a problematic tension between the idealised view of maternity as dissident, as it is presented in the articles of the 1970s, the analysis of maternal relations in her books from the 1980s, and the celebration of maternity as model for female genius in the 2000s. The notion of maternity in the books on love, melancholy and abjection, is coloured by Freud's Oedipal and melancholic definition of femininity. Such a view of maternity is far from the process of displacement that belongs to the radical subject of dissent. Given the Oedipal norm inherent in her writing, feminists have criticised Kristeva's apparent inability to handle feminine authorships. As Toril Moi and Judith Butler have shown respectively, the interpretations of women writers, such as Marguerite Duras, tend to identify femininity with melancholy and maternal fixation. Kristeva's subject-in-process is not as radical as it may appear. There is a normative view of the symbolic father present that counters the idea of the subject as open and appears restraining in the end.[54] Kristeva reifies maternity. When she claims that it can disrupt the symbolic, she merely displaces paternal law by an equally univocal signifier. In similar terms Anthony Ellliott argues that the troubling point with Kristeva's theory is that its notion of productivity can only unfold in a symbolic order that is inherently patriarchal: the mother referred to the pre-Oedipal sphere, the imaginary father becomes the point of reference to which the psyche opens up.[55] Object relation theory does not offer a way out of the impasse in which Freud places women in relation to their mothers: for subjects born and raised as women, the maternal fixation may turn into self-destructive pathologies. Some have argued that Kristeva, together with Klein and other members of the school of object relation theory, has contributed to a repressive reification of motherhood. Doane and Hodges argue that it is focused on the depressive 'dead' mother whom is it necessary for the child to kill. Especially women have a tendency to fail in this: 'Because women identify with the mother that they have encrypted within themselves, they too feel dead', conclude Doane and Hodges.[56] Kristeva's insights offer little help in finding a cure for female depression since, in their analysis, they remain in the framework of female pathologies: 'the Kristevan mother is silent or hysterical, suicidal or terrorist', with the subsequent consequences that follow for the daughter.[57]

From such a viewpoint, Kristeva's theory does not seem to make much of an advance on Freud. In 'Female Sexuality' from 1931, where the discovery of the pre-Oedipal sphere is held to be as important as the Minoan culture preceding the Greeks, Freud separates between a positive and negative phase in Oedipal development. In the positive phase, desire is directed towards the father. In the negative phase, which precedes the dissolution into the positive formation, desire is directed towards the mother so that the father becomes the rival. The great feminine trauma, then, is founded on archaic feelings of ambivalence and bisexual desires hidden underneath the adaptation to the heterosexual norm. The mother is both loved and hated, both revered and feared. Every object relation is coloured by the maternal relation and the vindication over castration. At the same time there is a component in the hatred that a daughter has against her mother – albeit at an unconscious level – which Freud cannot really account for.[58] The maternal relation and the kind of femininity it produces remains obscure.

Kristeva adapts the Freudian idea of an original bisexuality in women in defining a form of subjectivity that is inherently subversive. Maternity and femininity are both presented as forms of subjectivity that are split and open, challenging and productive of differentiation in relation to the social order. In her later writings, Kristeva returns to the idea of femininity as a form of dissent. *The Sense and Non-sense of Revolt* shows the deep rift between the pleasurable language of the semiotic and the symbolic language of representation. Destined to live in the phallic illusion in which language is representation and not pleasure, a feminine subject is more apt to reveal the foreignness and the gaps inherent in that illusion of totality than the male subject. She has no misguided idea of phallic monism as the sole bearer of pleasure. This means that the bisexuality inherent in her desire makes her close to the mysteriousness of knowing being and its resistances, meaning and its production, language and its erosion.[59] In other words, feminine bisexuality cuts through the illusion of the symbolic as a totality; bisexuality, then, is not to be understood as the totality of two sexualities, but rather as a ruptured form of desire, cutting through the illusion of phallic monism.[60]

The most problematic aspect of her theory of femininity as an original bisexuality can be seen in those writings in which Kristeva considers original bisexuality to have developed as homo- rather than hetero- sexual. In other words, the idea of bisexuality as radical dissent is only kept up in the heterosexual solution; when homosexuality dominates the outcome, cultural dissent is stifled and subdued. Her analysis of Marguerite Duras, for instance, perhaps one of her most exhaustive pieces on female sexuality all in all, is forged on that deep ambivalence invested in the maternal object that is presented as the 'malady of death' in Duras's introverted writings. Duras's women are representative of feminine sexuality in that the object beyond the male object of sexual attraction – the mother – is appropriating the drives and making them blank, depriving the subject of its capacity for pleasure and access to the symbolic at the same time. Feminine sexuality is one of 'ravishment' rather than pleasure.[61] The premises of such an analysis are in fact based on an uncritical acceptance of Lévi-Strauss's principle of exchange and his idea that elementary structures of kinship make up the differences that structure culture and give it meaning. Since these rules, fundamental to culture, are altogether erected on a patriarchal principle, the relation between mother and daughter is made depressed and impossible. The truth of the structuralist paradigm, in Kristeva's theory, lies in its Oedipal continuation in which the paternal figure is in fact made secondary; incest implies, for the girl as well as the boy, a forbidden return to the mother. Primary incest is always the sexual desire for the mother. All desire, therefore, begins in a fantasmatic act of transgression destined to failure. The acting out of such a transgression and of the tragedy inherent in the origination of the primary object of desire gives witness to a severe problem in phallic desire and its sublimation in language and thought.[62] In *Tales of Love*, Kristeva introduces one of the few discus-sions of this topic through the example of a female homosexual: in the story of Marie, Kristeva discerns a male object of desire in the discourse of a homosexual.[63] The androgynous dream, she argues, is really a homosexual, phallocentric dream; implying therefore that homosexuality is a symptom of phallocentrism and a way of foreclosing difference.[64] Such foreclosure is a psychotic trait induced through the complicated maternal bond. In *About Chinese Women* Kristeva discusses female homosexuality as a violent erasure of the initial dependence on the body of the mother, the outcome of an 'oral-sadistic dependence' resulting in an absolute foreclosure of the vagina. The lesbian, she argues, is a regressive form of subjectivity refusing the existence of the vagina in a jealous protection of the maternal, phallic mother, and is caught in a double-bind of absolute dependence that hinders her from discovering the alterity of her own body, and her own vagina: 'A melancholy – fear of *aphanasis* or evaporation – punctuated by sudden thrills marks the loss of this maternal body, this urgent investment of the symbolic with the sadistic.'[65] In *Black Sun*, the melancholic and the homosexual both share in the same delight in the killing of a sadistic maternal figure that has been introjected into the body of the melancholic self: 'I make of Her an image of Death so as not to be shattered through the hatred I bear against myself when I identify with Her.'[66]

Such passages, presenting the lesbian as an aggressive, regressive form of desire incapable of recognising alterity and femininity, tend to undermine a notion of femininity as dissent. They are problematic not just for their heteronormative assumptions but also for their failure to present femininity as subversive all in all. It may well be that Kristeva's discourse is presenting not only lesbian subjectivities, but also *all* subjectivities, as marked by a problematic dependence on the maternal body on the one hand, and the symbolic order on the other. Her presentation of the lesbian is particularly marked by a tendency towards pathologisation and has been justly attacked by critics such as Butler and de Lauretis. Kristeva's notion that the girl is incapable of fully separating from the maternal body, and therefore closer to the pre-Oedipal, she argues, leads to an immature and pathological view on female homosexuality. Unmediated female homosexual desire leads to psychosis, because it leads to the mother.[67] In Butler's view, the inherent pathologisation of female homosexuality in Kristeva is a weak point not only for its suspicious sexual politics, but also for its ultimate undermining of her theoretical construction of radical subjectivities all in all. Her positing of femininity as the outcome of an original bisexuality, and of an original, homosexual attachment to the mother is, ultimately, dependent on the paternal law in which such attachment and such desires are denounced and cast outside of culture. Therefore, the Kristevan theorisation of maternity and femininity as radical forms of subjectivities fails; it is in fact dependent upon a theoretical grid that has already deemed the maternal and the feminine to be politically and culturally impotent:

By relegating the source of subversion to a site outside of culture itself, Kristeva seems to foreclose the possibility of subversion as an effective or realizable cultural practice. Pleasure beyond the paternal law can be imagined only together with its inevitable impossibility.[68]

So is there a way in which we might face the complaints offered by Butler, de Lauretis and others that the Freudian and Oedipal grid that has been cast on her notions of femininity and maternity leaves her stuck in a model in which the radicality of her notion of subjectivity is undercut? Is there a way in which the very discourse in which her theory of femininity/lesbianism is presented might be cast in a light more consistent with the idea that femininity is a radical form of dissent? The answer to that is: only if the psychoanalytic discourse is looked at as a language beyond pathologisation might it be possible to theorise femininity differently. Both Butler and de Lauretis read Kristeva as arguing that the homosexual is outside of culture. But this view can only be upheld if one assumes the maternal, the pre-Oedipal, the pre-discursive, the semiotic, etc. to be outside of culture as well, and as we have persistently argued there is no such 'outside' in Kristeva's work. If we pursue that argument with a closer look at Kristeva's analysis of melancholy, that view is confirmed. Rather than setting up a grid differentiating the Oedipal from the pre-Oedipal, desire from drive, paternal from maternal, and a symbolic hierarchy in which the first of these pairs are considered to be forms of culture whereas the others remain subversive undercurrents of culture, her analysis of melancholy shows the subject to be conditioned by a radical form of negativity in which the question of the object is always conditioned by primary issues. The world of the melancholic is pre-objectal and pre-ontological; this makes it not an undercurrent of culture or subversive in terms of a pathology, but revelatory of those modes through which all forms of subjectivities are shaped.

In Butler's argumentation, Kristeva's notions of subjectivity and of sexual identity remain caught within a Lévi-Straussian/Lacanian framework through which notions such as the symbolic and the law clearly present us with the cut between an outside and an inside. But if one looks closer at the relation to the other, sexual identity and definitions of desire are rarely at stake. The relation to the other is barely ever shaped in accordance with a normative view of desire; all significant aspects of subjective life take place before a distinct form of desire has taken shape, whether that desire be hetero- or homosexual. In fact, the logic of desire is barely there, which is precisely why Lacanians have no patience with Kristeva and why some find her view of femininity depressing and misogynist. In accordance with Kleinian thought, the subject lives altogether in what Lacanians call the imaginary, incapable of rising to the world of desiring subjects. In this world the subject never fully leaves the realm of primary identification that Lacan tells us belongs to the imaginary, and that, therefore, psychoanalysis must traverse. Kristeva's analysis makes no such attempt at traversal. Remaining in the world of the pre-objectal, there is no answer to the question what might be the truth of my desire. The subject is never distinctly homo- or heterosexual. In fact, the question of sexual identity has little importance, since the object is never fully erected and desire never fully in place. There is no object present in melancholy. It is objectless. Instead, the melancholic drive is directed towards the pre-objectal shape called the Thing, a shadow beyond the object of primary of identification, centre of attraction and repulsion. The Thing is inscribed not as an object of alterity present in the subject, with which the subject can identify. Instead it must be understood as a traumatic splitting of discontinuity between self and other. Kristeva's Thing is the focus in an imaginary world dominated by affective impulses. Inscribed as hatred, not as love, the Thing of melancholy bears the traits of primary sadism. A form of subjectivity dominated by the death-drive, melancholy is a production of splittings and dissociations, in which the origin of the split between self and other is disavowed rather than affirmed. Fearing the loss of the object as other, as well as loss of the self, the psychic universe of the melancholic is dominated by a constant fear of annihilation.

Ewa Ziarek has presented us with the possibility of reading Kristeva's analysis of melancholy through a grid shaped by Emmanuel Levinas's notion of the ethical. Understanding femininity as melancholy (and thereby, one might infer, of female homosexuality as melancholy, since Kristeva tells us that femininity and homosexuality are configurations of a primary and never-ceasing identification with the mother) as a figure of ethicity rather than psychosis, she successfully moves away from the interpretative grid of pathologisation. Maternity, she argues, must be considered a paradigm of substitution in the Levinasian sense; the self gives itself over to alterity and puts the other first. Indicating such a figure of substitution through her notion of maternal introjection, Kristeva is uncovering an ethics of melancholy in *Black Swan*. Whereas mourning is a negation, melancholia is the denial of negation: an impossible mourning. Melancholy, Ziarek argues, bears witness to a crisis in symbolic mediation. Such a crisis consists of the impossibility of symbolising the other in the structure of a linguistic totality;[69] remaining unsymbolisable, the other (or Thing, as Kristeva calls it) is a form of alterity impossible to subsume as sameness or to negate as the other of the other. Melancholia reveals that the symbolic order is established only at the price of the loss of maternal alterity. Melancholy, therefore, reveals a breakdown in the possibility of representation and mediation. This looks like a Levinasian face-to-face encounter, an ethics where alterity is prior to the subject. However, Ziarek's Levinasian reading of Kristeva stops short of embracing its consequences and does not fully avoid a language of pathologisation. However, in *Black Sun*, the meeting with the maternal sphere is psychosis and requires violence as the only possible response: matricide. This confirms, argues Ziarek, identity and violence to be inherent in a Western metaphysics to which Kristeva adheres, sacrificing in the end to a Western socio-symbolic order that re-enforces the primacy of identity. Thus the political task of psychoanalysis, as represented by Kristeva, must consist of a consequent move away from such a solution, and 'a recognition of violence inherent in the neutralization of the other and a refusal of the necessity of that violence, without succumbing to a paralysis so characteristic of melancholia'.[70]

However, it is not clear that one should interpret melancholy as paralysis or even the 'psychosis' of the maternal realm as a pathology, that is as contrasted to another, more healthy kind of subjective solution. Although Freud clearly distinguished between a workable form of depression (mourning) and a form closer to psychotic frozenness (melancholy), Kristeva's melancholic is not stifled by his or her condition. As has been argued above, melancholy is a subjective formation that is part of culture itself; it is, as Kristeva argues herself, the preferred mode of the philosopher and of all those modes of language and signification in which questions of being, constancy and desire can be posed – without those qualities necessarily finding constancy themselves. Rather than asking for that which has truth, or that which has being, she is attempting to show the moods, affects, phenomena and *Stimmungen* leading to the possibility of asking any such questions at all. Thus it is only in remaining in the world where objects are but shadows or Things, and questions of truth and being are responses to the overpowering presence of that shadow, that Kristeva's notion of subjectivity may make sense. Her subject lives in a world not of the symbolic but of the pre-ontological; rather than asking the question of being, she is asking what makes possible such a question.

The melancholic, argued Freud, is stifled by a fundamental inhibition in his incapacity to mourn, in inhibition in which his self-hatred will prevent his very possibility of desire and love.[71] For Kristeva, however, *melancholy is a mode of sublimation*. The melancholic is always facing that gap in which signification arises, enforces into a position of splitting and dissociation that all signification carries the mark of, incapable of closing the gap between self and other so as not to lose his own life. Thus the melancholic may have a problem with love, but is driven by the negativity in which all forceful acts of signification find their hold. The melancholic can only find his resort in sublimation and in the language and signification of literature and philosophy, modes of thought that are closed to melancholy itself. The life of the Thing can only be maintained through sublimation. What is sublimated is, however, not the object of love and hate, but rather that uncanny, unrealisable and unsymbolisable Thing in which symbolisation finds its point of resistance. Philosophy is the language and thought of melancholy, in so far as philosophy must be considered a quest for the Thing beyond representation. In Kristeva's logic it is the melancholic disposition of disavowal, and therefore of doubt and perhaps even rejection of being that leads to the philosophical question of being itself, starting with anxiety in the face of the void of non-being: *Das Unheimliche*, the eruptions and fears of the uncanny. The language and thought of melancholy is, however, also present in the poetic attempt to reconstitute the shattered body of disavowal. The dark gaps of melancholy do not arise through our being towards death, but through the traumatising scission of the sign that cuts between self and other. For the melancholic, death is never a question of finitude, but the mode in which he himself finds himself in relation to that Thing beyond the object of desire, caught in the limbo of our fruitless attempts of resuscitation through love, hate, abjection, projection and introjection. Philosophical questioning takes shape in the return to a psychotic, homosexual and maternal realm. Beyond fear of castration another form of anxiety casts its shadows: the fear of losing the other or of losing oneself, which becomes one single fear, enforcing a volatile drive of destruction. The melancholic expression of that destruction is a rupture of the relation to the object.[72] Such a destruction, however, is not necessarily stifling or inhibiting. The rupture of desire brings the melancholic back to a preobjectal sphere, the realm of the pre-ontological, where he can no longer sacrifice to a phallic notion of unity and meaning. Beyond such a sacrifice he is capable of an incessant questioning and interrogation, out of which all philosophy is born.

The female genius is such a philosopher, thus overriding the issue of the fate of non-productivity that one would perhaps fear for the female melancholic. In the case of the female genius, the maternal position, rather than the transgressive position, serves to promote not only a singular work but also a promotion of the value of singularity as such. Whereas Beauvoir complained of culture's destruction of female genius, and the incapacity of women to transcend their corporeal position and therefore to the realm of productivity in culture and thought to which genius would have to aspire, Kristeva places the idea of genius not in transcendence but in an affirmation of the maternal position situated between nature and culture. Hannah Arendt showed that position to be politically poignant, in that it allowed for a rejection of universalist ideals in favour of an asymmetrical dialectic between singularity and plurality. Melanie Klein, in turn, discovered the world of fantasy in psychoanalysis through that position, showing the unconscious to be determined by a corporeal position in which the maternal realm will continue to keep its hold. The writer Colette, finally, created an *œuvre* in which the textual production is mothered and given birth to not as substitute for a child but through a metaphorical affirmation of the maternal position. The maternal position is thus one of dispersal and productivity, allowing for the depressive fear of the archaic mother to become a necessary component in the return that makes thought possible. Such a possibility of thought is, somewhat surprisingly perhaps, as connected to a philosophy of life in Melanie Klein as it is in Hannah Arendt; only in the face of the alterity present in the mother/child dyad is the affirmation of life and thus of thought and creation made possible. In Kristeva's interpretation, it is unimportant whether such an occultation takes place through childbirth or through the depressive return to a maternal body; the encounter with a primary alterity is also that which makes metaphor and thus thought possible. Fantasy in Klein, therefore, is not simply the unconscious submission under a symptom, but the corporeal metamorphoses of the experience of alterity into thought and language.[73] In this way, maternal identification is redeemed from being caught in the impasse between transgression or the white perversion of melancholic submission. The maternal, in Kristeva, must be considered to undo accusations of essentialism or Oedipal dogmatism, given its capacity to give way to the possibility not only of dissent, revolt or revolution, but to thought as such.

3

LOVE AND THE QUESTION OF IDENTITY

From recognition to *Einfühlung*

Kristeva's hollow universalism

In books such as *Strangers to Ourselves* and *Nations without Nationalism*, Kristeva takes issue with the politics of multiculturalism, racism and nationalism. The thesis propagated is, in brief, that xenophobia or fear of the other springs out of the unwillingness or incapacity to recognise the mechanisms of projection and introjection motivating hatred and resentment; an ethics of alterity where the other is as frail and faulty as ourselves would offer a bond of solidarity beyond projective identification. Such an ethics would be based on the experience of psychoanalysis and offer a new kind of cosmopolitanism. Having criticised the forms of universality through which the political subject has been defined in the modern European tradition, *Strangers to Ourselves* argues for a cosmopolitanism in which the Freudian notion of alterity is included; it could be called a hollow universalism since it aspires to rethink the bonds of modern society. Such a hollow universalism is not a negation of the particular, but the cut of alterity in subjectivity, an ethics aspiring, as has often been quoted, to entail a politics that would be: 'cutting across governments, economies and markets, might work for a mankind whose solidarity is founded on the consciousness of its unconscious – desiring, destructive, fearful, empty, impossible'.[1] The idea that the elaboration of the 'stranger in ourselves' – that is, of the unconscious – could offer a solution to problems of, for instance, xenophobia, may appear not only naïve but also dishearteningly reductive. But it may also appear as a powerful ethics of alterity offering a feasible notion of a politics of alterity. Therefore, rather than end this chapter with such a formula and repeat the way in which Kristeva ends *Strangers to Ourselves*, we will examine its premises and situate it in the context of modern political theory: first, through the question of universality itself and its place in a politics of negativity; second, through the concepts of recognition and social identity, and Kristeva's challenge to these concepts. Third, we will discuss the relation between recognition and love, and examine Kristeva's thoughts on religion as a basis for the construction of bonds in the community.

Modern conceptions of universality are abstract constructions, whether they be conceived of in terms of contractual implementations or through the universalisability of laws and rules. Kristeva problematises the modern conception of universality in several texts, but most interestingly in those that can be read as challenges to the sacrificial logic inherent in modern conceptions of identity: 'Women's Time', *Strangers to Ourselves* and *Nations without Nationalism*. There are, as we will see, two points of criticism to be accounted for when it comes to the sacrificial logic of what Kristeva calls the socio-symbolic contract. The first point of criticism, which will be discussed in this chapter, is directed against the reductive concept of identity in Western politics. The second, which will be discussed in the next chapter, is critical of the elimination of corporeality in that logic and aspires to reintroduce issues of embodiment in the political sphere.

The first point of criticism, directed against the politicisation of identity in contractual terms, is a direct consequence of her sustained critique of universality as sovereignty. The need for a 'hollow' universalism, based on Freudianism, is born out of the necessity to move beyond the modern ideal of universality as a metaphysical construction. Accordingly, *Crisis of the European Subject* argues against the metaphysics of the universal in the French Republic: 'the Republic has no other foundation other than the universality of the citizen', thus sacrificing differences.[2] Universality is a metaphysics, the tendency to think the one, assimilating the alterities of corporeality and sexual difference, an ideology of the unequivocal where 'every mental representation (sign, idea, thought) abandons, loses or sacrifices matter: the thing or the object to which the representation refers'.[3] An ideology of 'sacrificial universality' corresponds to the metaphysical idea of 'being for death', that is, a sacrifice committed in the name of universality, which has overtaken the resistance of heterogeneity, that is, of the singularity of the subject. The sacrificial logic of identification/ representation follows a European ideology of rationality, incapable of accounting for aspects of subjectivity that go beyond a narrow contractual framework of who is to count as a citizen, man, woman, etc.[4] The problem, argues *Nations without Nationalism*, is that man, since the enlightenment, has been defined as political through the declaration of human rights. The 'Declaration des droits de l'homme et du citoyen' says that man is born free and that his natural rights should be protected, but states also that the universal principle of his rights resides in his belonging to a sovereign nationality. This means that a person has to be a citizen in order to have rights. The enlightenment, aided by modern contract philosophies, develops a notion of universality in which the citizen is recognised as a political subject in so far as he belongs to a sovereign nation state. Sovereignty, in other words, is a condition for political subjectivity. Those that have no nationality cannot enjoy the freedom of political sovereignty. The notion of human rights is thereby subscribing to a notion of universality restrained by national sovereignty. In practice, all is included except the foreigner. Man can quote his rights through adherence to a nation, not through claiming universal laws. This insistence on nationality has made a victim of those peoples who have not had a nation state, argues Hannah Arendt. It is as if a 'naked' man is not a man, says Arendt, as if he is no longer a man when he has lost his qualities.[5] Arendt therefore wishes to abolish the separation between the rights of the citizen and the rights of man. Kristeva, however, argues further than Arendt on this point: we have to separate the abstract principles of the declaration from their perverted use. The same destructive tendencies that have perverted the historical destiny of nations have also ruined the psychic space, body and identity of individuals. At this point, she introduces the aspect of her political thought that truly distinguishes her from Arendt: only psychoanalysis can serve to unravel the causes of that ruin. The forces that make a Nazi Germany out of nationalism cannot merely be the object of contention for modern jurisprudence or political strategies. They are the objects of psychoanalysis because they are products of a drive economy. There are cases in history in which society has regressed to libidinal impulses like projection and introjection, and a paranoid imaginary world becomes transposed into social institutions. As Ewa Ziarek has observed, Kristeva shows an imaginary that may be institutionalised as drives, not through a repression of rationality but rather through a rationalisation of these drives themselves.[6] Such a rationalisation tends to use an exaggerated identification with the nation state as its motivating force. If one is to analyse Kristeva's reflections on nationalism, one would have to assess its role not so much on a historico-political level, but as a socio-symbolic economy of drives. From such a point of view, fascism is the outcome of the psychic space of a nation state aspiring to a projective form of identification through its citizens; its construction of identity is based on sacrifice of differences and ambiguities. It is an object of identification releasing an array of desires and drives, never a neutral concept but a symbolic body that is politically and culturally charged. In case the nation becomes an object of exaggerated identification, whether the terms of that identification be positive or negative – loving or hating one's country with an extraordinary personal investment – identity becomes based on an economy of the drive, which serves the abject rather than subject. Indeed, the nation itself can be defined as a space situated between the unconscious motivations of desires and drives, and that of legal institutions.[7] The logic of identity as sacrifice, such as it is imposed by the nation, is close to the sacrifice instituting enjoyment identified by Slavoj Zizek in his reading of Lacan: 'the subject does not offer his sacrifice to profit from it for himself, but to fill in the lack *in the Other*, to sustain the appearance of the Other's omnipotence or, at least, consistency'.[8]

If the nation is to serve any function in the formation of the subject's capacity of identification at all, then that function must be compared to that of a transitional object. Just as the transitional object paves the way for full and loving relations for the child, and prepares it for encounters with the outside world in a mode of safety and self-assurance, so the nation should be preparing its citizens for a wider sense of being, taken to a point at which identification is lost and replaced with an acceptance of identities as split and faulty. The nation is, in the best-case scenario, a good image of identification only to be traversed in the same way that a loving mother is. Its reversal into a bad object can have disastrous adverse effects through that same logic.[9]

At best, the nation is an instance in a greater international context, offering its citizens a reassurance of belonging that they can use for the benefit of a contemporary cosmopolitanism: 'the transitional nation ... offers its identifying (therefore reassuring) space, as transitive as it is transitory (therefore open, uninhibiting and creative), for the benefit of contemporary subjects: indomitable, individuals, touchy citizens, and touchy cosmopolitans'.[10] There is a decisive difference between a cultural nationalism advocating a universalist ideal, and a romantic nationalism that augments the drive of identification rather than offering transitory possibilities of sublimation. As a transitional object of identification, the nation is to be likened to Montesquieu's *esprit general*, offering a historical identity that can serve as a foundation for wider and more generous processes of identification. Such a wider possibility of identification offers its embrace and inclusive welcome also to the private sphere. One is not to feel alienated for being in one's own world, and the specific cultural, sexual and religious differences of individuals are to be respected through the law. Such an *esprit general* would counteract the regressive drives of nationalism, without effacing the value of possibilities of identification.

Cosmopolitanism offers a way of disinvesting the nation: no longer primary objects of identification, but transitory spaces, preparing the entrance into other, larger communities. Such a mode of existing may seem to offer little more than a watered out, upper-class variety of international solidarity, truly available only for a few, as 'cosmopolitan individualism' in the words of Noëlle McAfee. In her political argumentation Kristeva seems to forget her earlier description of the subject as 'an open system, vulnerable, deeply related to others, and "in process"'. In the political writings, McAfee argues, there emerges a picture of 'extreme individualism' where political relations are undermined or underplayed, and where the very construction of the political community has become the only question of any consequence: 'The citizen is a recipient of political goods, not a creator or actor within a political system.'[11] The definition of the political subject as cosmopolitan would, in other words, fail to account for the question of agency and the question of how transitional universalities are constructed.

One may, however, retort that the cosmopolitanism is, above all, a proposal to construct a form of subjectivity that avoids to define the political subject according to the sacrificial logic of representation in which exaggerated modes of identifications stand as possible outcomes. Fascism may be an extreme instance of this logic, but is nevertheless inscribed as a possibility in the very construction of the modern socio-symbolic contract. Cosmopolitanism offers little in terms of political argumentation, but shows a mode of identification in which the economy of the drive is eliminated. The modern nation threatens to overdo it and to catapult the subject into an exaggerated discourse of love or rejection, all directed to an imaginary object that may seem to offer everything, but gives little in return. The nation may present us with the extraordinary promise of a strong, symbolic order, but this is also what releases the dangers of a radical undermining of democratic ideals. The collapse of an imaginary space of unity, the space of protection and guardianship, into an imaginary space of projective identification, may be historically contingent and require many factors to be realised, but there is no doubt that the threat of an intolerant nationalism is built into the nation. When the promise of the nation is made too strong, or may seem too weak, the threat of a freefall beyond that promise arises. The fiction of a strong symbolic order appears transparent and faulty, producing rejection and hatred. In the modern world, subjects need to be capable of entering into communities where no simple forms of identifications are offered: communities of differences, where a variety of cultures co-exist, and the singular subject has replaced the subject of sacrifice and universality. Even if a concept such as cosmopolitanism does little to offer a trans-identificatory mode of existence, its ethical stance is motivated by the problem of an unavoidable nationalist economy of the drive that few political theories have recognised, let alone tried to solve.

Another notion of universality must therefore be conceived out of the declaration of human rights, not congruent with the body politics of the modern state that is counting all its citizens but not the foreigner. One could construe human rights through an ethics 'whose relation passes through education and psychoanalysis', steering away from classical humanism and instead producing a conception of human dignity based on 'the alienations, dramas and impasses of our condition as speaking beings'.[12] Such an ethics of psychoanalysis consists of an acceptance and respect for an alterity that prompts reconciliation with the irreconcilable: 'psychoanalysis is then experienced as a journey into the strangeness of the other and of oneself'.[13] Not to be taken at face-value as a banal solution to a general problem of xenophobia and racism, it is certainly not to be regarded as a simple injunction to 'know thyself'.[14] The ethical subject sketched by Kristeva does not coincide with a conscious self, and can never be 'known' simply through introspection. Only psychoanalysis is capable both of recognising the necessity of identity-formation, and the fact that identity is always only partial.[15] Recognising the abyss of the drives, we have to relinquish the idea of unity as an idealized version of the lost maternal continent that we have often and so fiercely wished to protect, as put by Jacqueline Rose: 'Death explodes inside the peace we thought to have absorbed (nirvana, intoxication, silence).'[16]

The subject of alterity can never be fully foreclosed; it is traversed by desires and drives produced in a politically motivated construction of communal bonds. The injunction that the stranger be recognised as part of our selves is a call for the stranger in all communities. Cosmopolitanism is a hollow universalism, a community of the uncanny where it is 'essential to respect what is *private*, or even *secret*, within a fully social domain that would not be homogenous but preserved as a union of singularities'.[17] A hollow universalism of the uncanny is a tie of non-belonging rather than belonging. Bonds are necessarily found through difference, not commonality. The encounter with the foreign in the midst of our community opens the uncanny experience of non-belonging. A superior human science, psychoanalysis manages to traverse non-belonging through recognition of the uncanny. A subjectivity based on such a hollow universalism is political rather than social, negative rather than positive, transformative rather than affirmative. In a contemporary world, social bonds should have little imaginary contour and substance, and offer no space for projective identification. An ethics of hollow universalism can be transposed into a politics that aims to reduce the space of projective investments, and prevent identificatory impulses from taking hold. It is therefore necessary to maintain a universalist ideal beyond the formation of the state. The function of such a universalist ideal is not only to create bonds between nations, but also more importantly to feed the psychic life of the subject. It is necessary that the symbolic fiction of the nation state is perforated by a hollow universalism through which an ethics of alterity may find a mode to function.

Porous identities – beyond recognition

Hollow universalism is not a nebulous identification with all nationalities and people, but an undoing of a metaphysical concept of universalism as unity. Although the West is no longer preoccupied with issues of universality but rather with identity, a modern politics of identity, recognition and emancipation still tends to be founded in a Western metaphysics of universality. A new kind of cosmopolitanism, supplanted with psychoanalysis, Kristeva's hollow universalism argues for the development of a subjectivity beyond recognition.[18]

Hegel showed that the political subject is not a 'political animal', but an individual of social awareness, introduced to and recognised by the community as having value in that community. The desire for recognition defines the emancipatory project of modernity, in which subjectivities are constituted negatively, through excluding what is other to it. Recognition, therefore, is bound up with a necessary foreclosure: it can only take place through a simultaneous negation of other and self.[19] The struggle to the death must overcome a certain relation to thinghood viewed in the other. Life is the object on which desire and work operate. Self-consciousness can never be an autonomous 'I', the being-for-self is always marked by alterity: not an object, in the Kleinian sense, but a moment of negativity. An example of such a negativity may be, as in the example with the lord and master, fear of death. Thus self-consciousness is constituted through the exclusion of an alterity:

> Self-consciousness is, to begin with, simple being-for-self, self-equal through the exclusion from itself of everything else. For it, its essence and absolute object is 'I'; and in this immediacy, or in this [mere] being, of its being-for-self, it is an *individual*. What is 'other' for it is an unessential, negatively characterized object.[20]

Charles Taylor's classical piece on 'Multiculturalism and the Politics of Identity' has, however, developed the Hegelian dialectic into a *politics of recognition* in an attempt to overcome, rather than follow, its exclusionary logic. Taylor, a Hegelian whose views on the identity of the political subject may be contrasted to those of Kristeva, departs from a notion of the self overcoming the Western logic of exclusion and foreclosure through the development of a new kind of universality. In modern contemporary society, Taylor argues, the self cannot be dissociated from cultural identities. We form intersubjective communities through which we identify ourselves. The community is a base for a cultural and social identity that can only be collectively determined and has little to do with personal character. The self is necessarily socially engaged: there is no self excluded from the social sphere. Although our identity may be open to change and development, it is necessarily determined by cultural belonging. Taylor makes intersubjective relations a major point in his argumentation on cultural identity. Identity, argues Taylor following sociologist George Herbert Mead, develops only in interaction with others; we acquire recognition either in intimate relations or struggles with others. Rather than remaining within the framework of the classical polity or social contract theory, modern social theory has to take into account ways of dealing with a state that cannot be exclusionary per definition.[21] In Taylor's argument, identity is related to value; it can therefore never be regarded simply as hollow or conflictual or transferential. It is something that we acquire in groups. Our horizon of self-understanding is shaped in a specific culture. A multicultural politics requires not just that we recognise the right for a variety of groups to exist, but the unicity of their value. A modern notion of universality could only be based on a politics of difference, allowing for and recognising the value of a heterogeneous net of competing identities. A democratic higher conception of universality and justice is developing beyond such a multicultural ideal, based not on abstract constructions of rights and recognition but on a communal development of social and cultural ties as differentiated and unique.[22]

Let us, however, scrutinise the argument through the parameters set up by Kristeva where the question of identity can never be approached without taking the Freudian experience into account. Kristeva does not presume that identity politics would be misguided or mistaken; there is not necessarily anything wrong with its practice. Her argument would, however, contain a conviction that political agency is not to be equated with social identity and as a consequence that the field of the political must be recognised as heterogeneous and irreducible at the same time. Arguing for a porous identity as the foundation rather than the limit of human solidarity, *Strangers to Ourselves* sketches a hollow universality coming out of a negative and enigmatic element in all identities: the unconscious and its mechanism of negativity. The stranger in everyone is a moment of inescapable alterity challenging self-consciousness in its Hegelian form. The stranger is in everyone and has its origin in the place where we all recognise ourselves not as belonging to a community but rather as being foreign to it.[23] This does not imply that modern man is alienated, but rather that alterity cannot be foreclosed and that political subjectivity is never dominated by ideals of self-interest. The other is never merely other, but an object of introjection and projection, of drives and desires. Hegel's model of universality, identity and recognition must be supplemented with the drives. Post-Hegelian philosophies such as Marxism, forgoing the idea of negativity as a form of unconscious, have made the mistake of positing coherent identities. In this, it fails the ethics of hollow universalism. All attempts to exclude alterity from subjectivity will effectively promote projective and abjectal forms of identification. The stranger invokes fascination as well as rejection in us. The fascination and rejection of the other that belongs to the symptom of xenophobia, for instance, is an actualisation of the part that invokes the uncanny in us: death, woman, the drives.[24] The fact that the female organ is the prototype of the uncanny is not only due to fear of castration, but also to its intrinsic relation to the maternal womb. In this sense the uncanny constitutes the key to the limit between the psychic and the biological.[25] The experience of the other is emotional, affective and phenomenal, making me accede to that which is strange in me.

> Also strange is the experience of the abyss separating me from the other who shocks me – I do not even perceive him; perhaps he crushes me because I negate him. Confronting the foreigner who I reject and with whom at the same time I identify, I lose my bound-

aries; I no longer have a container, the memory of experiences when I had been abandoned overwhelm me, and I lose my composure. I feel 'lost', 'indistinct', 'hazy'. The uncanny strangeness allows for many variations: they all repeat the difficulty I have in situating myself with respect to the other and keep going over the course of identification-projection that lies at the foundation of my reaching autonomy.[26]

The shock of the stranger has an effect of depersonalisation. At the same time, however, its uncanniness announces the possibility of an opening. The split subjectivity of the foreign is capable of unknown pleasures:

Living with the other, with the foreigner, confronts us with the possibility or not of *being an other*. It is not simply – humanistically – a matter of our being able to accept the other but of *being in his place*, and this means to imagine and make oneself other for oneself … Being alienated from myself, as painful as that may be, provides me with that exquisite distance with which perverse pleasure begins, as well as the possibility of me imagining and thinking, the impetus of my culture.[27]

Living between cultures, between tongues, like an orphan without parents, the foreigner is as exposed as he is exposing others to the arbitrariness of all our origins.

A hollow notion of universality demanding that we recognise the stranger in ourselves, for all its simple beauty, appears to offer a merely banal formula as solution to the pressing problems in the multicultural debate. But Kristeva's negative notion of identity is above all a provocation to all political theories assuming the political subject to be coherent and rational, motivated both by self-interest and common goals. A concept of emancipation assuming such a notion of subjectivity is therefore not possible to apply. Given that Kristeva's subject can never be a coherent identity, a politics based on recognition of identity as having value cannot be reconciled with her thought. Emancipation in the modern world, argues Kristeva, can only lie in the giving up of desire for unity, in the affirmation of conflict and alterity forming our lives and our minds. The unconscious is not easily reconciled with socio-political demands for rights, recognition and empowerment. Social identity is a restraining and binding influence that may become the target of forces of negativity unleashing the process of destabilisation.[28] Kristeva is not content with the definition of the social that stays with the notion of a unified subject of desire, a subject of the family, of work and of the state. It is a mistake to discuss the subject of the social world as a subject simply of desire, since in that capacity, we repeat:

man remains an untouchable unity, in conflict with others but never in conflict with 'himself' he remains, in a sense, neutral. He is either an oppressing or oppressed subject, a boss or an exploited worker or the boss of exploited workers, but never a *subject in process/on trial* who is related to the *process* – itself brought to light by dialectical materialism – in nature and society.[29]

Some feminists have used Kristeva in order to argue for a kind of politics of difference, beyond recognition. Drucilla Cornell has coined the concept of an imaginary domain: a space where the person is formed, sexually, politically, ethically. The state can never impose restrictions or definitions of that space. The problem is how to define its boundaries, since it is cast under the influences of the symbolic and the real that will distort or displace it.[30] Noëlle McAfee, in turn, wants to substitute a politics of identity for a notion of relational subjectivity. The question of who we are with is not so interesting as that of investigating the way we are with others, and the way in which we are formed as open systems with alterities already in us. The fact that the subject is an open system is also a motor of subjectivity as such. It makes possible a form of deliberative democracy beyond identity politics; because the subject is always already with others, it is constituted in a community. The question of what differs between the public and the private then no longer appears to be so poignant. Subjectivity is formed in and through a plurality serving to supplant others in their faultiness and shortcomings.[31] Here, Kristeva's theory of the subject supplants Habermas's theory of the public sphere. Rather than assuming that the subject-in-process is a concern for the 'private' sphere, it fulfils the criteria of political agency that Habermas has set up, including making politics into an intersubjective issue, and capable of spontaneous will-formation informing the legislative bodies. This is so because a subject that is an open system is not inclined towards the private sphere, but has already integrated the issues of the public in itself. One may therefore link Kristeva's notion of subjectivity to a classical notion of plurality: 'speaking beings are always constituting a civil society and inclined to create political public spheres'.[32] McAfee, therefore, recognises the alterity in us, as elaborated by Kristeva, to be a political category. The dread of the foreigner is an ontological possibility; it could be transformed into the welcoming of difference.

Alterity is an opening, but also a deep and disturbing uncanniness, not only welcoming but also threatening. Cosmopolitanism or 'hollow universalism' is based on the same radical negativity as the subject-in-process. Rather thank linking the subject to the social sphere through desire, as Lacan does, Kristeva thinks of it as negativity and negation. The subject she sketches is potentially a cannibalistic one, set on the path of destroying differences, 'swallowing' the other on the way, making alterity part of a self-consciousness that is always trying to supersede the other. The

Hegelian movement is, in the eyes of Kristeva, the movement of a paranoid subject trying to overcome the schizophrenia of the split inherent in self-consciousness. In other words: there is no 'neutral' ground on which these splits can be thought; they are always caught in the paranoid movement of becoming, always part of a continuous process of introjection and projection. When the subject is reduced to a subject of the state and of religion, the paranoid moment is foreclosed. A dogmatic form of materialist dialectics has informed an all too simple understanding of negativity as subordination under a social and economic order, rather than as a movement of subjectivity, refusing to accept Hegel's challenge to all forms of stasis. Rather than referring to subjectivity as revolutionary activity, such dogmatism tends to speak in objectivist and psychological terms, or dismiss subjectivity altogether.[33] But while nineteenth-century political movements have striven to work with the unity of identity, it has been reopened in the aesthetic practices and in psychoanalysis.

In her book on Kristeva, Patricia Huntington criticizes her open subject for being anti-social.[34] Kristeva's dilemma is the fact that she proposes society to be constructed on the violence of drives that are asocial to their very nature, a proposition undermining her attempt to distinguish 'cathartic transgression from socially productive strategies of liberation'.[35] According to Huntington, Kristeva fails to see that the subject is immersed in social relations, and in the world, in such a way that it is necessarily open to alterity and difference without necessarily longing for the gap or truncated subject of alterity to close. But whereas Huntington criticises Kristeva for her emphasis on catharsis and transgression as being anti-social and counter-productive, it must be noted that catharsis is not relief. It is, for Kristeva, transformation, transposition, a catharsis of the drives from the meaningless to meaning. As we have seen in previous chapters, the unconscious is not a repressed content but a process of displacement and condensation (the 'dreamwork') operating in all our symbolic activities, whether they be visual or linguistic, a factor of instability affecting not only the production of language but also the perception of the self and the fantasies involved in the formation of desire. A subject of splittings and dispersions, the corporeal subject is living with and in a body always remaining foreign to it, given to affects and affections, projections and introjections. It is therefore disqualified, per definition, from edifying an identity that would be coherent and whole.

Strangers to Ourselves is certainly the work in which the political theory of early Kristeva is joined most clearly to her psychoanalysis. There is, however, a tendency to ascribe political aspects to domains that would perhaps be called ethical in other contexts. Marilyn Edelstein has coined a new concept – *poléthique* – in order to highlight the lack of difference between ethics, feminism and politics. There are no totalising metanarratives in the intertwining of psychoanalysis, motherhood, love and religion.

As Edelstein remarks, these domains are also marked by a lack of teleology that also makes them unsuited to the goals of emancipation that have been set up in the modern tradition but which ultimately may appear constraining: 'they can be liberatory, just, and ethical – or not'.[36] Transgression, and deconstruction of identities, of boundaries, etc., are all examples of a new, postmodern poléthique. The poléthical aspects of Kristeva's of the subject would necessarily force a confrontation with a social theory such as that of Taylor's, for instance, without necessarily refuting it. Perhaps it is a necessity, as Taylor argues, to take group identities seriously as the basis for recognition in multicultural societies. But what are we to do with that part of the subject that is to be found beyond a given cultural and social identity, taking the open aspect of the subject into account? Iris Marion Young has, successfully to my mind, argued that Kristeva allows us to form a politics that contains a sustained questioning of the idea of a coherent identity. In *Justice and the Politics of Difference*, Young argues against a notion of discrimination called *aversive racism*, where people from other groups and races are separated and avoided. Such aversive racism includes not only people from other races but also other groups as well, including elderly, disabled, homosexuals and so on. Young explains aversive behaviour with the notion of the abject. Abjection cannot fully explain aversive group behaviour, which is always culturally constructed, and historically and socially contingent. However, Young, like Ziarek and Fanon, assumes the possibility for projective behaviours to become socially instituted through abjection: 'the association between groups and abject matter is socially constructed; once the link is made, however, the theory of abjection describes how these associations lock into the subject's identities and anxieties'.[37] Many people belonging to these groups still tend to identify with the oppressor and assume a split subjectivity, Young argues: 'A way out of culturally defined racism, sexism, homophobia, ageism, and ableism ... is to push all subjects to an understanding of themselves as plural, shifting, heterogeneous.'[38] For Young, then, Kristeva's idea of a heterogeneous self is very important. The idea of a unified self encouraged in our culture creates a fear of loss that in turn creates a culture of aversion.[39] If one is to follow the consequences of the argument of Young, the way out of such institutionalisation of aversive behaviours would lie in a politically and legally flexible approach to the notion of identity whilst recognising the political reach of a modern economy of the drive. The most important issue to be addressed for a modern identity politics, then, seems to concern not the various strategies that one may develop against a sustained foreclosure of or aversion against the other, such as has been systematised in racist countries or institutions for instance. One would need to move beyond the Hegelian and post-Hegelian concepts of universality, recognition and social identity in order to be able to fully explore other kinds of political subjectivities.

70

Sara Beardsworth has interestingly argued that Kristeva's ethics of psychoanalysis fails to account for true alterity, and ends up repeating the logic of the same in which it has been conceived. Based on the Freudian conception of alterity, it ends up repeating a trauma that disallows for a move into a realm where an ethics may fruitfully be conceived in relation to politics.[40] Kristeva's refusal to essentialise difference is, in my conception, a move of displacement rather than a philosophy of alterity. Unlike Beardsworth, I do not interpret Kristeva's notion of alterity as a return to the same within a narcissistic economy of the drive. The alterity accounted for, rather, is on the one hand that of the unconscious, which in the Kristevan theory equals the dreamwork and the processes of displacement and condensation, and on the other the corporeal site of the drives that is the site where the object is introjected, projected, abjected, etc. In the same vein I do not consider the economy of the drive to be a repetitious return to the same, but rather as a repetitious return of continuous displacement (the psychoanalytic concept of narcissism referring to an original alterity as giving birth to the ego, rather than referring to a mirror of the ego). The most important work of transformation or revolt is going on in the field of motility where meaning is being fixated. In this viewpoint, Kristeva comes close to that of the theory of radical democracy, as represented by Ernesto Laclau and Chantal Mouffe. For Laclau and Mouffe, all subjects are subjected to a plurality of positions that co-exist.[41] The problem is, for radical democracy, the continuous conflict between an interior and an exterior of every society. While it is possible to promote equality, for instance, every notion of equality will leave something outside, a 'them' that is impossible to include. Hegemonic struggle, aiming to allow the 'them' or the outside to form themselves as political identities and make emancipatory demands, must therefore proceed from the notion that identities are discursively constricted and constructed. Arguing that there is no substantive notion of the subject, no substantive notions of equality, no substantive notion of justice, and so on, these notions can only be decided in a discursive field where different identities are constantly being articulated and rearticulated.[42] An emancipatory politics must also primarily be concerned with the question of identity and its other; the question of emancipation needs to move away from modern narratives of representation, which necessarily moves the question of emancipation to concern the partial and the particular of society. Only through restoring a kind of universality through which the logic of emancipation proceeds through the positing of its own ground and a simultaneous logic of exclusion and inclusion can the question of emancipation regain its dynamic: 'Without the emergence of the universal with the historical terrain, emancipation becomes impossible.'[43] Universality, however, is not to be understood as the totality of particularities, or as the totality of society. It can only be posited as the simultaneous presence and absence of the ground through which emancipatory discourses produces its 'other'. All identities are constitutively split through the simultaneous positing of its outside: the relation between universality and particularity is unstable and undecidable. If we are to bring this back to the case of feminism one may perhaps argue that the emancipatory potential of the signifier 'woman' could only lie in the embrace of a strategy where the universality of the political category of 'women' could only be embraced in its absence.

Laclau and Mouffe's proposal that universality/particularity can never be kept fully distinct entails a refusal to essentialise differences, and keeps the question of identity open and mobile. As we have seen, one may perhaps look at Kristeva's proposal that identities are symbolic positions and not, as has been argued, social ones, from a similar perspective. But Kristeva's politics presents an alternative to that of Laclau and Mouffe: not only are political subjectivities always split and challenging to the distinction between universality/particularity, but they are also elusive to the kind of signifiers that try to designate them because the political subject is not an identity, but the unconscious. The question to pose from a psychoanalytic viewpoint is: what happens with the part of the subject that remains unacknowledged from *any* discursive point of view, that is not designated by a signifier? As we have argued before, the distinction inside/outside is not really relevant to Kristeva's politics, since the consequences of her theory bring with it that no political society can successfully produce an outside. It can never foreclose the relation to an uncanny alterity that it is trying to distance itself from. Kristeva's hollow universalism is paired with a notion of the political that can only be researched at the level of the particular, or at the level of an uncanny alterity marking singularity.[44] Rather than proposing singularity as the other side of plurality, and rather that conjoining the two, she replaces the question of communal bonds with that of a modern cosmopolitanism of fear and dissolution. The fact that the singular body is submitted to a contract, which is secondary to the social contract forming the body politic, submitted to it and not represented by it, is a feminist issue. In so far as women take part of the modern state, they would still need to be recognised in their difference, which makes their participation sacrificial only to a degree. Such a participation cannot be based merely on demands of equality but would have to promote singularity: 'A singularity that remains, today more than ever, beyond equality and, with it, the goal of advanced democracies, that is, those based on consent in the negotiated handling of conflicts.'[45] Such a non-sacrificial logic of identity is problematic as well as inspirational; problematic because, as we have seen, it would threaten to undermine social bonds in its insistence on singularity, and inspirational because it throws light on other kinds of bonds. A politics of singularity makes differentiation, not sacrifice, the sustaining wheel of democratic bonds.[46] Psychoanalysis, argues Kristeva, is a superior science of the human because it focuses on differences, and sexual difference in particular; every important issue in ethics and politics have to be considered in the light of it. This is why a politics of identity ought to be replaced with studies of singularity.[47]

Perhaps we can, with Jacques Rancière, propose that Kristeva's subject is one of disidentification rather than identity. A political identity must take shape through a kind of disidentification with its natural description. In this sense, modern politics reopens the question of the *who* of political subjectivities (such as it has been described by Arendt, although this is not an open reference made by Rancière); the subject of experience or the 'who' of the natural order is always denatured and unacknowledged in the political order.[48] The formation of political identities through radical disidentification with natural and social identities is the moment where the political truly begins, Rancière argues, with the exposure of the miscount between the various parts of the political community, and the emergence of identities formerly lacking voices.

What truly distinguishes Rancière's argument from Kristeva's is her focus on the unconscious which shows that the 'who' of the political is not merely an excess of freedom in relation to its social construction, or produced through a form of subjection. The 'who' of political subjectivities is not produced through the gap or split between the social and what society recognises as having a political voice, as Rancière argues. The 'who' is rather that which attaches the subject to an inescapable alterity and a domain that lies beyond the idea of politics as the public space of negotiation and recognition. In her focus on subjectivity, rather than social, racial or class-based identity, Kristeva follows Hannah Arendt's critique of the materialist tradition when Arendt argues that it tends to 'overlook the inevitability with which men disclose themselves as subjects, as distinct and unique persons' even when the material world and its objects are at stake.[49] All communication is formulated through speech, which is a disclosure of the 'who' and not merely of the 'what'. Who we are becomes clear with others, but it is hidden to ourselves, a part of our *daimon* life:

> the 'who', which appears so clearly and unmistakably to others, remains hidden from the person himself, like the *daimon* in Greek religion which accompanies each man throughout his life, always looking over his shoulder from behind and thus visible only to those he encounters.[50]

If we are to follow our interpretation of Kristeva's notion of political subjectivity as a contrast to a politics based on social identity, the 'who' gives us a clue to what she is referring to. The *daimon* identified by Arendt becomes, in Kristeva's interpretation, the unconscious, a demon of alterity produced by the forces of negativity and the mechanisms of introjection and projection that have taken hold there. Such an alterity is disturbing, because the 'demon' appears as a threat, and can only be experienced with apprehension. And while the experience of such a threatening alterity is intimately connected to the singularity of the subject, it is not to be understood simply as individual or personal. The *daimon*, rather, is what disturbs an identity that has been formed in and through a collective; it is the disturbing otherness that forces us to confront the outside of a communally formed identity, 'that apprehension generated by the projective apparition of the other of what we persist in maintaining as a proper, solid "us"'.[51] The 'who', in other words, appears to be that which disturbs and threatens any socially formed identity in Kristeva's conception. It is that part which is singularly attached to subjectivity as such, and which is excessive to every form of social identification. Every formation of identity will produce its own dispersion, its own projection, and its own fears; there is no escaping the *daimon* operating at the heart of social identity. The who or the *daimon* is the stranger in ourselves, the split subject that no social institution can ever heal. Thus one may draw the conclusion that the political subject, for Kristeva, is precisely that aspect of subjectivity which can never foreclose its other, unlike an identity formed through social identification. And since the political in this sense becomes excessive to the socially instituted dynamic of recognition, the political subject is that which can neither be recognised nor foreclosed, withdrawing in its alterity and persisting in its threat. The *daimon* of politics can, however, be disclosed in its truths; and this is why the domains of psychoanalysis and art, where such a disclosure may take place, become domains relevant to the definition of the political itself.

Love, recognition, *Einfühlung*

For Hannah Arendt, love is radically anti political. It may disclose the 'who', and possess an extraordinary power of revelation for both the self and other 'because it is unconcerned to the point of total unworldliness with *what* the loved person may be', uninterested in the worldly kinds of evaluations through which a person's value tends otherwise to be judged in the social sphere.[52] The fact that love discloses the 'who' and not the 'what', however, does not make it a politically viable force, but rather the opposite: 'it is not only apolitical but antipolitical, perhaps the most powerful of all antipolitical human forces'.[53] This is so because love is inherently unworldly, and it can become a dangerous force when it crosses the line out of that state to levels of pretension where it becomes a weapon of political use, pretending to be a weapon of change and salvation.[54] In contradistinction to Arendt's rejection of love as politically irrelevant, there are at least two possible ways of considering love within a political context. The first one is linked to the function of recognition. In a sound

74

relation of love, the argument goes, two subjects mutually recognize the independence and autonomy of the other. Satisfaction of primary needs becomes a condition for personal security and self-esteem, and eventually also for the capacity for moral and political judgement. This position is represented by Axel Honneth, for instance. Intersubjective relations are responses to the other, and recognition is intertwined with the process of individuation. Honneth's position contends that fulfilling, primary relationships incorporate normative practices that should be protected in and through the legal system. Here, the link to the political may lie in the assumption that a person cannot be emancipated, that is, win political freedom, unless he is recognised as an autonomous agent. Such a recognition requires that a process of individuation takes place, in the sphere of the family to begin with, but also through the recognition of the individual as a subject with legal rights. Psychoanalysis is taken to throw light on certain conditions of subjectivity and intersubjectivity, which are taken into consideration in order to understand more of the ethical and the political function of the subject. Psychoanalysis (in the form of object relation theory) is applied in order to throw light on the intricate relation between dependency and autonomy, the process of individuation, and the function of recognition. Recognition, in turn, conditions the goal of emancipation. Such a view, however, necessitates that we presume the subject to be one of self-consciousness, integrity, awareness and steadfastness. Another way of approaching psychoanalysis and politics, represented by Kristeva, takes psychoanalysis to counter and question that view. A symbolic demarcation line between self and other is always in place, rather than introduced through a gradual process. Arguing that the human subject is constituted through an original alterity, this position is less concerned with the quality of the relation to a human other and considers original alterity to be inscribed through instances such as the law, language, death. Replacing recognition with love, Kristeva brings the latter into the domain where the transformative aspects of subjectivity are being evoked together with the alterity of the 'who'. The political aspect of the other is not translated into normative implications of social practices, but a foreign aspect of the subject at work in all relations of love, empathy and care, not allowing for a function of recognition proper.

Hegel's description of the struggle between master and slave develops out of another, earlier description of primordial relations of dependency – relations of love. Even though love is not comparable to the struggle for recognition, the similarity lies in the fact that man can think of himself only in relation to a 'soft' human object. In both cases, subject and object exist for themselves only through the other.[55] Consciousness, therefore, arises in relation both to matter and to persons. In a relation of dependency such as love, however, the thought of self transcends consciousness as a property merely of the subject and becomes a matter of mutual recognition:

75

'True union, or love proper, exists only between living beings who are alike in power and thus in one another's eyes living beings from every point of view; in no respect is either dead for the other.'[56] Love is not finite, and it excludes oppositions. Hegel thinks of love as a sense of life, from a living subject to a living object. There is no matter, only a living whole. The position of early Hegel is recounted by Axel Honneth, who argues that object relations may provide a vehicle for the understanding of the particular conditions of that which Hegel called the ethical order. Honneth's *The Struggle for Recognition* is focused on Hegel's early political philosophy, and is more concerned with the base of intersubjective attitudes than his later writings. Like Aristotle, Hegel thinks that there is something in human nature that unfolds in the community: the organic coherence of society lies in the recognition of the particularity of individuals. Hegel therefore interprets social struggle as an ethical moment. Neither the state, nor moral convictions, can replace its importance. The struggle for honour is more than a metaphorical description of the replacement of natural power: it affirms the integrity of a person. In his later philosophy, Hegel loses the ethico-political dimension of intersubjectiviy. Instead recognition becomes universalisation and integration. The notion of an original intersubjectivity has disappeared. In *The Phenomenology* recognition is reduced to concern consciousness and labour. The practical questions of moral struggle and intersubjective relations are never developed.[57] The ethical order is constituted by the practices and habits of a community seen in its entirety, from family life to the installation of law, but intersubjective relations are not considered. Honneth uses psychoanalysis in order to throw new light on the intersubjective aspects of primary relations: or, in other words, love. His model for recognition incarnates the ideals of a modern family politics. Honneth's question is taken from Jessica Benjamin's *The Bonds of Love*: how can a mother–child relation where there is no differentiation become a relation of mutual recognition, where the individuals are separated and individuated. For Honneth, recognition can only be won in stages. First of all, we need recognition in the intimate sphere, by what Winnicott calls a 'good enough mother' satisfying the need for love, food, intimacy and so forth. Love serves as an introduction to the normative order as constituted by positive values: justice, rights, etc. In other words: in order to become ethical subjects, we need to satisfy the primary need of love.

According to Hegel, love is a reciprocal relation of knowing oneself in the other. It is recognition, but only of natural and not of social or legal individuality: 'love is the element of ethical life, but not yet ethical in itself', Hegel writes.[58] Honneth's interpretation of this claim is that Hegel refers to:

> the emotional conditions for successful ego-development: only the
> feeling of having the particular nature of one's urges fundamen-

tally recognized and affirmed can allow one to develop the degree of basic self-confidence that renders one capable of participating, with equal rights, in political will-formation.[59]

Consciousness of rights develops through the consciousness of self and the self-esteem produced by a loving relation. There is an element that cannot be controlled, and it cannot be extended beyond primary relationships. Love relations are dependent relations, and therefore exposed to abuse and transgression. This means that love will have an element of 'moral particularism' in it. Nevertheless, both Hegel and Honneth hold it to be 'the core' of ethical life. It is only the symbiotically nourished bond to that which Winnicott calls 'the good enough mother', which produces the degree of 'basic individual self-confidence indispensable for autonomous participation in public life'.[60] The law that gives its citizens rights, thereby recogni-sing him or her, is continuing the work of the 'good enough mother'. Self-realisation is dependent on legal recognition and the freedom and autonomy it represents. Recognition, overall, is a condition for a positive relation to one's self: 'the prospect of basic self-confidence is inherent in the experience of love; the prospect of self-respect, in the experience of legal recognition; and finally the prospect of self-esteem, in the experience of solidarity'.[61] The individual identifies with the values of the law: justice, rights, etc., and love serves as an introduction to the normative order as constituted by values such as equality, freedom, justice, the right to have rights, etc.

From a psychoanalytic viewpoint, however, a subject's relation to the law presents itself wholly otherwise. Rather than being the object of an identificatory relation, it is a scission; rather than producing coherence and continuity, it produces splits and conflicts. The fact that the psychoanalytic 'law of the father', which incarnates the fact of scission more violently than any other law, must be considered quite differently from other contingent laws does not make a difference for the argument as a whole: no law can be detached from that primary splitting function. The relation between love and law, also, presents itself as a production of split and alterity rather than as identification. There is no doubt that love is a necessary component in the successful introduction of the individual to the social sphere. But the love that socialises the child could just as well be called care, or perhaps loving care, which is not the complex and ambivalent bond called love in psychoanalysis. Seen from a Freudian point of view, love originates in a narcissistic instinct aimed at the preservation of the self, which makes the relation to the other an ambivalent mixture: he comes to represent both help and threat.[62] There is reason to set the demarcation line between love and care. Love is not just ambivalent sometimes, but is so *always*, because it is a function of an original alterity in the subject itself. Whereas Honneth may be right in his description of the socialising function of loving care, it is less evident that love should have an emancipatory function, or serve the introduction to autonomy and freedom.

In Kristeva, there is no originary symbiosis between mother and child, but an original situation of differentiation internal to the subject itself. From such a point of view, the political potential of maternity does not lie in a continuation of the process of individuation, serving an emancipatory capacity of solidarity and awareness of rights for both oneself and others. If maternity occupies a privileged space in her politics, it is because it forces us to take issue with that which escapes the socialisation of political subjectivity. Bonding does not simply produce an identificatory basis but an *awareness of the risks and depths* of all loving relations.[63] Love is a relation of transference introducing an ethical relation through lack or negativity. There is no assertion for any moral goods to persist through that relation. If there is identification, it is immediate in Hegel's sense: the subject presenting itself for an object, *parousia*. It is reflection doing away with itself, replaced by *Einfühlung* with a primary object that cannot be spoken of in terms of identification. The object of primary identification or *Einfühlung* is neither father nor mother, not a partial object but a metaphorical one. It does not yet exist; it is the emptiness in which we have to raise an illusion of unity that the child is mimicking, transferring onto, bordering between the psychic and the somatic, idealisation and eroticism. In *Strangers to Ourselves*, *Einfühlung* is a capacity to grasp the strange, the uncanny, that alterity within us that prompts an ethics of psychoanalysis as reconciliation: 'psychoanalysis is then experienced as a journey into the strangeness of the other and of oneself, toward an ethics of respect for the irreconcilable'.[64] The symbolic instance that makes primary identification or *Einfühlung* possible is not the mother but rather the third party that the mother respects as coming between her and the child. In this way, it serves as a protection against the maternal body as phallic and devouring. The narcissism of *Einfühlung* has a ternary structure: the mother, the child, and the third party of alterity that could be described as that fleeting shadow towards which maternal desire is directed. The child identifies not with the mother but with the mother's desire. Capacity to desire is constituted as transference directed towards the maternal site of negativity. The first other is introduced in an instance of split and the object of primary identification is neither father nor mother, but a metaphorical object. *Einfühlung*, unlike the process of individuation, is a fragile state that will never produce a stable ego. Love – or the transferential relation to the paternal metaphor, which does not coincide with the real love of a parent – does not primarily give us the ground for any affirmative identification with justice and the good. What love can do would rather be to prepare the subject for a constitutional homelessness and alienation. But it is precisely in that constitutional homelessness that the political subject, marked by an alterity irreducible to social identity, comes to be. The subject, constituted by metaphor, is in fact, per definition, not a simple being but a 'being who acts', in Kristeva's own words.

> The being who acts gives its all in subjective experience, and this is even truer in the love between two subjects – that climax of destabilising–stabilizing identification. There is no act, just as there is no sexual act, outside of love, for it is in the constituent violence of its field that the subject's signifying structure is shaken, drives and ideals included.[65]

The language of love challenges the desexualised discourse of normativity, the symbolic, the discourse of universality and recognition. But love is also the language of the subject *per se*. Overall, there is no well-adapted subject to contrast with the pathological mode. The subject, for Kristeva, *is* this very break with the normative. In so far as there is subject, it can only exist as symptom, or not at all. The subject of love emerges as resistance against, rather than identification with, normative values. Political change is therefore intrinsically intertwined with the very process of becoming of a subject that *cannot* be recognised because it does not fit into a given social or cultural category. The alterity of the stranger is something that cannot be fixated: a fleeting movement. At the same time, it is impossible for anyone to deny being the stranger. The commonality of the community is altogether made up by bonds of solidarity created of the hollow and negative universality. Such a notion of the political forces us to consider domains that are not commonly regarded as relevant to politics. While norms and codes are constituted as laws of universal validity, there is, in Kristeva, a radical break between the ethical and the normative. Transference is, unlike the process of individuation, a fragile state, and emptiness lurks behind. There is no assertion for any values to persist outside of the relation to a metaphorical relation. There is, in other words, no relation between the ethical experience of love and the normative claims of justice, right, good or bad. Not only is such resistance indiscriminate and blind to ethical values such as justice and the good, the intersubjective link is simply the unleashing of the forces of negativity. This may seem like a real weakness in her work; the other is an aspect of the subject, rather than the representative of an ethical relation. Patricia Huntington considers Kristeva's account of the metaphoricity and metonymy of love to be an idealisation of hysteria. However, she also sees that affective investment in the real (metaphoricity and shared meanings) is also an affective investment in a peopled reality.[66] In other words, the social and the affective are simultaneous, and therefore: 'Kristeva reifies the desperate longing for idealized identification as a necessary compensatory mechanism for loss of immersion in corporeal and libidinal immediacy.'[67] Whereas Huntington's point is perceptive it seems to me Kristeva's conception of loving identification and idealisation departs from a narcissistic split, which means that it does not presume the subject to be longing for anything, since it conceives of the split as primary to the subject of *Einfühlung*. Love, therefore, is not a fantasmatic relation but produced through the gap or void presented through the shadow of an object. In contending the subject of love to be a political one, Kristeva explores an aspect of political subjectivity that has perhaps been overlooked in much political theory: rather than presenting the political as a sphere into which the subject or individual is allowed or not allowed, a space of autonomy and recognition, she presents it as a space of negotiation immediately linked to a gap or void, an immediate function of the failings of the subject to identify with political power as incorporated in the form of paternal, phallic representations. The only power recognised by Kristeva is the flexible, floating power represented by those objects towards which transference is directed. Kristeva calls the transferential relation to a metaphorical object a stabilizing apparatus; an educator, a family authority, or maybe a psychoanalyst may mediate the paternal metaphor but never incarnate it. Such a figure is an: 'an intermediary who becomes a fixed point of support and confidence and who permits the individual to find his capacities for play and for construction'.[68] The political space to be negotiated, the space in which representation of the symbolic may appear, is situated in the gap between the ethical function of love, of corporeality and sexuality, and the universal function of rights. The relation needs constant renegotiation in the metaphorical sphere of language. In this, she points to the gap situated between the functions of corporeality, sexuality and affectivity, and the symbolic order. The relation between these domains needs constant re-negotiation. The political is a form of being and speaking, an ongoing process explored in practices that traditional theories of the political regard as too private to really concern them.

Reviving a non-secular ethicity

What Kristeva is doing, then, is much more than showing the infamous unreliability and intricate distortions of the subject of desires and drives. In fact, her theory moves from the diagnosis of pathologies into a more forceful and speculative area that still remains to be explored. Her ethics can be universalised without becoming normative. And this is precisely where one of the most interesting points of Kristeva's theory appears: we seem to be situated at the limit of our own (Western, European) secular *ethos*. The argument of *Strangers to Ourselves* closes at the point at which it has shown that the deferral to a universal imperative of rights is not longer possible, arguing that a multicultural politics can no longer simply refer to a secular ethics; principles of sovereignty and universality may serve national strength as well as international solidarity, but they also inspire mechanisms of foreclosure that they are unable to address. Given that, it seems obvious that we must formulate a new kind of ethics, leaving the universalisation of justice, right and equality of Western nations behind, and accept instead an ethics of weakness, ignorance and exposure. The interesting aspect of the conflicts that keep arising in a multicultural society is, as Kristeva has shown, that its dysfunctions in the form of racism for instance continue to prohibit acceptance of other ethicites and identities than those that are recognised. We must therefore aim towards the realisation of a new political subject, leaving the imaginary sphere of recognition behind, preparing instead to reform and transform under the sign of constitutional weakness and porosity.

It is from this perspective, as advocating the need to found a new political subject based in a non-universal form of ethicity, that Kristeva's interest in religion should be seen. Her advocating a non-universalist ethicity is in fact aiming towards the reinvention of a non-secular ethics in the service of the political. This is also what has led some commentators to consider the religious and/or moral dimensions in Kristeva to be more interesting than her politics.[69] But there are at least two ways of approaching religion in Kristeva's work, ways that simultaneously seem to support and cancel each other. In one instance, religion is an imaginary support of the subject of *Einfühlung*. In another, religion seems to enforce the perverted fixations of a split subject. As we will see, these two characterisations of the effects of religion in the life of the subject do not necessarily cancel each other out. They both relate to the pertinent question of how meaning is produced, and society's imaginary constructed, in contemporary life.

In *Tales of Love,* the necessity to produce meaning is put forward as an ethical imperative. In her recent work, however, Kristeva has stressed the fact that giving meaning is not just an ethical gesture, but a political task. Making sense, no sense or non-sense are not just artistic gestures without further implications. Literature acts as a substitute for religious meaning in that it reproduces the tertiary structure of transference and metaphorical support in which meaning is produced. More importantly, however, meaning is a product of conflicting forces, and a matter of politics in itself. A politics of meaning consists of the challenge of, the breaking down and the reconstitution of the imaginary field that defines a society. The language of literature is one of displacement and reconstruction of the imaginary. Meaning is neither a product of contingency, arbitrary signs and plays of differences, nor a return to originary practices, but a product of conflict between the subjective sphere and the normative order, in which Kristeva stresses the transformative potential of the subject in relation to the norms and codes of language. Ever since *Revolution in Poetic Language* Kristeva situates the production of meaning in a sphere strictly attached to the radical negativity of the subject itself, as we have seen in the first and second chapters. Meaning is the product of transference, created through the investment in an object of love, hatred, fear, etc. Rather than confining the notion of transference to the psychoanalytic clinic, Kristeva makes it into a preliminary for the creation of meaning as such. Psychoanalysis repeats the Christian form of meaning construction. Psychoanalysis could even, at least to come extent, be said to have taken the place of religion. After theology, psychoanalysis studies how language produces meaning, through the notions of transference and counter-transference. Rather than being a science, or a question of truth, psychoanalysis is faith. Its object is also a question of the imaginary. Transferential discourse has produced a new kind of love, defining a new era where it is not only the symbolic – aspirations to universality, unicity of meaning, etc. – but also the semiotic – cosmopolitanism, ambiguity, etc. – which defines the way signification is produced.

In order for meaning to be created we must postulate the existence of a relation. In other words: the subject only comes to be when desire is transferred onto something. This 'something' is what Kristeva calls the 'Thing'. It is not an object in the full sense of the word but the shadow of an object: that shadow of metaphoricity towards which transference is directed.[70] The Thing represents both a limit and a possibility, constituting a necessary gap between ourselves and the world. In the psychoanalytic description of the subject, it could be translated as a necessary lack. If neurosis is marked by a lack or a constitutive absence in the picture that stands for our own incompleteness or castration, then perversion is a structure where the lack is eradicated. For the subject living in a 'blank' perversion, such as melancholy, something is failing in the interaction with the world. The failure to transpose a world into language turns around the inability of metaphorical transference; linguistic impoverishment affects the ability to experience difference, distance and space – language creates the depth and weight of the world of experience. Metaphor stands for a necessary gap between thing and word, or perhaps, to speak with Freud, the representation of the thing and the representation of the word. Together with metonymy, which binds the links of the linguistic chain, metaphor is creation. The closure of metaphor affects the space of perception, and the depth of vision gradually shrinks towards a final collapse. When the mobility and flexibility of symbolic language becomes impoverished, the experience of world is replaced by an obsessive delusion. The missing alterity cannot simply be interpreted as the absence of another human body or subject. The depth of alterity is represented not by other subjects or bodies but by the metaphorical cut between word and thing, the lack or incompleteness that guarantees mobility and space. Metaphoricity substitutes the paternal phallus, coming into being without allowing for a hypertrophied symbolic dimension. An instance of alterity represented in and through speech needs to be introduced, however, for the flesh of creation to develop. In the Christian religion, faith is connected to the trinity and the co-existence of father and the holy spirit. Metaphoricity is thus already present. In psychoanalysis, alterity can only be represented through another *with whom we communicate*: with interlocutors, respondents, other speakers. The notion that space is represented not just by another body or another gaze, but by another speaking being, explains the lack of meaning in the perverted structure of foreclosure. Metaphor makes it possible to explore the gap between word and thing, thus for flesh to unfold. With the loss of speech, the gap closes and causes the collapse of the world of experience. This is why a tertiary structure needs to find symbolic support in every culture; such structures have their primary model in a Christianity affirming the metaphorical rather than anthropological quality of paternal law. In other words, Kristeva's turn to the interpretation of the function of paternal law in the Christian tradition is applied also to the tertiary structure of Oedipus, offering an alternative to the Lévi-Straussian interpretation when the law of the father is applied strictly to prevent incest and to found a sexualised, possessive form of desire. For this reason, Kristeva assures us that 'the father is never spoken of enough'.[71] The Freudian, Oedipal paradigm is not introduced as a cultural foundation, but as the continuation of a politico-religious ethics that Freud rethinks and displaces in other terms. The Oedipal revolt, as well as his mistake or fault, is a structural necessity of the subject. This is not because it inscribes desire according to a given socio-economic model, but because Oedipus is dependent on the religious idea of the father as an absolute authority and as a guarantee of the law. As such, however, he can only be thought of as an absence: the father is always dead.

In Kristeva's version, the tertiary structure of the Oedipus complex indicates that the subject comes to be through a kind of primary transference:

> This 'direct and immediate transference' to a form, a structure, or an agency (rather than a person) helps to bring about primary stabilisation of the subject through its enduring character; because it is a gift of the self, it both encourages and hinders the disintegrative and aggressive agitation of the instincts.[72]

Psychoanalysis, like religion, works in the mode of a transference directed to a paternal metaphor, but its mode of operation may appear to have changed radically from that of religion. A rejection of faith must bring with it a certain repression. In a first instance, psychoanalysis appears as nihilism. Interpreting man as a sexualised being, psychoanalysis prevents both unification and destabilisation of the subject. It describes a new relation to the body, but also to the ideal: introducing the unconscious, the ideal is no longer mere transcendence. Psychoanalysis may appear as nihilism because there is nothing but the subject. It is a kind of atheism because with its description of desires and drives, and its stress on the corporeality of all signification, it can never refer the production of meaning to a transcendent sphere. However, psychoanalysis is in fact an antidote to nihilism. But the kind of faith psychoanalysis introduces is a new one. It believes the subject to derive from an alien form of significance that moves it and overwhelms it: produced by the unconscious.[73] Freud's notion of the unconscious would perhaps even allow us to see something 'divine' in the other. But this is something Kristeva hesitates to conclude. For her, Freudian alterity has a political rather than religious impact. Her working through of the Freudian concepts, however – the law, the production of meaning, transference and so forth – relies at heart on a religious paradigm that she displaces and rewrites in political terms.

The same goes for another aspect of the new ethics of psychoanalysis that can be approached to the Christian tradition: that of *forgiveness*.[74] In forgiveness we may find another sign of the fact that political issues are being displaced from a locus of universalisability to the singular.[75] Psychoanalysis is to a large extent a practice of forgiveness, precisely through its capacity to give meaning. But it can never do so in the reliance of transcendence. It must do so in the recognition of man's internal conflict, and in the recognition of the fact that meaning is embodied and corporeal, displaced and transferred. As we have seen, for Kristeva the introduction of the unconscious in the political sphere brings with it a new emphasis on singularity that makes the production of meaning immanent rather than transcendent, embodied rather than spiritual. Psychoanalysis allows for the analysand to discover an irreconcilable conflict, a splitting that detaches him from desire for unity. Emancipation in the modern world can only lie in the giving up of desire for such a unity. Freud has clearly shown us that the psychic universe of Western civilisation can never be thought beyond the splitting of the subject, or beyond repression and guilt. These are phenomena inherent in the thinking and being of modern man as such.[76] What psychoanalysis can do, however, is to introduce the possibility of reconciliation through insisting on an imaginary sphere of meaning beyond the split, a sphere governed by the imaginary father or paternal metaphor of *Einfühlung* that has been described above. The ethicity of forgiveness implies another kind of politics, a politics of meaning, where the imaginary is making meaning happen, the creation of meaning as a new kind of politics.[77] As has been noted by Kelly Oliver, however, Kristeva's notion of forgiveness is not restricted to the transferential relation to an imaginary domain that is to be set in a transcendental dimension, beyond the corporeality of the subject. Transference always involves the relation of one body to another: 'as the agency of the meaningful relation between two bodies, transference itself gives pardon; it is not given by one subject or the other'.[78] In order for the paternal metaphor of forgiveness to emerge, then, it can only be thought through a form where the corporeal existence of the subject is involved rather than overcome; it can only be produced through the very desires and drives that keep the subject fettered, guilty and suffering.

This brings another aspect of Kristeva's Christianity to the fore, one that may be more subdued in her later writings. Beyond the paternal metaphor that gives us flesh, meaning and forgiveness, there is another and more chaotic religious dimension to evoke in the new 'Christian' ethicity in the life of the contemporary subject. This dimension is the feminine sacred. In order to clarify the nature of this dimension, Kristeva uses Arendt's separation between life as *zoë*, which has traditionally been connected to the feminine sphere, giving life, and *bios*, the story of life, the capacity of giving meaning, which has been a male privilege for a long time, in order to evoke a kind of divinity presenting itself beyond the tertiary structure. Evoking feminine ambiguity versus the idea of a paternal God, she argues for the understanding of a sacred realm that goes beyond that of the unifying function of paternal metaphor. This is a maternal love, or sacred love, which does perhaps not immediately present itself as love but rather as corporeality and as body.[79] In this sense Kristeva's notion of the sacred is not an equivalent to that of Western theology. As Jean Graybeal has rightly pointed out, Kristeva has used the notion of the sacred to look for the separation of the subject beyond identity: in this case, religion becomes not sheltering but a splitting open of the gap in the subject.[80] In this context we may be reminded of the fact that early Kristeva has argued that religion is situated at the intersection between sublimation and perversion.[81] In her book on the abject, religion and the rituals of defilement accompany any institution and maintenance of a social order. Sacrifice fulfils several purposes. One is to exorcise the abject, that which threatens the distinct borders of the community and of the self. Another purpose, no less powerful, is to link the subject to God. God is not divination and union, but separation, order and rules:

> A religion of abomination overlays a religion of the sacred. It marks the exit of religion and the unfolding of morals; or leading back the One that separates and unifies, not to the fascinated contemplation of the sacred, from which it separates, but to the very device that ushers in: logic, abstraction, rules of system and judgement.[82]

In the Freudian mythology the foundation of the social order is, as we know, religious. The social links are formed through the mutual sacrifice of the paternal name. In this instance, paternal law wins over maternal ambiguity, metaphor over the chaotic quality of the sacred. The meaning of the primal killing, according to Kristeva, is this: it is necessary because it is the condition of the ritual transgression of authority, which, according to Kristeva is fundamental for all religions. The transgression can be lived in several ways: as a representation of murder, as a *passage à l'acte*, or as sublimation. A religion of the sacred (rather than that of metaphor) does not so much implement order as it affirms the fundamental ambiguity of subjectivity as being both pure and impure, subject to persecution and revenge. A function of the fundamental perversion inherent to all subjectivity, religion adheres to its obsession and to its paranoia. All that ambiguity is incarnated in the flesh of the Christian, always already eagerly doomed to transgression, through which he is promised spiritual life in the end. Defilement, abomination and sin are all part of the ritual whereby the sacred is approached, through the transgression towards a limit that in actual fact serves to maintain the promise of redemption. According to Kristeva, all religious bonds are formed through the separation between the maternal and carnal, the symbolic or spiritual. The logic looks like this: in the first instance we find a purification of a contamination deriving from the maternal sphere. In the second instance we find the murder of father, reaction against tyranny and exclusion, installation of symbolic pacts in which paternal authority is introduced.

So how are we to link these two aspects of religious ethicity: the sacred, ambiguous maternal sphere and the paternal metaphor of forgiveness? In contemporary secular societies the investments that motivated religious practices have been displaced into those of art. Practices of art are in many ways more true to the motivations of libidinal investments and transference, as well as to the affirmation of the polymorphous body of pleasure than religious practices. Art, like religion, is incarnation and regression. At the same time, it is made meaningful through the metaphoricity of transference. Art, also helps form social bonds through the metaphorical character of its practices.[83] Whereas religion may serve as a repressive instrument of desexualisation, art has liberated a space where *jouissance* and metaphor, transgression and meaning, are kept alive in a unique combination.

4

BODY POLITICS

Pleasure, abjection, contamination

Challenging the socio-symbolic contract

Kristeva's hollow universalism challenges the ideals of sovereignty, universality and equality as being the most important sites of political negotiations of the modern state, transposing the political to areas such as literature and psychoanalysis. Such transposition takes place, most importantly, through the *chora*. The hollow universalism of constitutional weakness will help develop the notion of a body transgressing the boundaries not only of social practices but also more importantly of language and thought. Feminists such as Toril Moi, Seyla Benhabib and Nancy Fraser have observed the progressive potential in Kristeva's theory of a destabilising and displacing element in subjectivity. At the same time they are protesting the lack of social and political definition: how are we to form new conceptions of solidarity out of a theory celebrating destabilisation and transgression? Judith Butler has written off Kristeva's 'body politic' as a dead end: her notion of subversion relies on there being a sphere beyond the paternal law against which the subject reacts against. At the same time such a subversive sphere, which is supposedly corporeal, is dependent on the law it reacts against. Rather than deny it, we must affirm the productive capacity of the law:

> If subversion is possible, it will be a subversion from within the terms of the law, through the possibilities that emerge when the law turns against itself and spawns unexpected permutations of itself. The culturally constructed body will then be liberated, not to its 'natural past' nor to its original pleasures, but to an open future of cultural possibilities.[1]

Kristeva's strategy of subverting the law is fruitless, because it remains within the parameters of the symbolic. It is unclear in what way the drives would serve a subversive purpose. Even if the drives are considered heterogeneous they are in themselves subjected to the symbolic since the

87

law is merely prohibitive. One is therefore unable to see the way in which the law actually produces desire. The subversive (female) is in fact still produced by the law that posits it as transgressive:

> In order to avoid the emancipation of the oppressor in the name of the oppressed, it is necessary to take into account the full complexity and subtlety of the law and to cure ourselves of the illusion of a true body beyond that law.[2]

Butler implicitly criticises the body as 'pre-political' or 'pre-discursive' as a form of naturalisation. What is natural is, however, always already given and Kristeva's body is never given, but produced negatively in relation to the sign. A Freudian rather than a socially instituted negation makes possible a play of the semiotic in the symbolic, challenging any kind of fixation as well as any illusion of a natural past. If one looks more closely at the theoretical construction of the *chora* – which is the domain of the pre-Oedipal – one may observe that it opens a site of theorisation where concepts such as transgression become irrelevant. The definition of the body as pre-Oedipal, pre-linguistic and so on does not exclude it having a distinct cultural and political quality. A pre-Oedipal notion of corporeality is however, in spite of its apparent transparency, rather difficult to assess. It is not obvious what kind of body we are dealing with. Is it a vehicle of flesh that is merely lived and felt? Is it a body defined by archaic and infantile qualities, naïve vessels of impulsive affects preceding the context of discursive and cultural practices? If that is the case, such a concept of the body would be one of naïve naturalism and be theoretically uninteresting. But Kristeva's bodies are not prediscursive, and nor are they defined by discourse; the pre-discursive or pre-Oedipal body is one of negativity, differentiation and transformation. Although construed according to psychoanalytic concepts relating psychic experiences to the somatic sphere such as the drive and affects, the scope of Kristeva's body cannot be exhausted in psychoanalytic terms. Taking recourse to Plato, the *chora* is a model of the body not representable as object.

In her critique of modernity, Hannah Arendt has shown that abstract, universalist ideals may have adverse effects on the spaces of the political. Only the principle of natality can account for the frailty of human affairs, which a politics of modernity has targeted but failed to cure. The lack of boundaries surrounding every human action overruns the modern project to contain the political within abstract ideals: 'while the various limitations and boundaries we find in every body politic may offer some protection against the inherent boundlessness of action, they are altogether helpless to offset its second outstanding character: its inherent unpredictability'.[3] Linking the *chora* to Arendt's notion of the political as an activity challenging the boundaries of the community and its conception of itself as an autonomous maker, John Sallis has shown that the *chora* of the *Timae* has political signification. One could say that it challenges the definition of the limits within which a politics is supposed to determine the collective investments and wishes of a people and of a nation. A politics of the *chora* will never be a simple linear discourse as John Sallis puts it in his reading of Plato:

> a politics of the *chora* will never provide a prescription for making or remaking the polis; it will never issue a paradigm in reference to which that degraded politics of which Arendt writes would then set about fabricating the polis, looking to the paradigm so as to make the *chora* in its image. Rather, a politics of the *chora* would look instead to the limits of every such *poiesis*, and would undertake to think the difference, the displacement, correlative to these limits.[4]

The question of the political, such as it could be posited through the notion of the *chora*, Sallis shows, is not a question of making, but of the transformative powers of becoming. The *chora* is the inherent lack of boundaries with which every political action is pregnant.

In Kristeva's theory, the *chora* is the economy of drives of a corporeal subject, representing a notion of embodiment transgressing the problematic restrictions of the social contract. If the political sphere is dominated by an abstract body then it will restrict itself through given demands of sacrifice and exclusion. The *chora*, on the other hand, is a site of becoming of subjectivities, tied together through processes and experiences that are not usually recognised as being politically relevant. Such a body is also one of affectations. Rather than adhering to the modern pathology of *jouissance* that is produced by an authoritarian and/or perverted symbolic order, Kristeva's bodies lend themselves to pleasure, sadness and joy. The conception of the body is intrinsically interwoven with the critique of identity as a sacrificial contract, forcing the loss of embodiment.

Moira Gatens has shown the need to probe deeper into the relation between the body politic, such as it emerged in the modern discourse of the social contract, and the singular body. Discourses on the body and discourses on the body politics share a vocabulary in such a way that it necessarily will have an effect on our understanding of political practices – terms from each other, she argues: 'A philosophically common metaphor for the appropriate relation between the mind and the body is to posit a *political* relation, where one (the mind) should dominate, subjugate or govern the other (the body).'[5] This order, argues Gatens, implied for instance the rule of men over women. Women were not considered capable of rational thought, or as autonomous minds in relation to their bodies, as opposed to men. The problem for Gatens is to find a way to *embody* the modern notion of a body politic that has come to be constructed on the notion of disembodiment and rationality. Feminist theory often argues that Western thought is governed by dualisms between nature and culture, body and mind, passion and reason, family and state. Gatens adds another: that between body and body politic. Modernity, in the guise of the social contract, has submitted the singular body to abstract constructions of representation. This means that the singular body is submitted to the body politic rather than represented by it. The social contract is, in fact, representative only of a certain kind of body, usually male, white, employed, and so on. The modern contract of a body politic is always exclusionary and restrictive.[6]

There is a gender problem deeply embedded in the socio-symbolic contract according to which identities are formed in the West, as Kristeva noted already herself in 'Women's Time'. European universalism promotes a logic of identification consistent with rationality that in turn relies on a sacrificial logic: part of the subject must, in this way, be foreclosed and made inaccessible.[7] As we have seen, the demand of foreclosure causes a vindictive return of alterity in paranoid and projective forms. The tendency to sacrifice differences in the name of universality and representation includes a disdain of corporeality: 'the body, and with it sex, gives way, or rather is assimilated, to the One'.[8] Rather than accept such a sacrifice one must consider identity otherwise: the founding separation of the socio-symbolic contract as *internalised* rather than defining the subject through social and sexual status. The contract will then institute differentiation rather than sacrifice. A Freudian contract would demand the sacrifice of the body in relation to the sign. However, if the socio-symbolic contract is internalised it becomes a condition for subjectivity without fixed representational forms. Certain practices, such as religion and art, demystify and transgress the symbolico-linguistic representation of gender. Such transgressions, argues Kristeva, are motors of social transformation. The body of the subject-in-process is not gendered or defined in social terms. Through its open character it presents a challenge to a body politic operating in terms of domination and exclusion. The most poignant consequence of the theory of the subject-in-process, cast under the drives of the *chora*, is its reconfiguration of the political citizen from an abstract, subjected body to a lived body of experience and affects.

The pleasure of women

The pleasure of the female body, defying castration, is the most radical form of subversion. Rather than accepting that pleasure has to come to an end, woman perversely attempts to prolong it. Nowhere does the subversive potential of pleasure come out more unashamedly than in writings on the mythical erotic domination of Chinese women. *About Chinese Women*, a controversial work from 1974, is not an anthropological study of China but a critique of the West as seen through the perspective of China, its other. *About Chinese Women* is a book rarely referred to in contemporary writings because of its exoticism and uncritical mythification and mystification of the life of Chinese women. Her view of China has been accused not only of orientalism but also of making multiplicity into one, a univocal signifier, as Butler calls it.[9] Forgetting or suppressing the blood and violence of the Cultural Revolution, this is, however, a work where Kristeva presents the most powerful, original and theoretically inventive critique of the phallocratic society of the West. For all its shortcomings in comparison with political consciousness of today, *About Chinese Women* attempts to redefine Western societies and women's place in them. The male universalist subject is dethroned and the patriarchal family put in question. Kristeva's interest in China, where she also travelled, offers a crucial experience for the understanding of a radical, transformational politics; partly because of the women's movement that is active there, and partly because Chinese culture is repressed in the West.[10] China offers the possibility to study the other in a double sense: the other as woman, and the other as a nonphallic culture of enjoyment. Kristeva's reflections on Ancient China argue for a political order constructed on feminine enjoyment, rather than phallic representation: based on an erotic economy dictated not by Western ideals of love but the 'explosive, blossoming, sane and inexhaustible *jouissance* of the woman', a 'permanent flight' that prevents narcissistic fixations.[11] In no other text does Kristeva present such uncompromising politics of pleasure, or such a decisive challenge to the phallic spectre inhabiting psychoanalysis. The psychoanalytic fixation on the phallus is criticised as an unfortunate echo of a logic pervasive in all aspects of Western society: family life and political life as well as the subjective experiences of pleasure and sexuality. The limited usefulness of phallic logic can be seen in, for instance, Western conceptions of power, caught in an impossible double-bind. Ideologies on the right tend to exalt it as a primary principle and as a 'peerless, primal, absolute force' whereas the left 'denies it in anarchist rage or in the naiveté of humanist spontaneity'.[12] The same kind of double-bind is explored in 'Women's Time' where Western feminism is shown to be suffering from a patriarchal dialectic where they have to choose between either going along with existing power structures, or overthrowing them altogether. The West, with the help of psychoanalysis, holds the domination of the phallus to be a 'necessary and internal limit of the social animal'.[13] Psychoanalysts fail to recognise the political determination of phallic power, and tend to mistake it for an absolute, rather than realising that phallic power is politically negotiable, and a contingent cultural and social form of power. Focusing on woman and her erotic power, which appears decentralising and productive rather than centralising and authoritarian, *About Chinese Women* argues that power may be incorporated but not represented. The desires and drives of the female body

91

incorporate an erotic economy defying castration, and the possibilities of a revolution without sacrifice or victims.

In order for the sacrificial logic of the West to be contravened and under-mined, one would have to theorise new kinds of contracts between individuals, families and society. In the article 'Les Chinoises a "contre-courant"' the readers are assured that women are the primary forces of the Cultural Revolution. The Chinese perspective serves to unravel the contin-gency of phallic structures. Its ancient matriarchal cultural history (whether this is accurately described by Kristeva or not) shows other forms of kinship to be possible. The revolutionary project promoting new forms of kinship and family formations is a continuation of an ancient tradition. In fact, it has succeeded in politicising areas of life that were not considered political before: reproduction, the family, the relation between the sexes.[14] In *About Chinese Women*, the family politics of new China is presented as a triumph not only over the ancient patriarchal customs of the country itself, but also over Western structures. Indeed, the book presents a critique of a Eurocentric naturalisation of family, a naturalisation present in the Western philosophical tradition from Hegel to Freud.[15] The modern nuclear family has wrongly been depoliticised. Individuals are not products of their family, above all, but of their relation to society.[16] The West, however, has failed to see that the family is a politically negotiable institu-tion. Instead, the relation between subject and society has been fixed in patriarchal family structures and frozen in a pattern that has proven detri-mental to women above all. The revolution, argues *About Chinese Women*, must begin in the intimate sphere; in modern China the Westernised notion of the family is taken apart, all to the advantage of the status of women.[17] The Marriage Law adopted in 1950 undermines the symbolic support of patriarchy. Moreover, the law recognises the right of the wife to take plea-sure, which is quite in line with old customs. The marriage law is therefore superior to that of European ones, argues Kristeva; it makes the family an ethical rather than economic institution, and undermines a marriage contract that has kept the submission of women as its clause. Most impor-tantly, the family is considered not an autonomous unit but as an intermediary between the individual and political society. The Chinese family has passed from one form of contract to another. In this process, women have gained unprecedented autonomy. Chinese women, therefore, embody a new kind of contract in which the female body is no longer to be excluded or sacrificed. Instead it has become the focus of new kinds of experiences and new kinds of subjectivities.[18]

The body of fantasy

In works such as *Black Sun*, *Powers of Horror* and *Tales of Love* psycho-analysis is used in order to examine the religious, social and political condition of the singular subject. It may seem that the Kristeva of the 1980s, no longer talking about the revolution of poetic language, is devoted to a conformist practice dedicated to rehabilitation.[19] If we consider her theory of the subject, however, we find a different picture. Shifting the emphasis from revolution to pathology, these works offer a cultural criticism where the subject becomes a symptom of a given society and its history. Overall, there is no conformist, well-adapted subject to contrast with the pathological mode. The subject *is* this very symptom of the unconscious, breaking with the symbolic. In so far as there is subject, it can only exist as symptom, or not at all. Poetry and psychoanalysis represent not the unconscious symbolism of cultural repression, but the breaking point between a given order and its negative pole. Always suffering the risk of contamination, a cultural community will produce obsessions and fears, and thereby exclude, ban and create taboos. It will never wholly succeed, however: no society may prevent the emergence of sites where historical and cultural conflicts will be enacted and embodied. Culture is both integral to the social sphere and acting as its critical conscience.[20] As we have seen, art and literature are produced as a constant challenge to society's norms and limits, and the truth of the subject is to be found in the discourses of society's weak points (or its pathologies) rather than the ideological illusions it promotes. Culture, for Kristeva as for Freud, is primarily a product of unconscious fantasy formations and drives. Art incarnates the very forces that will disrupt and challenge a society, the unconscious and more in its revelatory status. Mixing literary analysis with patients' stories, the work from the 1980s points to the fact that pathologies are not only causing suffering and lack of adaptation, but they are also inherent to the production of meaning, such as literature and psychoanalysis. The pathologies of modernity emerge as resistance against, rather than identification with, dominating discourses. Such resistances also participate in a continuous process of change where the subjective mode of becoming is necessarily symptomatic.

In her work on melancholia, abjection and love, the human body itself holds a central position. Not only is such an analysis called for by the psychoanalytic concept of the object, but it is also motivated by the artworks that are to be found at the centre of attention. Holbein's Christ has a central position, as well as Bernini's sculptures of motherhood. The pathologies of melancholia, abjection, narcissism and so on will dissociate thing and word. The human body, however, comes to mediate in that blank space. The focus on the human body takes its inspiration from Melanie Klein for whom the relation to the world is defined in the pre-Oedipal phase. Infantile fantasies produced by a presymbolic death-drive will produce partial objects invading an inner world – torn breasts, ripped-up stomachs, detached penises, excrement. The other side of infantile dependency is aggression, directed towards the body of the life-giving mother who is perceived to be invaded, or pierced, by a damaging paternal phallus. For Klein fantasies are perceptions where inside and outside are not yet separated, a psychic reality not yet cast under the rules of language and meaning. They also stand for an omnipotent will to control psychic reality. The child of fantasy has not been castrated. He or she does not live under the rule of the phallic signifier – the patriarchal economy of frontiers, restrictions and limits, which governs the life of the adult.[21] The Oedipus complex, according to Klein, brings a resolution to the free play of anxious and aggressive fantasies, which later become repressed, socialised and symbolised. For boys it ends with paternal castration and the giving up of genital desire of the mother, for fear of retaliation. For Freud, the Oedipus complex is the beginning of desire and love towards other women. But for Klein, the shadow of a hateful mother of revenge, or loving mother of gratification, continues to cast its spell. 'Early Stages of the Oedipus Conflict' (1928) describes a boy passing through a feminine phase before the Oedipal drama. During this phase, which is mingled with fear, the boy fantasises about depriving the mother of the father's penis as well as the inner organ of the womb and her capacity to bear children. Comparing it to the castration complex for girls, Klein calls it the 'femininity complex'. A boy's fantasmatic development will be dependent on the frustration of not possessing feminine organs:

> The tendencies to steal and destroy are concerned with the organs of conception, pregnancy and parturition, which the boy assumes to exist in the mother, and further with the vagina and the breasts, the fountain of milk, which are coveted as organs of receptivity and bounty from the time when the libidinal position is purely oral.[22]

Klein considers the generalised, cultural hatred towards women to be related to this phase of jealousy and frustration whereas the dissociation of the Oedipal phase entails the renunciation of that hallucinatory destruction of the inside of the mother. There will always be something left of the initial aggression motivating the infantile aggression towards the mother that Klein speaks about, corresponding to a kind of violence that goes on in the outside world, and that is related to patriarchy. Fear of castration draws upon a violence that is built into patriarchy itself. Separating *savoir* and *connaissance*, truth and knowledge, Klein's notion of fantasy makes it possible to analyse a form of knowing proper only to the world of fantasy, where the truth of the subject is the enigmatic truth of castration.[23] At the same time, Klein's fantasy is tainted by the historical traumas of her own time (the war, Hitler, etc...). The hatred and the aggression the child directs towards the body of the mother is culturally overdetermined. Klein also puts the death-drive, or rather the consequences of its effects, in a gender perspective. The lust to kill, the will to tear apart, the tendency to destroy, is initially, for Klein, not a male, but a human drive. Nonetheless, violence is a pre-eminently male behaviour. Klein explains this in psycho-analytical terms – the man directs his aggressions towards the maternal origin different from himself that he necessarily has to reject. Klein did not have any theory of the symbolic to counter the idea that drives are a natural part of the organic subject of psychoanalysis. In her practice, however, she shows that the hatred and aggression directed towards the maternal body is culturally overdetermined and not just an infantile defence against separation. As a psychoanalyst active in the upheavals before and during the Second World War, Klein discovered that the domi-nation of the death-drive and the hatred cast upon the maternal body had an immediate relation to the violence of her age, although they were natu-rally to be interpreted as fantasies. Fantasy gives witness to an ongoing disintegration of her cultural framework.

Bringing Klein's critique of the Oedipal complex up to date and showing the increasing hollowness of Oedipus in the twentieth century and beyond, Kristeva's psychoanalytic work makes the father a weak and problematic representative of the law. She thereby reverses the Lacanian idea that 'woman' is the non-entity that keeps patriarchal culture and its correlation in the Oedipus complex together. Instead, that non-entity is the absent, imaginary father. Concepts such as desire, the symbolic and the Oedipal are all on the side of the father, and are weaker categories than their maternal counterparts: the drive, the semiotic, the pre-Oedipal. Still, woman is an overdetermined figure that has to be 'eaten', discarded, negated or violated, since she threatens the limits of the symbolic. But the disruption of the maternal, semiotic sphere into the symbolic is produced by the fragility of the symbolic itself, and not merely a symptom of such weak-ness. The conflict between the semiotic and the symbolic is not just to be interpreted in terms of poetic versus normative language. It is intertwined with the processes of history, ideology and religion where woman intro-jected as the threatening, fantasmatic *inside* is recast and projected as a fearful and contaminating *outside*.

Abjection: an aesthetics of contamination

As Kristeva herself points out, the internalised object in Klein is theoreti-cally impure, which is also what makes it so fruitful in the clinic. The first inscription opening us towards an exteriority, as well as the interiority of the internalised object, is the other body, or more accurately the body of the other. The distinction subject–object is constituted through the encounter with another body that also serves to open a relation to the other as such. Freud, in his first model of the psyche, 'Entwurf einer Psychologie' (1895), describes the ego not as kernel, but as a protective shield, encircling the organism in order to counter excitations from the

inside and the outside. The ego learns to channel the experiences of pleasure and displeasure that stems from the organism.[24] The Freudian
imagery leads us a bit on the way, when we say that it could be possible to
change the metaphorical sense of contamination, to steal its negative associations from ideologies of purity. We need a minimal border against the
outside world, and our fear of contamination stems from the fact that this
border is attacked. While the object of affects (such as the good or bad
breast) belongs to the imaginary in Lacan, it is made out of images, sensations and substances in Klein.[25] The Kleinian notion of fantasy could be
described as a chiasmic reversal between the relation of mental world and
body. The psychic meaning has been thrown out from its mental place
and placed in the body. The unconscious fantasies involved are always
related to another body: the trace of another person being inscribed in an
experience wavering between pleasure and displeasure, crossing the
borders inside/outside. Affects and sensations become part of the same
universe, carried by an inevitability that seems to strive towards an erasure
of the border between psychic world and body. It seems, then, as if Klein's
world is striving towards contagion, or contamination, an energy or power
making bodies infectious to one another. The drive motivation of fantasy
breaks down the differences that keep them apart.

Such a notion of the body holds contamination not as a risk or disease
but as an immanent possibility of openings and becomings. Kristeva's
aesthetics in the psychoanalytic work, such it has been influenced by her
reading of Klein, could be described as an *aesthetics of contamination*.
Contamination is the breaking down between inside and outside, an
aesthetics of contamination a phenomenon through which I am moved or
touched, by my fellow being. The touch appears with intensity and fever-
ishness where the separating limit between inside and outside runs most
thinly. Is this the reason why we also see a new interest for that which has no
shape or form but which can still be related to the object of a human other,
phenomena such as blood, guts, bodily fluids? These liminal phenomena
can be read as manifest expressions of the fact that the other encountered
in a work of art may have an infectious function. Rather than being mere
products of fantasy, art and literature catches the 'beyond' of fantasy.

In Aristotle's *Poetics,* tragedy has been theorised as a form of contamination or *miasma*, balanced in the work through *catharsis*. In the ancient
world, the idea of contamination is related to the collapse of a certain
social and cultural order, where certain categories that should not meet
have infected each other, such as the plague coming to Thebe as a punishment for the Oedipal fate. With contamination, chaos follows and a ritual
purification is demanded to compensate for the social breakdown,
catharsis restoring the balance and the order.

In tragedy's staging of an original contamination, the ritual expulsion of
that which is foreign becomes the bond of the social and cultural commu-

nity; art replaces religion as the unravelling of expulsion. In Kristeva's aesthetics, as in ancient tragedy, there is no substantial difference between the experiences of expulsion at an individual level and those of the community. In the sphere of tragedy, concepts such as *miasma* and *catharsis* cut across individual and political bodies. The powerful concept of *abjection* does the same with contemporary art.

One of the most potent expressions of Kristeva's aesthetics, it cannot simply be equated with *l'informe* to use Bataille's expression: an indeterminable phenomenon that is impossible to contain within our traditional categories of intentionality and understanding.[26] The term of abjection is not simply synonymous with expulsion. Contamination must be avoided. At the same time, however, we carry a secret desire within us to erase borders. Abjection is produced in search of a new kind of knowledge and therefore a motor of social transformation. Kristeva finds the production of a transfomative inner experience in her reading of Bataille. The realisation of what Bataille calls inner experience puts the object in question and produces a new kind of knowledge, not an object. Such experience cannot be theorised in the same terms as a material object. The abject is not simply something that is outside of us, and that we are disgusted by. In being neither 'subject nor object' it seems, first of all, to threaten the borders of the self. In difference to the object it does not give any support to the subject; it is a 'fallen object, which pulls me to the point where meaning collapses'.[27] Abjection is exclusion or rejection rather than denial or denegation, which means that it is not detached from the body at a symbolic level: the abject has not been repressed through a process of negation but can be traced back to a rejection that has taken place before the subject of judgement is fully developed – 'I' reject myself and comes to be in and through this very rejection. Abjection is the other side of perversion: it is repressive, and anchored in the superego, creating the shield of a fragile ego and destroying the psychic space of the subject at the same time. The shield of the self is dominated by feelings of disgust. On a subjective level, corporeal rejection marks a differentiation between inner and outer world, the body of the self creating its contours, the abject being a remainder that has to be cut off in order for the self to be kept 'pure'. The abject is, however, a confirmation of the fact that the subject can only be conceived of as a heterogeneous construction that is always already contaminated. Bodily fluids mark a separation between inner and outer world, which is why the body acquires a fragile contour through disgust. The problem, however, is that the self is expelled in the same process. In this way, the logic of abjection follows that of the superego in Klein. It is not a moral but a persecutory instance in the ego.[28] Instinctive rejection prevents the process of negation and symbolisation from performing its function, since the object of primary repression (the phallus) is denied. Primary repression of the forbidden object, the maternal body, has never taken place and never been replaced by the paternal signifier. There are lives, according to this logic, that are not sustained by desire. Rather than being produced through the dialectics of negation and negativity, such lives are driven by exclusion: forcing the subject into a perpetual position of defence. Abjection is not an obsession with filth, but the compulsive search for the in-between, not respecting borders, positions and rules. It may become enjoyment when it appears as the object of the other, i.e. as subjection to a strong symbolic law such as God, the country, etc. In this form it may revere the other and appear repulsive to itself and dejected. The abject of such enjoyment will remain in a fascinated disgust that is both introjected and projected, not capable of separating between self and other.

Abjection is not just an affair of the subject. It accompanies the sacrifice that, as we have seen, is a prerequisite for the installation of the symbolic. Rites of purification and defilement are all playing with the border between inside and outside that is co-extensive with the social and symbolic dimension of society. Sacrifice is fundamental to culture, from which follows that the phenomenon of abjection is universal. Its cultural signification will vary. But there is one trait in common to be seen: the cult of phallic powers will always appear threatened by the feminine, the seemingly unbound feminine aspects of the body.[29] The abject, then, can take on many forms: it is the holy abject of fascination and ritualistic defilement, such as food in certain religions. It is menstrual fluids, such as blood and semen. It is corpses, between the human and inhuman. The abject is waste, excluded from our culture and yet haunting it through the need for ritualistic purifications. In contemporary literature, the abject is a substitution for ancient religious rituals of purification. Contemporary literature of the Judeo-Christian tradition, mixing the pure with the impure, prohibitions and sins, morality and immorality, shows a fascination for that which is prohibited and dirty. On a subjective level, the corporeal rejection marks a differentiation between inner and outer world, the body of the self creating its contours. The abject is the symbolic treatment of rejection, at the limit between inner and outer, a remainder that has to be cut off in order for the self to be kept 'pure', the persecutory other. Bodily fluids mark a separation between inner world and outside world; the body acquires a fragile contour through disgust.

Modern pathologies such as racism and xenophobia, for instance, are in one way or another functions of abjection. Racism is a privileged example in Kristeva, in that it constitutes perversion of political subjectivity in its denial of necessary 'castration' demanded by the social contract: racism projects the foreign rather than accept it as a necessary component of the political body of the state. Racism is also a liminal area of society demanding a political analysis that takes the need for a radical non-phallic and anti-patriarchal stance towards issues of violence and rejection. In its most consistent form, patriarchy is a closely knit system with converging values in religion, politics and the social sphere. In Kristeva's cultural history, there is a direct relation between the fragmentation of these values, and patriarchy's disintegration into perverted forms such as fascism, racism and religious orthodoxy. The pathologies linked to it are those of psychotic forms of narcissism and abjection. Incapable of containing the maternal, patriarchy institutes its own grains of disintegration. In *Powers of Horror*, the immediate relation between the abjected maternal body and paternal fragility is highlighted. The representations of the unconscious are conditioned by history and ideology, reinforcing certain so called 'archaic' fantasies of evil and dark feminine forces. The language of abjection is less caused by an inherited fear of these forces than imposed by a culture of violence. But more importantly, the abject is a reminder of life itself: the fluids and smelly products that are deflected by the body. An instinctual process of rejection allows for the limits of the body to constitute itself against the threat of its own rejects. The abject is the symbolic treatment of such a rejection, a remainder that the self may attempt to cut off in order to be kept 'pure' from an alterity that is already part of itself, perceived of as a persecutory other. Such an other is, then, not the other with whom I identify but an other who 'precedes and possesses me, and through such possession causes me to be'.[30]

There are two possible causes behind the abject. On the one hand there is a relation to an other (a maternal relation) that is too strict and restrained, while on the other hand to an other that is too weak. Abjection, then, appears as an attempt not to kill the other but rather to gain life, as an attempt to create an object out of a pit where there is none. The state of abjection sticks with the same repetitive enjoyment thrust under the superego as perversion: '"subject" and "object" push each other away, confront each other, collapse and start again – inseparable, contaminated, condemned, at the boundary of what is thinkable: abject'.[31] At the same time, however, the experience of abjection is present in all signification: 'Language learning takes place as an attempt to appropriate an oral "object" that slips away and whose hallucination, necessarily deformed, threatens us from the outside.'[32] The formation of the object, in Freud's theory, is correlative to the drives. The object is a retroactive construction and response to the narcissistic drive of the subject. The subject of the drives has a capacity of eroticising language, a capacity that is indifferent to symbolic issues of sexual difference. Dominated by the abject, identification of such subjects becomes fleeting and elusive. They become empty, fortified castles, whose desires are shallow and determined by social norms rather than the unconscious object formation of the Oedipal structure. The abjected body is estranged and numb not just in relation to object choice and sexuality, but also language itself. The process of signification is being invested with drives, of imprints of visual impressions as well as the sound-making process itself. The object presented and re-presented in language is always shot through by the drives, and makes its appearance in conjunction with affects, a result both of the drives and the intellectual operations accompanying the process of symbolisation. When the object collapses, the process that has been condensing word, image and sound is undone. The fragile self is turned inside out and spat out as the content of which it would try to purify itself from: waste products of the body such as urine, blood, sperm and excrement become the privileged images of phenomena that are not quite representations or symbols, but existing only in the realm of fantasy, attacking the limits of the self as well as the contour of the other. The abject is the eroticised content of a maternal inside, a fantasy shielding the subject from the castration and loss it has to suffer. It is also the experience of a world beyond that loss, putting in question not just the ego but also the object of any affective experience.

Hating your country

It is telling that abjection has become an aesthetic of fascination in contemporary culture. The cultivation of abjection as art was particularly strong in the 1980s and 1990s, at least in part as a result of the coining of Kristeva's own concept.[33] As a phenomenon it is a returning feature of Western culture, exploring the limits of the socially acceptable. George Bataille's work, provocative and challenging in its fascination with that which lies beyond, both in terms of social norms and in terms of perception, could be regarded as a source of this feature of contemporary art. The strategy of invoking the abject does not seem to have lost its grip on artists who want to provoke the invisible limits of the acceptable and unravel the slow process of normalisation in which we all seem to be caught. But what kind of revolt is abjection if it can be reduced to a symptom, caught in the auto-destructive pangs of narcissism? As we have discussed above, Kristeva's aesthetics is not a project of emancipation in the traditional sense. Critics (Eagleton, Fraser, Rose, Butler) have complained about the emphasis and romanticisation of transgression in Kristeva's work. As we have shown earlier, however, there is little said of transgression. Overall, there is no conformist, well-adapted subject to contrast with a transgressive mode. Given the inherent pathologies in any society, a politics of negativity will always open towards experiences that are neither ethical nor particularly constructive. There is no edifying basis in Kristeva, no heroism and no remedy for nihilism.

Fascism and Nazism are discourses where the abject is rationalised: a systematic and ritual exclusion of real or symbolic dirt. These ideologies are expressions of hatred, rejection and disgust, and may appeal to a subject where the inclusion in a totality with distinctive borders between the pure and the impure appears as a rescue from an experience of dissolution and fragmentation. The French writer Céline, a fascist and anti-Semite, has served to illustrate the phenomenon of abjection better than anyone else. Céline, Kristeva says, *is* this discourse. His desire for an unbroken symbolic, which would substitute for the faulty and frail one in which he is living, lies behind his own fascism and anti-Semitism.[34] Catapulted to fame with *Journey to the End of Night* (*Voyage au bout de la nuit*, 1932), inspired by his own experiences as a soldier during the First World War, Céline lived a good part of his life as a traitor to his country during the Second. After the war, he was shamed and exiled.[35] In the 1970s, the *Tel Quel* group rediscovered the works of Céline, taking interest in his writings because of his strange style and syntax. His idiosyncratic text was considered to be elaborations of a new subject emerging as a reaction against a stale literary institution.[36] A medical doctor, Céline showed a strong interest in and fascination for bodily fluids. His novels are catalogues of death, disease, mental and physical illness, vomiting, bad smells and so forth. The body is an unreliable, transparent and perforated vehicle for living, through which the traumas of the twentieth century, most notably the two world wars, find their way. His stories of injuries, craziness, murders and broken bodies do exactly what Kristeva tells us that the abject must do: challenge not just our tolerance, but also our feeling of a secure self and identity. Abjection is situated in a relation between subject and culture where neither could be looked at independently of the other. The voice of abjection is heard in the inhumanity of 'horror, death, madness, orgy, outlaws, war, the feminine threat, the horrendous delights of love, disgust, and fright'.[37] In fact, all literature is abyssal in one sense or another, written at the limits of a discourse between subject and object: 'double, fuzzy, heterogeneous, animal, metamorphosed, altered, abject'.[38] Abjectal art is a challenge to ideologies of completeness and totality that in turn fosters racism and misogyny. It has strong political implications in ways that are contrary to anything like a coherent political message. Céline's nihilism reveals a void of values and sense. There is no point in Céline's story of hatred and persecution at which one would find something worth attaching to: nothing to hold up as symbol of value, and nothing to repress either. What we must do is to take Céline's revolt against symbolic institutions seriously, and acknowledge that 'Céline had the right to be angry about the aspects of symbolic institutions that are unjust, repressive and arbitrary in the name of universalism, goodness and tolerance.'[39] It is, in fact, the very nihilism of his art that may serve to make it potent. In *Journey to the End of Night*, the narrator, Ferdinand Bardamu, is a young doctor fleeing from his duties or responsibilities first as a Frenchman, and then as a doctor. The two themes are intrinsically intertwined: it is impossible to understand the rejection and disgust of Céline if one does not look at the symbolic function of France in his work. Bardamu is supremely uninterested in saving lives for the nation. He is also unwilling to risk his own life for the nation. This does not mean that his life carries any value, as is shown in the narcissistic reflection on and of the self that permeates the language of the novel. He may detest homosexuals and Jews, but he is himself the most hated object of disgust.[40] Abjection in Céline, notes Kristeva, is closely related to frustration with a law that is binding, restraining and weak. 'The law is the great "Luna Park" of pain', he says, speaking about a situation in which he throws himself under laws that he does not understand but that appear to haunt his life.[41] Céline wants to replace these incomprehensible and impotent laws with another one, which would represent a promise of completion and fullness, a kind of 'mystic positivity' as quoted from Céline himself:

> There is an idea that can lead nations. There is a law. It stems from an idea that rises toward absolute mysticism, that rises still without fear or program. If it flows in the direction of politics, that is the end of it. It falls lower than mid and we with it … we need an idea, a harsh doctrine, a diamond-like doctrine, one even more awesome than the others, we need it for France.[42]

Such a law would then be a remedy for the frailty and incompleteness that governs the human condition, degraded and humiliated. A harsh doctrine would replace the discourse of France as a good mother, ridiculed and detested throughout *Journey to the End of Night*. The maternal abject is incarnated by a character with the name of Branledore above all, a war hero celebrated for his extraordinarily high morality. Branledore is, says Céline, the image of what the good mother requires of its children … an extraordinary patriot, living and dying for France. A metaphor for high morality and patriotic values, the image of France's beloved child, has to be juxtaposed with another one: a wreck with perforated intestines, a destroyed and smelling remnant of a human being.[43] Céline's fascism is a kind of hate speech, directed towards his country, his fellow being as well as himself. The question is, of course, how the abject is produced: in a maternal prehistory with a contingent relation to political ideologies or as an ideological necessity, produced in a culture with a certain historic and political disposition, independent of its subject? When Kristeva says that Céline *is* his discourse of hatred and exclusion the claim is forceful: it is not just fuelled by hatred of Jews and homosexuals and so forth, it is a *hatred of the symbolic itself*. What makes Céline's abjectal discourse so poignant is that he hates France not because it is strong and oppressive but because it is weak, frail and failing to resist.

One may pursue the argument of Kristeva further. The phenomenon of hating one's country is not rare among intellectuals in the twentieth century and perhaps even a motive of underestimated importance in modern European literature.[44] Céline incarnates a position where an exaggerated *hatred* of the nation is reversible in relation to an exaggerated *love*, as incarnated in the dream of a strong, potent nation. An exalted reverence of one's origins can result in a discourse of love of one's own and hatred and exclusion of the other. The reverse is also true. Repression and hatred of one's origins can result in hatred of the self but also a form of abjection that can easily turn into hatred of the other.[45] Céline's extreme and fascist form of subversion is less interesting than the logic of his abjection: all his judgements relate to his identity being determined by an authority into which he projects the capacity to recognise him in the fullness of his being. Dreaming of a 'mystic positivity' that would save him from his suffering, his longing is not only a symptom of fascism, but also a common modern illusion, produced by ideologies of nationalism and the erroneous belief that identities may become strong through a direct identification with a strong symbolic order such as the nation. Hatred or love of the nation are reversible afflictions resulting in similar symptoms.

The 'drive-foundations' of fascism are an economy where libidinal impulses are intertwined with the (Kleinian) death-drive and rationalised as ideology. However much we may be repulsed by the nihilism of Céline, his writings are revealing of what could be found beyond the imaginary world of revolt as disgust.[46] The domination of the abject is produced through an Oedipal crisis where the feminine stands for an alterity that may well be interchangeable with that of the Jew. Woman is eroticised partly as dominatrix and partly as victim. Motherhood, too, becomes sexualised, through the painful and dangerous act of giving birth that Céline makes part of a grotesque human comedy where the humiliated feminine subject becomes the victim of her own capacity to procreate. Women are to be pitied, but at the same time their sexual capacity is powerful and threatening. The father, on the other hand, is merely a shadow, easy to demobilise and to ridicule. What we find, then, is a world where images of masculinity and femininity are exaggerated and derided, serving a libidinal economy where the most hated object is the author himself. That self-hatred is epitomised in the Jew, an abject of fear and fascination whose correlative is, of course, the writer himself. Both the narrator/writer and the Jew are, equally, feminised and rejected.[47] That which produces rejection is, one may conclude, ultimately transposed from the sphere of femininity and everything connected with the feminine; Céline's anti-semitism, as well as his abjection, is but the other side of a misogyny born out of an ideology that serves to foster such views.

As is well known, the figures of focus in Kristeva's work all tend to be marginal in one way or another. Whether they are homosexuals, women, displeasing intellectuals or dandyish poets they all push the limits of the acceptable. The theory of marginality is often evoked as a revolutionary idea of subversion, or a postmodern notion of ethics. Marginal existents, however, are not necessarily heroes. The objects of Kristeva's studies are neither particularly revolutionary nor particularly ethical. They tend rather to be unheroic at best, like Proust and Baudelaire. Sometimes they are tragic, like Duras, or unsympathetic, like Rimbaud. At worst, they are fascist and misogynist, like Céline. Given the inherent pathologies in any society, language will always open towards experiences that are neither ethical in the normative sense nor particularly constructive. The problem that must be asked, then, is if the radical separation between the ethical sphere of love and transference on the one hand and the normative values of justice on the other should be upheld, even when it comes to 'marginal' discourses. This point of view is consistent with a refusal to replace one symbolic order with another. Art does not necessarily help construct a better or more just society. Quite the opposite: the force of art consists in a relentless and often nihilistic challenge to symbolic structures. The occupation with themes such as violence and obscenity is not a window to the unconscious, but gives witness to the inherent weakness and instability of a given society or nation. Literature challenges the desexualised and sublimated discourse of normative language, injecting the drive and reinvoking heterogeneity.[48] And at the same time, it defines the subject per se. There is no well adapted subject to contrast with the pathological mode. The subject of art, rather, is this very break with a stable discourse. In so far as there is subject, it can only emerge as resistance against, rather than identification with, a normatively instituted language, such as it has been instituted in a certain mother tongue, for instance. But there is no specific goal attached to the resistance. The subject of art does not have an emancipatory goal; it is not a political reaction but a productive and differentiating force, resisting all strong symbolic structures such as nationalism.

Subversion of the body: *The Idiots*

The obsessions of Danish filmmaker Lars von Trier are as dubious as they are relevant to the issues of abjection and sacrifice. The themes of unconditional love, feminine sacrifice, childish gestural provocations and victimisation are contrasted with the neurotic fears of normality and authoritarian abuses of power. In relation to political discourse, Lars von Trier's films are politicising an elsewhere that has also been the focal point of French philosophy from the 1960s onwards. Julia Kristeva, Gilles Deleuze, Alain Badiou, Michel Foucault and others have all evoked a politics of transformative practices against a normative discourse. As discussed in the first chapter, Roland Barthes evokes a politics of pleasure in his attempt to demythologise pleasure as a simple and rightist concept.[49] In fact, the case of *The Idiots* is interesting not least because it stages a return to the ideas of the revolt of the 1960s, which also saw the birth of contemporary art forms such as situationist performance, a radicalisation of the surrealist desire to shock with an outspoken political intent. Rather than the feverish excitement of Paris of '68, *The Idiots* is situated in the sleepy

Danish suburbia of the 1990s. The kind of revolt that is staged is however a return to the gestures of a pleasurable transgression that was part of the alternative ways of thinking for the political of the 1960s and 1970s. In fact, von Trier has himself explicated the film as an expression of his own hatred of the living experiments of that epoch: alternative communities and families only cover the pathetic side of dogmatism in suburbia.

Revolt as return offers a certain commutability with the regression staged in the film, and allows us also to consider the highly ambiguous effects of that return. Kristeva's view of the abject already makes it 'situationist', since abjection is theatrical, a demonstrative act of separation that takes place, as she says, 'not without laughter'.[50] Whereas the politicisation of another scene has been an interest among most of the radical philosophers in France of the 1960s, few have emphasised the neurotic and perverted pleasures of that revolt and the ambivalences that are already inherent in it; in doing so, Kristeva is not just endorsing a politics of pleasure but also bringing it to its impossible endpoint. Because of its language, Kristeva's ideas of the political dimensions of expression become relevant too. The rules of 'dogma' filmmaking require technical minimalism: no artificial lights, no make-up and a hand-held camera among other things. The result is a cinematic language where the technical devices are no longer made invisible, but rather allowed to dominate the screen. The graininess and shakiness of the image are features that could be called a cinematic language dominated by the semiotic. It creates a perpetually fleeting viewpoint that makes perceptual space uncertain and fleeting, and the borders between perceived object and point of view become compromised and ambiguous.

In *The Idiots* the semiotic language of the film is impossible to detach from its theme; a group of people deciding to live together and act out 'the idiot' inside themselves, both in the bourgeois neighbourhood in which they live and with each other. Replacing speech with sounds, experimenting in touching each other without inhibitions, they are looking for the moment of *spassing* when mimicry of regression has been transposed into a genuine state of enjoyment. There is no aim with the provocative gesture, except for the provocation and pleasure taken in the revolt through *spassing*. The group goes to restaurants, to job interviews, to a home for retarded people, on field trips, acting out the gestures and sounds of retardation only to be received with a mixture of consideration and condescension. The provocation lies in not just the challenge to social norms in behaviour. *The Idiots*, inept at communicating or acting in conformity with linguistic and social norms, clearly threaten not society so much as the identity and sense of self of the people they are encountering. Their enjoyment is the embarrassment of others. Consequently, the first half of the film is quite funny, showing the fear of bourgeois suburbia in the face of such boundless pleasure. The mood changes, however, when the group inverts its efforts to transgress towards its own members and becomes increasingly menacing. Gradual disintegration ensues. A girl, who has fled from her home, is collected by her father because her psychosis is not just enacted, but real. The main female character, who has been attracted by the group in a state of vulnerability after the death of her child, is slowly falling apart to the point of 'idiocy' and continues to *spass* after the group has been dissolved. The subversive gesture of the Idiots reveals itself as a blind alley, undoing not just repressive norms of society, which is trying to rid itself of those that are different, but also those norms that serve to tie the bonds of love and protection. The leader of the group is revealed as a fanatic with no consideration for weakness and gives witness to the kind of dogmatism that Kristeva from early on has diagnosed as political perversion, a symptom of denial rather than intellectual force. The fascination transfixing an individual to a political idea is, she argues, in fact of the same kind that attaches an individual to a perverse fixation. What lacks in this experiment, as in perverse fixation, is the moment of sacrifice in which pleasure in given up: there is no decapitation of the revolt.[51] The experiment is, instead, escalating to the point where a harsh doctrine of enjoyment replaces the pleasure taken in the transgression of phobic social norms, indicating that there is no possibility to 'tame' pleasure and avoid its continuation into the perversity of enjoyment. In that regard, there is in fact not that much difference between the compromised position of a fascist like Céline in prewar France and the subversive gestures of the Idiots in 1990s Danish suburbia. Political perversions are all commanded by an ideal that refuses reality in favour of libidinal or sublimated forms of gratification. As has been recognised from early on in Kristeva's work, there is a direct link between the refusal to give up on gratification and the persistence of the abject, shooting through the demarcation line between subject and object, fascination and horror, heroic subversion and disintegration. The gestural provocation of the group of 'Idiots' is allied to the aesthetic of Kristeva herself. The idea of there being an invisible symbolic order, comprised primarily of linguistic and social norms, against which art is 'revolting', is not far from von Trier's vision of the Idiots upsetting sleepy suburbia. And von Trier's vision could perhaps be said to recall the criticism directed against Kristeva for her belief in the semiotic: it is precisely in its own efficiency that semiotic transgression may appear politically useless and self-destructive. The majority of Idiots, safely lodged in the house of a well-to-do uncle, are not really putting anything at risk; they are merely enjoying their transgression. But for the subjects who really are exposed to the disintegration of the invisible limits between 'normality' and psychosis, the experience is a disaster. In the end, the transgressive gesture does not disrupt social norms, only those who are already crushed by them.

The question would be then: in promoting a politics of pleasure – another word for politicising those other spaces of corporeality and art promoted not only by Kristeva but also by Deleuze and Foucault for instance – are we really putting social norms at stake or are we merely enforcing other kinds of divides? Do we respond to the upset with new fetishist fixations, or are we capable of accepting the ambiguity that any politics of pleasure must be prepared to sustain? Although Kristeva's body politic is indeed open to such criticisms, perhaps one could argue that the body of pleasure is not hedonistic but a site of all those processes of displacement and transposition that Freud has called the primary process, processes that tend to overshoot the sacrificial logic instituted by the models of political representation. A revolt of pleasure is not an event, or a vision, but a gradual process of displacement and condensation that takes place in and through the corporeal subject, rather than in the organisation of social and political institutions. In order to avoid new fixations such pleasure must be supplanted by sacrifice. As has been discussed concerning the semiotic revolution in the first chapter, the body politic of Kristeva will waiver between pleasure and sacrifice. It is pleasure because all transgression involves a return to corporeal processes of symbolisation. It is sacrifice because all revolutions must end with decapitation, which in this case involves a temporary stasis or halt in the movement of destabilisation: the body is recuperated only to be lost again.

Jouissance of the stranger

The stranger is a being of *jouissance* and irresponsible pleasures rather than alienation. The fact that dissonances of our identities would appear in symptoms such as *jouissance* and melancholia, and that mechanisms such as projection and introjection are at work in our relation to others, is an effect of the sacrificial logic we have been discussing. Since such dissonances are part of our identity, the stranger acquires a pivotal role in Kristeva's theorisation of a politics of pleasure. As Ewa Ziarek has noted, Kristeva's notion of the stranger is the point at which the ethics and politics of her work form a significant relation. The foreigner incarnates an irreducible social antagonism that is inherent to the modern nation state.[52] Ziarek herself argues for an ethics of 'becoming', based on Levinas's and Irigaray's model of the body as intrinsically other to the ethical subject, and therefore as a model of an ethics of responsibility for the other, not only allowing for differences but also productive of them. The other is irreducible to the image of the ego ideal or the fetishist embodiment of the abject in social relations. Difference cannot be sacrificed for justice and justice cannot be allowed to transcend difference as a normative criteria either. Such a social antagonism makes perceptible that a democratic politics, argues Ziarek, has to examine the potential of *jouissance* as well, whether it be destructive or not.[53] The importance of Kristeva lies in her theorisation of the imaginary powers that steer hegemonic formations, and in her emphasis on enjoyment as a mode of being that transgresses the boundaries between ethics (the question of alterity) and politics (the community of differences).

It is, as I have argued above, necessary to differentiate between a form of enjoyment that is pleasure and embodied and the kind of enjoyment in which the body is given up in favour of perverse fixations. For this reason immature gestures such as those presented to us by *The Idiots* – a film enacting the ritual returns to such origins if any – becomes truly challenging. And such gestures are not new; they are, as Kristeva herself has shown in *Strangers to Ourselves*, dateable to the origins of sacrificial notions of political representability itself. Already Hegel had a reading of Diderot's *Le Neveu de Rameau*, published in 1805 in Germany, and 1821 in France. The novel is a dialogue between a self that is a philosopher and the awkward *He*, an ebullient body acting out everything that is being said in a distorted fashion:

> He was prostrate at my feet, his face on the ground, and seemed to be clutching in both his hands the tip of my slipper. He was crying and sobbing out words ... He jumbled together thirty different airs, French, Italian, comic, tragic – in every style. Now in a baritone voice he sank to the pit; then straining in falsetto he tore to shreds the upper notes of some air, imitating the while the stance, walk and gestures of several characters; being in succession furious, mollified, lordly, sneering. First a damsel weeps and reproduces her kittenish ways; next he is a priest, a king, a tyrant; he threatens, commands, rages. Now he is a slave, he obeys.[54]

For Hegel, the text shows that individuality is unstable until it becomes 'universal'. The nephew is the incarnation of the perversity of court culture or 'pure culture', where consciousness is estranged from itself and split, beyond possibility of being reconciled through universality.[55] For Kristeva Diderot's texts insist on the specific pleasures associated with the split subjectivity of the foreigner: 'Being alienated from myself, as painful as that may be, provides me with that exquisite distance with which perverse pleasure begins, as well as the possibility of me imagining and thinking, the impetus of my culture.'[56] Living between cultures, between tongues, like an orphan without parents, the foreigner is exposing modern man to the contingency of his own identity. In Kristeva's reading, it is not by chance that the nephew's cosmopolitan idiocy is contrasted with universalist demands. The nephew, in fact, tries very hard not to be a citizen, not to be subjected to sovereignty or indeed to the sacrificial logic of any contract. He is from many disparate places and origins; a cosmopolitan not through travels but through the dispersal of his many positions as subject. Such a strange man, spasmodic to the point of idiocy, she argues, is in fact a reaction against the shortcomings of political institutions and their incapacity of embodying symbolic power. In fact, the worse the symbolic institutions seem to function, the more the idiocies seem to multiply.[57] Ultimately, the political stance incorporated by such a strange personality is, of course, a rejection of the sacrificial logic instituted by the new universalism. This is in line with the argument that we have proposed: there is no project of emancipation properly speaking in Kristeva's work: The subject of intimate revolt is rejecting freedom and autonomy in the name of universalisable models, aiming instead to release forces of productivity and differentiation, where the site of the political is displaced from universalisable representations to non-representable subjectivities. Given that logic, we may perhaps look at Kristeva's politics with new eyes, such as it has been enacted by idiots in Hegel's time as well as our own: the return of pleasure.

5

REVOLUTIONS OF OUR TIME
Revolt as return

Revolt and return

The term of revolt is, as Kristeva underlines in her first chapters of *The Intimate Revolt*, not a moral concept but a temporal one. Re-volt is *retour*-return, *retournement*-return, *deplacement*-displacement, *changement*-change: return in the sense of repetition, not of the same but in the form of a continuous displacement. Only in the field of the arts is it possible to fully affirm a displacing return to an elusive origin; art is the return of a language to its past and to those elements that are most archaic to it – fear, passion, abjection, etc. The revolt of the unconscious is serving to uncover a domain that continues to withdraw from the normalisation and levelling of the dominant culture, the domain of *intimacy*. Intimacy is not privacy, but a form of interiority in which the body is being reinvoked as part of the mind: not a psyche but a *psukhe*, as in the Greek word for a soul of sensibility.[1] Describing modernity as a flight to intimacy, Hannah Arendt has warned against reinforcing an emphasis on intimacy that allows for social bonds to overtake the dimension of plurality that marks political society.[2] Arguing that intimacy has become excessively severed from the political domain, Kristeva, however, makes it into the privileged domain of revolt. Since the political is cut off from the private, it has become stale, abstract, and elongated from issues of daily life. The intimate is not the same as the private, but has evolved as a domain in which issues of life may be negotiated in a productive manner: the intimate is a domain of signification where the subject may share the questions, affectations and sensations that relate to a certain society at a certain point in time. It is thus a domain of sharing that may be directed to the public (in the form of art and literature, for instance) but still exist only in the singular. The intimate is a sphere of singularity, irreducible to the private. The intimate revolt is in fact the only possible revolt, intimacy being that which is the most profound and the most singular in us; the political having become too technocratic, too totalitarian and conflated with the social, the intimate domain evolves as a response.[3] The *revolt* is an irreconcilable conflict

110

between the subject-in-process and the normative order, demonstrable as an ongoing process of questioning and thinking in art and philosophy. The realm of interrogation in philosophy, psychoanalysis and literature is in fact a more potent political field than actual political negotiation in itself:

> it is not exclusively in the world of action that this revolt is real-
> ized but in that of psychical life and its social manifestations
> (writing, thought, art), a revolt that seems to me to manifest the
> crises of modern man as much as the advances.[4]

All subjects will in some way cultivate an ambivalent relation to social and linguistic norms. Though determined by these norms, part of the subject will withdraw from them. This phenomenon is, for Kristeva, the most important mark of the condition of modernity: it makes possible a space where subjectivity is continuously challenged and reconstructed. The intimate is all those phenomena and experiences that concern the subject on its way to becoming: aggression, love, melancholy, and so on, the return of elements that are most archaic to it — affects, desires and drives. An experience of the intimate, psychoanalysis recasts the soul/body dichotomy, and reintroduces the body into the life of the mind. This is done through transference, not representation. Only through transferential signifying practices such as art and psychoanalysis is it possible to fully affirm a displacing return to an elusive origin: revitalising the singularity of human life.

The idea of a process of thought and language continuously traversing representation has gone under different names: inner experience, negativity, the semiotic, the abject, transference, and so on. All these phenomena have something in common. They refer to the life of the subject excessive to a linguistic and social order. The pre-subjective, pre-Oedipal, etc. is not a temporal or biographical dimension but the irruption of timelessness in subjectivity. The notion of there being a pre-subjective sphere inflected in subjectivity, beyond history and discourse, which produces the politically challenging aspect of the subject, is by far the most criticised assumption in Kristeva's thought. Lacanians, feminists, Marxists, etc. have all found fault with it: for remaining in the imaginary, for romanticising transgression, for individualising the political, etc. Therefore, what makes Kristeva's latter work so interesting is that she has come to reconsider, or perhaps elaborate, the temporal aspect played by the notion of the pre-Oedipal. Works such as *The Sense and Non-sense of Revolt* and *The Intimate Revolt* argue that one of the most important aspects of modernity is the eruption of the uncon-scious in thought and language, an eruption of timelessness overcoming and liquidating time itself. For Freud, the unconscious is timeless, which means, as Kristeva puts it, that death is overcome; the unconscious cannot be talked about in terms of negativity, but as a kind of immanence of dead time, irrupting in conscious time.[5] The timeless unconscious makes itself known as memory-traces, moments of breaking and splitting in thought and language, serving to uncover the dynamics of the dominant culture. It is the pre-subjective, pre-Oedipal irruption of enjoyment in the life of the subject, overcoming the finite disposition of subjectivity.

The definition of the subject through intimacy is a contrast to Lacan's concept of *extimacy*, where the subject is constituted in and through that which is radically foreign to it: the Thing that is foreclosed in the space of the real.[6] Recasting that foreign entity as a thing of *intimacy*, Kristeva reverses the perspective on its irruption in subjectivity. Rather than relying on the symbolic order and its correlative the real as keys to the structure of the subject, and hence to its extimate organisation as symptom and *tuche*, intimacy refers to the Kleinian experience of a foreign entity taking part in the life of the subject as an interiorised object. If Lacan's notion of extimacy is a challenge to the idea that the subject is a form of interiority, then Kristeva's notion of intimacy challenges the Lacanian idea that the structure of the subject is based on foreclosure. The extimate thing of foreclosure can only be known as symptom. The thing of intimacy, however, is lived through language, thought and art. Not a product of foreclosure but of transference, the thing of intimacy transpires through experiences of the foreign and through an enjoyment that marks the singularity of the subject.

The intimate structure of subjectivity reveals itself not only in literature and psychoanalysis but also in philosophical thought. Touching the frontier of absolute negativity, *re-volt* is a permanent element of thought. Being is revealed not through insight but in the form of conflict and contradiction. In Hegel, this is obvious: the negativity of being gives birth to the dialectic. In Sartre, negativity shows itself as freedom. Freud, in his text 'Die Verneinung', links the function of negativity to naming and thinking. The being of Heidegger's Dasein is shown through anxiety or sensations that are in themselves experiences of such a negativity. Dasein becomes, in Kristeva's reading, not an alternative to the subject but rather an alternative form of unconscious subjectivity. Like the subject of psychoanalysis, Dasein understands itself in relation to that which is foreign to it. The subject of unconsciousness, like Dasein, is other also to itself. For Heidegger, the examination of being throws Dasein outside of itself, towards structures that are both escaping and defining it. Such a transcendental intuition of the other, argues Kristeva, will show itself as revolt. In forcing me towards the other in me, it will push me towards an alterity that will force me to question, interrogate and think, activities that in themselves must be considered the beginning of all politics.

Having defined the subject as the alterity of the unconscious, Kristeva approaches Dasein to the Freudian subject. In psychoanalysis, the Oedipal structure of the unconscious indicates a subjectivity that can only fully be understood through its specific temporality, just like Dasein reveals the human subject as a primarily temporal being. Interpreting the temporality of Dasein in terms of repetition rather than historicity, as disruptive rather than projective, Kristeva identifies Dasein through another kind of temporality than the one examined by Heidegger himself. Beneath the kind of temporality that is revelatory and projective lies the repetition of the drive that forces Dasein onto the question of his being: the repetitive re-volt or return of the drive through which all questioning is carried. In Kristeva's provocative reading of Heidegger's approach to Hölderlin, these issues are being illuminated. That which is foreign to Dasein is not what Heidegger himself called the Greeks, or the negativity revealing itself as being through poetry, but rather negativity revealing itself through the language of psychosis. Heidegger's notion of the foreign is worked out in his encounter with Hölderlin's poetry because the question of truth is opened not where language is revelatory of the being of Dasein, but at the point where language ceases to work and the process of symbolisation collapses. Nothingness in Heidegger presents itself not as nothing, but as being. In Heidegger being announces itself through *Stimmungen*, reinterpreted as affects by Kristeva. Where nothingness presents itself as repulsion, expulsion and fascination, a form of being comes to the fore.[7] Heidegger's recourse to affects in his analysis of language gives witness to this fact through the 'eradication of the distinctions between subject and object, the attack of the drive, language becomes "tonality" (*Stimmung*), memory of being, music of body and of matter'.[8] In Hölderlin's poetry language reaches the end of the work of negation-symbolisation. In this, it incarnates the alterity of the unconscious, showing that the temporality through which the question of being can be posed is the temporality of the unconscious itself. Rather than interpreting the limits of language as foreclosure of the symbolic, Kristeva shows it to be a point of displacement. The temporality of the revolt must be understood as a challenge to thought *without* being reduced to the traditional terms of dialectics, or as the historical transformations of consciousness. The revolt is, instead, a function of displacement. In its radical questioning of the unity of meaning, Freudian psychoanalysis has announced the kind of revolution of thought and language of which philosophy and literature are other kinds of realisation. 'L'avenir d'une revolte' or the future of the revolt is not futural or a projective vision, but the establishment of a displacing return, a permanence of the function of negativity, questioning and interrogating, challenging and reconstructing given presuppositions.

In this psychoanalysis has suggested another kind of politics, where the radical alterity that splits society open is continuously affirmed rather than suppressed.[9] Like Heidegger, Kristeva stresses the open character of political commonality. Since all subjects are determined by alterities we will never arrive at a total community. While *Mit-Sein* is a form of commonality of singularities, in which the alterity of the other will appear through the alterity of the self, Oedipus is the coming into being of a subject through double negation: self and other oppose each other in an infinite series of splits.[10] In Kristeva's reading, the Heideggerian analysis of *Mit-Sein* is positing the co-existence of singularities in an open community. The Freudian analysis of Oedipus could also be said to imply a form of commonality beyond the individual destiny. Both modern philosophy and psychoanalysis have, according to Kristeva, touched the limit of frontier of absolute negativity in recognising an unapproachable alterity in the midst of the community and made the *re-volt* to a permanent element of thought.

The time of the revolt

Like Hannah Arendt, Kristeva organizes the political around a notion of temporality that emphasises the corporeal aspect of political action. The frailty of human affairs, as Hannah Arendt has argued, comes out of the principle of natality, every human action lacking boundaries that would make it finite in space and time. Arguing that such frailty marks not only actions but also the institutions that are the product of human relations, such as the law, Arendt asserts that modern political institutions are but illusory protections against a frailty of which the ancient had a more lucid understanding: 'while the various limitations and boundaries we find in every body politic may offer some protection against the inherent boundlessness of action, they are altogether helpless to offset its second outstanding character: its inherent unpredictability'.[11] The principle of natality, or birth as Kristeva prefers to call it, is not simply transposed into the concept of re-volt, since re-volt implies return and displacement rather than production of something new and unpredictable. What Kristeva has in common with Arendt, however, is a notion of temporality that takes maternity as its given model, although they interpret the maternal aspect of human action in opposing manner: whereas for Arendt maternity is giving birth to, for Kristeva it is the site of alterity and ambivalent drives. Re-volt is not only return to an archaic origin, but a word connoting disgust and horror, thus forcing the displacement of the political from the public sphere of discourse to the intimate sphere of affects, desires and drives.

The temporal dimension of such a displacing, intimate revolt would dispute the traditional definition of the time of modernity, described as infinite progress, where new sets of values are continuously being established in favour of old ones.[12] The temporal dimension of return, which has been described by psychoanalysis as repetition, is not only a symptom of modernity in Kristeva's description, but also its very modality or mode of being. As Sara Beardsworth has convincingly shown in *Julia Kristeva; Psychoanalysis and Modernity*, modernity, for Kristeva, is not only an object for analysis of psychoanalysis, psychoanalysis is itself part of the issues defining it.[13] The question must then be asked to what extent Kristeva's thought is compatible with post-Marxist thought, which tends to be dismissive of psychoanalysis because of its individualistic stress on the subject. In A Singular Modernity, Fredric Jameson argues against the idea that modernity could be described as narrations of new forms of subjectivity. Such narrations usually posit the separation between subject and object as a distinct feature of modernity, traceable to the operations of the Cartesian cogito. In this version, modernity begins as consciousness of something, in the form of a subjective cognition of an object. The positing of cognition in this form is, however, not without its problems. Jameson finds the positing of the cogito to be imbued with ideological presuppositions. He does not consider capitalism to be a new form of consciousness. Capitalist ideology, rather, is a structure transposing issues of knowledge to the subject, and is inherent in the epistemological presumptions that structures an object in relation to a subject. Modernity can never be reduced to forms of subjectivity or forms of consciousness. Modernity must not be considered as the introduction of the thinking subject but rather as the transposition of knowledge towards issues of representation. Jameson follows Heidegger in positing modernity as intro- ducing repre-sentation as the focus of a knowing subject.[14] The valid discourses on modernity must concern forms of representation, not forms of subjectivity. Modernist subjectivity such as it can be found in the arts is nevertheless radically working through representations so that they become 'allegorical of the transformation of the world itself, and therefore of what is called revolution'. Revolutionary change, therefore, never begins in the subject, but in a present that finds its 'figuration in such unique psychic allegory'. In Jameson's ontologisation of the present, modernism is never a sign of subjective metamorphosis but of the demands placed upon the subject by the world, a world that can never be interpreted outside of the capitalist system and the technocratic orders that are being imposed in its wake.[15] No thinker can afford to forgo the question of capitalism in their description of modernity. Rather than aptly theorise modernity, or remain stuck in the allegorical mode of a revolutionary psyche, theory must move beyond the aestheticisation of modernity and aptly criticise the ideology of modernity that has been so involved with capitalism. For Jameson, the revolutionary language of modernism has little to do with affects or sensations, or even with ideas or thoughts. If literary language has any political significance it is because it is already imbued with the changes transforming the world.

An analysis focusing solely on representation, however, does not tell us how the limits of representation can be theorised if we are to bracket the subjective and pre-subjective processes that forego it. As a conse- quence, subjectivity and its correlative in affects, ideas and thoughts becomes possible to study only as allegorical representatives of the ongoing transformations of the modern world. That which Jameson posits as a world is detachable and possible to isolate from subjective experiences. It is not surprising that Jameson, for whom the subject and therefore anything called pre-subjective is uninteresting, in his survey of thinkers of modernity and modernism fails to mention Kristeva. A radical detachment between subjectivity and representation would, however, be refuted not only by Kristeva but also by Adorno, who in *Negative Dialectics*, argues for a move towards the subject of the materialist critique. The problem with the subject–object divide, Adorno argues, is that it tends to spiritualise the object as cognitive content, or to reduce it to the transcendental structures of subjective cognition. The only resistance against such spiritualisation or subjectivisation is the fact that all cognition has a somatic moment in it:

> The fact that the subject's cognitive achievements are somatic in accordance with their own meaning affects not only the basic relation of subject and object but the dignity of physicality. Physicality emerges at the ontical pole of subjective cognition, as the core of the cognition.[16]

That physicality, however, can never be reduced to a primal set of facts or sensations, but must be considered through the antagonistic coupling of subjectivity and objectivity that makes it impossible to simply posit the body as the mind's other, or the mind as the body's other. The outcome of that antagonism must, in Adorno's mind, be the precedence of objectivity, since there is no way in which we can spiritualise the somatic impressions that determine cognition. On the other hand, it is precisely because the object has precedence that it is impossible to do away with the subject, as Heidegger and Marxist materialism has attempted, although for different reasons. Whereas Heidegger's ontological analysis does away with ideology and the possibility of critique, Marxist materialism is unwittingly reproducing idealism in its denial of subjective reflection. As manifested in the history of philosophy, the dialectics of thought prevent us from doing away with the subject as an inherent factor of its own movements. Adorno, who theorised the gendered implications of the subject–object divide, has taken recourse to the questions of the unconscious, fantasies and desires imposing themselves in critical theory after Freud. Adorno, like Kristeva, has found reason to examine the processes of cognition that forgo representation in order to illuminate the dialectics of thought. Adorno, however, disallows a notion such as the pre-subjective, or the idea that there could be anything having precedence over the subject–object divide of reflection itself. In Adorno there is no correlative to a notion such as the *chora*, displacing and transposing the elements inherent in thought and representation before they become conceptual or figural. Negative dialectics cannot allow for the pre-objective, pre-subjective, pre-symbolic, pre-Oedipal, etc., because it would assume a layer of signification both anterior to and inflected in thought and language: an impossibility, since thought itself proceeds through a movement of negativity that precludes the assumption of anything exterior to it. In Adorno's description of early modern materialism, all elements that are heterogeneous to thought, such as pleasure and pain, are but remainders of a physicality demanding to be overcome. Both pain and pleasure evoke the possibility of a suffering threatening to the survival of the community: society must be organized so as to

> negate the physical suffering of even the least of its members, and to negate the internal reflexive forms of that suffering. By now, this negation in the interest of all can be realized only in a solidarity that is transparent to itself and all the living.[17]

This view presents itself also in the discussion of the reality of Auschwitz, where a fate more terrifying than death presents itself in the genocide and human suffering through which history seems to be accomplished. As is well known, Adorno sees metaphysical questions live on in the quest for the meaning of life, while history itself seems to have emptied the possibilities of finding an answer: our metaphysical faculty is paralysed, because it can no longer be joined to experience. Therefore, the course of history is undoing metaphysics, enforcing a materialism that for Adorno is irreducible to the Marxist categories of the market.

> The integration of physical death into culture should be rescinded in theory – not, however, for the sake of an ontologically pure being named Death, but for the sake of that which cadavers expresses and we are fooled about by their transfiguration into 'remains'.[18]

In Adorno's negative dialectics, therefore, the only point at which radical heterogeneity presents itself is through a suffering immobilising the capacity of representation. In presenting Auschwitz as the end of history in the modern era Adorno introduces a moment of foreclosure through which the idea that history is a continual development in which poverty and suffering is overcome is eclipsed and undone.

Perhaps Kristeva's abject could be regarded as a response to Adorno's call for a reintegration of physical death and corporeal remains into theory, thus theorising the leftovers of modernity's technocratic rule in the twentieth century. In order for such reintegration of death to occur, however, Kristeva introduces another function of negativity: denial rather than foreclosure. Crossing the lines between subject and object, body and affect, abjectal art denies the necessity of castration but does not foreclose it. In her psychoanalytic readings, death is contaminated by sexuality. Death is not foreclosed or impossible to represent; it is attached to the object that is introjected or incorporated in ourselves, caught in the limbo of our fruitless attempts of resuscitation through love, hate, abjection, projection and introjection. Beyond our fear of castration a more powerful form of anxiety casts its shadows in which the fear of losing the other has become the fear of losing oneself. The dead object is therefore maintained in a volatile and endless form of resuscitation.[19] This is also why negativity operates otherwise in her work than in Adorno's. There is no point of foreclosure; instead the dead are contaminating the living, the inside contaminating the outside, the other contaminating the self through, for instance, melancholy, love or hysteria. The difference between Adorno's dialectics and Kristeva's systematic displacement could be seen in terms of their highly diverse understanding of negativity. Whereas for Kristeva the term of negativity connotes a contamination of rather than a separation from alterity (such as the unconscious, or the libidinal object of fantasy, or, most importantly, the maternal object), for Adorno negativity is a moment of separation and ultimately foreclosure of the other.

In the early writings, Kristeva's notion of heterogeneity is introduced through matter. This means that her subject, although it may be split and determined by the unconscious, cannot be reduced to a psychic topology: it can never be thought outside of the body.[20] Dialectical materialism can be reduced neither to Marxist nor Freudian formalism. The terms of the dialectics – subject, object, signifier – do not simply negate each other but are traversed by an unconscious situated in the liminal dimensions of the body: the unconscious is always produced in and through a corporeal subject in conjunction with the effects of a signifier.[21] Kristeva's own notion of something radically heterogeneous to thought – corporeality, the unconscious, the semiotic, the *chora*, the object of intimacy are some of the names for that heterogeneity – must be considered challenging not only from the point of view of ontological questioning, or dialectical materialism, but also from the position of negative dialectics represented by Adorno. The temporality of the unconscious challenges not only that of Heideggerian Dasein but also the temporality of modernity such as it has been presented in the narrative of dialectics. The latter relies on an erroneous notion of time as progress where human subjects are continuously striving for something new and better. The idea that modernity is to be considered an overcoming of unnecessary suffering and death is made, if not invalid, then at least insufficient in Kristeva's thought. She takes up the challenge of Adorno, overcoming the foreclosure that has been installed after Auschwitz through theorising not only the irruption of death in subjectivity, but also the matter of death itself, through her theory of abjection. Most importantly, however, the psychoanalytic notion of temporality is consistently avoiding a description of modernity as a time of strife, against which death presents the only moment of rupture. For Kristeva the question of representation begins with horror, fascination or love, not with death. If modernity, therefore, is determined by the irruption of the un-conscious it means that it is determined by irruptions of timelessness overcoming and liquidating time itself. Death is overcome as the other of subjectivity, the body taking its place.

The body is always contaminated and contaminating. The maternal with which it is infused opens up a space of revolt that is not to be confused with the dialectics of protest caught in the paternal axis of symbolic laws; as has been discussed in Chapter 4, such a protest would be considered caught in the double-bind of the socio-symbolic contract. Politics is constituted as a field of contradictions and struggles that cannot be dissociated from the contaminating effect of the body itself. A revolt would thereby have to return to Freud and to 'an analysis of the political instance neglected by Freud, an instance in which the plural strategies, dominated by the struggle of contraries, seems similar to the lack of being in the subject in relation to the signifier'.[22] Referring to the Freudian hypothesis of maternal divinities as being more archaic than paternal ones, Kristeva's thought is not only traversed by the impulses of the Freudian/Kleinian maternal body, but wholly produced by that body. No other post-Marxist theory would recognise a pre-discursive or corporeal notion of subjectivity having precedence over the discursive conditioning of the subject. As Laclau and Mouffe put it: 'subjects cannot ... be the origin of social relations – not even in the limited sense of being endowed with powers that render an experience possible – as all "experience" depends on precise discursive conditions of possibility'.[23] Laclau and Mouffe argue that not only is a subject a conglomerate of discourses articulating various interests and needs, and therefore a point of dispersion rather than a singular identity, but it is also an overdetermined entity, the representative of a number of a historical, political and economical points of interests coming together at a certain moment in time. But even if Laclau and Mouffe are directing their interests precisely towards such subject-formations rather than representations and objects, no body is contaminating the discursive formations of such subjectivities. The question of how we are to regard Kristeva's notion of the political cannot be detached from the corporeal determination of what she calls the fourth term of the dialectic: the drives of the embodied subject, which determines the temporal quality of signification. Although reminiscent of Laclau's notion of political antagonism, it adds a decisive corporeal dimension that in turn determines its temporal quality. Although both Laclau's political antagonism and Kristeva's fourth term of the dialectics are terms of resistance situated outside of the traditional materialist dialectics, Kristeva adds a quality that situates in the body of the subject. For Laclau political antagonism is a rupture from the outside, and a contingent form of dislocation.

For Kristeva, the fourth term of the dialectic is a drive of differentiation and displacement that cannot be considered outside of its corporeal conditioning. Such corporeal conditioning produces the temporality of the revolt: an incessant and repetitive return, productive of the *jouissance* that marks the singular quality of human life. This is also what makes the notion of an embodied subject of the drives and of the unconscious so powerful: it institutes a temporality unconcerned with the 'new', with progress, or with the creation of new imaginary collectivities. The time of the revolt is a time of pleasure, produced through an incessant return. Revolt gains its political power in the displacement produced through such a repetitive turn.[24]

The limit of representation: the beheading

In 1998, Kristeva participated in the curation of an exhibition at the Louvre to which she had also chosen the theme: 'Visions Capitals', an exhibition on decapitation.[25] As clearly stated in the exhibition catalogue authored by Kristeva herself, the theme was clearly evoking a feminine experience. Although the images that were exhibited depicted both women and men, a beheading implies a wide array of literary, psychoanalytical and philosophical questions that take on particular significance in relation to women. In Kristeva's novel *Possessions*, the story of the travel of a Parisian journalist to an imaginary country and the ensuing murder of her friend, the narrative opens in the following way:

> Gloria was lying in a pool of blood with her head cut off. The ivory satin dress, the rounded arms, the long manicured hands, the Cartier watch, the diamond on the ring finger of the left hand, the sun-tanned legs, the shoes matching the dress – no doubt about it, that was Gloria. There was nothing missing except her head. 'My sexual organ', as she laughingly used to call it, referring to the cerebral pleasure she got out of her work as a translator and the equally intense pain she suffered from her headaches.[26]

A motive in painting from Leonardo da Vinci to Caravaggio, the decapitated body marks, says Kristeva, the limit of the visible: 'the deepest depths of horror can't be seen...'.[27] Given its long tradition in the arts, it seems as if that very limit has prompted a fascination that has been inspirational for some important women artists. What does the beheading of a woman come to mean in a feminine or even feminist discourse? We may think, for instance, of legendary Italian painter Artemisia Gentileschi and her images of Judith and Holofernes's head from the seventeenth century. Or we may think of French artist Louise Bourgeois, whose elegantly sculptured organs range from hands, arms and genitals to heads displayed without bodies, opening their mouths in the surprised gaping of the newly guillotined victim. As if to complete them, she has also created whole bodies lacking heads, like *The Arch*, the figure of a woman violently bending backwards in convulsions. We may also think of Cindy Sherman's reworking of Hans Bellmer's *La Poupée*, the taking apart of a mannequin's body and the almost ritual replacement of her head in these images. Kristeva does not comment on these motives in contemporary visual art, but shows the insistence of the theme from archaic times onwards. The decapitated head suggests the limits of representation since it is associated with death, which is impossible to represent, and the feminine sexual organ, which evokes castration. The most archaic image of a decapitated head is that of the Medusa, the feminine head whose gaze must not be met, or the viewer would be paralysed. The figure of the Medusa is analysed by Freud as the monstrous head of the female organ, forbidden to the eye. Kristeva, in turn, notes that the phallic power of the head increases the fear it evokes. The only possible way to represent the phallic femininity connected with the head is through decapitation.[28] In Colette's work, the decapitation is that of the evil mother and a form of displacement of the decapitation of herself. Such decapitation relates to her work. The image suggests the forced cut that separates her from the monstrosity of her own work.[29] Still the beheading is more important for its undermining of the logic of representation than it is as a sign of hatred for the monstrous, archaic mother. Referring to the claim of an analyst the narrator of *Possessions* reports that women's dreams about heads are astonishingly frequent and speculates that 'women are eternal mourners of castrated corpses, passionate only about a guilty, that is, severed phallus'.[30] Inferring from the psychoanalytic logic of Kristeva we must conclude that such mourning is typically produced in a phallic culture that, as Kristeva points out elsewhere, is not necessarily obsessed with the representation of the phallus but rather with the 'unrepresentable', or the veil that covers the mystery of that which cannot be represented.[31] In a culture dominated by the fantasy of phallic monism the limits of visibility are therefore doubly determined: on the one hand by a veil covering that there is nothing to be seen, while on the other by the fantasy of a castrating violence beyond that veil. Such a castrating violence is then repressed in the aesthetic idealisation of the female corpse by Poe and others, and exposed in the feminist undoing of that idealisation in the work of, for instance, Artemisia Gentileschi, Louise Bourgeois and Cindy Sherman. A feminist undoing must, necessarily, be critical of the aestheticisation and fetishisation of that veil which is but the other side of the unconscious fantasy of phallic power.

As has been shown by literary historian Elisabeth Bronfen, the aestheticisation of dead women is inscribed into the modern history of literature; according to Edgar Allan Poe a woman's dead body is the most poetic subject in the world.[32] Such tendency to poeticise feminine death is not necessarily reducible to psychic projections as argued by Bronfen, who wants to show that a dead woman's body, situated at the limits of culture, is an archetypal image of abjection. The risk with such a reading, however, is that it may reduce the use of psychoanalysis to symptomatology and become oblivious of the issues raised at the limits of representation. As a contrast, we may evoke Heidegger's reading of *Antigone*. Antigone's being towards death, Heidegger stated, is 'the purest poem of all' because it indicates the limits of representation. Striving towards the limit of a finitude to which man is already given, Antigone poeticises the impossibility inherent in that strife, but she does not represent it.[33] This brings us back to our reading of Kristeva: in what way does her theory account for that which traverses representation? As we mentioned earlier in this chapter, modern thought has elaborated the separations between word and image, subject and object, thought and representation, since Descartes. In Heidegger's critique of such separations, poetry becomes the means of undoing them. Replacing them with the terms of appearance and concealment in *The Origin of a Work of Art*, Heidegger shows that the limits of representation coincide with the temporal and historical conditioning of Dasein. In his analysis of the poetic language of *Antigone*, Dasein can be seen as given to a projectional form of return to a finite disposition. What Heidegger does not do, however, in the critique of modernity that is implied, is to link such a notion of finitude to the corporeal disposition of Dasein. It is not by chance that the poeticisation of Antigone is focused on Sophocles' 'Hymn to man', stopping short of the sexual disasters in the tragedy's 'Hymn to Eros'.[34]

Evoking psychoanalysis, Kristeva elaborates a corporeal conception of temporality that in turn can be seen as a key to her critique of the fixation on representation in Western thought. Discussing the limits of representability in her comment on Sartre's concept of the imaginary, *Sense and Non-sense* reflects on how a representation is conceived. The symbolic demand on representability in the West is clearly linked to visibility. The image is not the same as representation, but all images are representations. The question is to what extent the image tends to co-exist with the symbolic; since Western thought is based on images it tends to kill the negativity at work in the capacity to imagine.[35] Both Heidegger and Sartre have identified the nihilating function of imaginary capacities; in going beyond the world through such a nihilating function the transcendental quality of the imaginary space may be affirmed. Kristeva's thesis is that the symptoms of today's 'maladies' are produced through an incapacity to affirm the nihilation through which imaginary spaces may appear. The limits of representability must protrude in the visible spaces that surround us. If it does not, the society of images becomes a threat to the possibilities of politics. When negative and nihilating functions are no longer allowed we are run over by 'images without imagination', killing consciousness and the capacity to think and feel. Since that capacity is in peril, a threat emerges that is more radical than 'the banality of evil' denounced by Hannah Arendt, argues Kristeva: the threat of destruction of psychical space. Freud's fantasy, on the other hand, allows for forms of representations in which negativity is at work. If the imaginary is to regain its potential, i.e. the capacity to create representations in which thought is productive it must affirm a form of negativity. Representations, whether they be images, words or other forms of expression, must be produced in the same intimate space of the unconscious as fantasy.[36] In its affirmation of the realm of fantasy, psychoanalysis allows for the function of negativity to reopen:

> Psychoanalysis only works on objects (fantasies, bonds, drives) that are already representations, afterimages (nachträglich, Freud says) of things and experiences that are intersubjective and 'negativised', 'unrealised', 'liberated' from the start in the essential freedom not only of consciousness but also of desire. In other words, psychoanalysis works on the constructions that are always already on the mode of not being, and it is here that it reveals the essential freedom of the speaking being.[37]

In operating with fantasy and thereby the processes of condensation, displacement, etc., psychoanalysis helps the imaginary. Art and literature in particular may fill the same function. Psychoanalysis has a privileged place in this argumentation, however, since fantasy is fully affirmed as both necessary and unreal, necessary since it serves as support of desire, and unreal since the very experience of psychoanalysis must consist in traversing it. In psychoanalysis fantasy is 'asserting itself as indispensable and in this sense real' but at the same time 'it poses its own necessity to dissolve like fantasy in order to appear in its essence of nihilating, liberating unreality'.[38] Kristeva is thereby identifying the Freudian fantasy with Sartre's view on the imaginary, and holds it to be the best protection available against the assaulting and mindless imagery that dominates consumer society.

The critique of thought as representation must be seen in context with her notion of the subject as embodied and as dominated by the drive. The Freudian subject is a subject of dead time rather than finitude, of repetition rather than event, of expulsion rather than separation, phenomena that must be conceived of as corporeal effects of the drive. The subject of intimate revolt is continuing the work of the subject-in-process, such as it was presented in the 1960s and 1970s, determined by the situation of corporeality itself: of the *chora*, as suggested in her early work, of the displacing movement of repetition, as suggested in the latter work. Such a time is explored in philosophy, art, literature and the practice of psychoanalysis. Completing the quotation from *Possessions* from above, Kristeva indicates the way in which the question of representation is being recast from its visual or phallic framework in her own poetics: 'the deepest depths of horror can't be seen though perhaps they may be heard'.[39] This important remark opens up another trail of thought: any beheaded body evokes the head of Dionysus, who by the German romantics was considered to be the same mythological figure as Orpheus: severed from the body but yet continuing to sing. Orpheus–Dionysus flows down the stream after the *sparagmos*, metamorphosed into the flesh and blood of the poem. That aspect of the myth of Orpheus has, however, not been accepted in the modernist discussion of the orphic problem of poetry that refers to the fleeting and defiant character of poetic representation. The time of Orpheus, such as it has been depicted in Paul de Man and others, is that of the allegorical reading, avoiding the relation between meaning and figural representation ever to be fixed and arguing that the resistance of such fixation is produced through the temporality of the reading subject in the encounter with the text. In the introduction to his essay on *The Gaze of Orpheus*, Maurice Blanchot argues that the night enveloping Orpheus at his descent in the nether world is evoked through an art that alone has the power to welcome him into that second night in which his work is concealment rather than appearance. The art of concealment possesses the enveloping power of feminine intimacy:

> Eurydice is the limit of what art can attain; concealed behind a name and covered by a veil, she is the profoundly dark point towards which art, desire, death and the night all seem to lead. She is the instance in which the night approaches as the *other* night.[40]

The other night is, beyond the representation of Eurydice, the exclusion of intimacy: the night of her refusal rather than her welcoming, the strange encounter with her closed body and face. Assuming a dead woman to be the most poetic subject of all, Edgar Allan Poe, Heidegger and Blanchot may well be uncovering that which is concealed in the other night, as Blanchot calls it, thereby undoing the separations that they perceive as problematic – between word and image, subject and object, thought and representation. But Blanchot's recasting of these metaphysical separations, through uncovering and concealment, immediately introduces yet another veil beyond which Freud has taught us to face a philosophically more dubious question: that of the unconscious and the processes through which it affects the life, desire and apprehension of the world by the subject. Appealing to horrors that can be heard but not seen, Kristeva indicates that the covering and uncovering of the veil is still caught in the phallic question of representation. Her theory of the semiotic is an attempt to overcome the idea that meaning is fixated through symbolisation as representation. Instead, it is a form of poeticisation, an intertwining of negation (symbolisation) and negativity (the undoing of or resistance to symbolisation). From such a point of view, 'the other night' to reuse the expression of Blanchot is experienced not only by finite being but also above all by an unconscious subject caught in the pulsating movement of negation and negativity, sublimation and repulsion. Both Kristeva and Blanchot evoke the origin and end of the artwork through the fleeting figure of a human body, but the signification of that body is conceived in two significantly different ways: in Blanchot, the figure of Eurydice becomes a representation of the work, detachable from the writing subject. The work becomes an object, detached from the subject through a kind of sacrifice that becomes all the more painful when that body of work, object or 'woman' closes her face and becomes a figure of death rather than a figure of intimacy. In Kristeva, however, the work of art or the text is conceived of in terms of a process of corporeal identification and as a process in which the boundaries between object and subject are never fully in place. In her readings, the object of art is transposed onto the object of the other and back again, invested with desires and drives. It is of course not by chance, then, that Kristeva's choice of works is focused on human forms and bodies. The body is affecting language and thought through the displacing processes of the *chora*. The processes of negativity and negation that can describe signifying practices are always produced in and through a corporeal subject with a complex history of somatisations and symptoms. The process of symbolisation as produced through the *chora* is therefore radically recasting the so-called orphic problem of representation that has occupied the theory of modernist poetry for such a long time.

A politics of displacement

At the heart of Kristeva's reshaping of an old-fashioned form of a materialist dialectics lies an unease with dialectical thought as such. To some extent dialectics is inescapable: political thinking itself can never escape the dialectical conditions in which it has been imbedded ever since the imposition of European universalism and the socio-symbolic contract that followed in its wake. Universalism will produce singularity as its negation, no matter what the aim of the universalist claim will be; it is impossible to merely impose a model of solidarity, feminist politics, equality and so on in modern society without suffering the revolt which that model will spark. This does not mean that political work is an impossibility but that any political project will typically produce resistance. Such resistance will not, however, express itself as conflict, but as displacement. Kristeva's psychoanalysis of symptoms such as narcissism, abjection, melancholy and so forth is the outcome of such a notion of displacement. Whereas the collective or society remains untouched in her writings, the fact that she keeps the subject in focus should not be mistaken for individualism. The symptoms of a singular subject is a product of displacement in relation to society and its history.

Kristeva's model takes its cue from the abstract universalism in Rousseau's social contract and its development in the negating processes of Hegel's historicism, resulting in the hollow universalism offered in works such as 'Women's Time' and *Strangers to Ourselves*, where the sacrificial logic of the socio-symbolic contract of modern society is replaced by a Freudian contract, making positive identification impossible. Rather than promoting an apolitical and naïve belief in artistic revolt, which she has often been accused of, her theorisation of the semiotic, of the pre-Oedipal, of the intimate, etc. draws the consequences of a sustained displacement of the political from the universal towards the singular: art and psychoanalysis.

The revolt that is being acted out in and by these domains is not to be regarded as forms of transgression, but as a displaced response to the violence present in a universalist organisation of society. Freud's notion of the unconscious serves to displace the dialectics in which the socio-symbolic contract has been caught since it came to dominate Western forms of society. Any social contract will be based on a form of violence, as Freud taught in *Totem and Taboo*; although the taboo, which is the founding prohibition of a socio-cultural order and exceeding any ethical or religious implication, is of unknown origin, one may infer that it has been imposed with violence in previous generations.[41] Psychoanalysis, together with literature, serves to displace the pleasure and sacrifice that any dialectics will necessarily introduce. The revolt, as we have seen, is necessarily prompted by pleasure, the enjoyment of the overcoming of sacrifice imposed by the socio-symbolic contract. Rather than positing pleasure and pain as affects and therefore as irrelevant to politics, one must look at what makes it so dangerous.

The enjoying woman has her head cut off. A decapitated woman with the head severed from her body is all too bluntly shutting us out from the intimacy of that other night. The motive of the beheaded woman does not present the irrepresentable as a veil, but changes the issue of representation from *what* is to be seen to *who* is seeing. Such a change is also explicitly performed in the orphic death introduced at the beginning of this paper: Orpheus becomes a 'you' and Eurydice an 'I', a reversal challenging to the logic of the orphic problem of representation in its traditional version. A beheaded woman such as the Medusa inverses the gaze and undermines the phallic fixation of visuality. Undoing the fixation on representation, Kristeva replaces the shadow of Eurydice with the negative glow of Orpheus. The figure turning around on his way out of the underground evaporates, and prompts a search for a whole new sensibility: using touch, voice, etc. In turn, the shadow behind the figure turning around, Eurydice herself, has not disappeared out of sight, but rather lost her sight. What is most important, however, is that the temporal logic of the orphic problem is reversed with this gesture: the fleeting representation to be captured is replaced with the glow of the subject to be. The text grapples not with the gap between signifier and signified, or the fleeting character of representation. What we find is not a subject in search for the object of desire. The negative glow of the poem is rather presenting us with a text in search of its subject. The involvement of the body of *aesthesis* in those terms offers an experience of intimacy in the very terms of which Kristeva is talking: rolling back and recovering a corporeal affectivity, fragile and reclusive. We are here being transferred to a domain of corporeality altogether. Any image of a beheading points to the highly charged status of corporeality as such. The body is not so much an object of thought, or representation, as a form of contamination following every process of symbolisation. The only freedom that psychoanalysis can offer is the realisation of life as a process of perpetual rebirth in which the body is nihilated through the sign and then recuperated again.[42] If the revolt has a temporality of its own, it is precisely in terms of corporeal frailty that it must be thought. The dialectics of such a revolt moves through pleasure, decapitation, displacement and return. Return to where, return from where? Perhaps to and from that through which we have found ourselves capable of the greatest pleasure: the polymorphous, sensuous body that still has so many secrets to be uncovered.

NOTES

CHAPTER 1

1 Kristeva herself tells this story in 'L'Hyperbole de ma mémoire' (1983b). Describing the atmosphere in the intellectual circles in France as a mixture of universalism and xenophobia, she gives an interesting background to the climate she arrived in.

2 As stated by Kristeva herself in 'Mémoire' (1983b).

3 Derrida cannot be considered a part of it. Although he published a couple of texts there, his relation to the *Tel Quel* group quickly became troubled in the non-ending game of positionings that went on among leftist intellectuals. Philippe Forest, who has written an exhaustive history of the story of *Tel Quel*, dedicates part of his research to the ambivalent relation between Derrida and the other Telquelians. Forest 1995, pp. 401–3.

4 Trans. by author, *Théorie d'ensemble*, 1968a, p. 10. The idea of finding a politics linked to such a non-representative idea of writing was not confined to one method or theory; at this point the group welcomed Derrida's critique against logocentrism as well as Roland Barthes's semiology, Kristeva's sémanalyse and Foucault's discourse analysis. The manifesto is one of the few documents indicating a common project among these thinkers

5 Sollers 1968, p. 70.

6 Kristeva 1968a, pp. 84–5.

7 The books have been edited and reworked into a scholarly format, whereas the articles often contain a more raw and prodigious material. These articles, moreover, demonstrate Kristeva's position in the group and in the leftist context in general. Many of the articles published in the reviews are discussions and transcriptions of debates where positions are challenged and contested, therefore Kristeva's own ideas appear more clearly but also in a more extreme form. This could be explained by the genre; as *Tel Quel* historian Marx-Scouras has argued, the very form of review invites a more political discourse than books, since a review has to keep up with actualities and make itself seen and heard. Marx-Scouras 1996, p. 2.

8 Trans. by author. See also 1968a, where Kristeva argues for the new science of semiology, researching the 'social text' of which literature is but one variety.

9 Kristeva 1970a, p. 126.

10 Kristeva 1970a, p. 124.

11 Kristeva 1969, p. 17.

12 Kristeva 1971d, p. 37.

13 Kristeva, rather than celebrate realism, which was the style traditionally favoured by Marxists, deems it to be a sign of a society in crisis and/or stagnation, and directs her attention to the avant-garde. Kristeva 1971d, pp. 37–8.

14 Forest has noted that Kristeva in particular was made the object of derision over *Tel Quel*'s 'theoretical delirium'. Not only was she slanted by the conservative establishment, but also by fellow Marxists. The critique was particularly fierce in the group connected to a competing Marxist review, *Change*, which was launched in 1970 and led by Jean-Pierre Faye. Forest 1995, pp. 345–6.

15 Kristeva 1970a, p. 133. Niilo Kauppi has observed the exchange with Ronat (of the group *Change*) and pointed to the fact that other linguists share Ronat's concerns, that of Kristeva never reaching the 'other' of the text and staying at a rather superficial level. Kauppi 1994, p. 256.

16 'Our work is situated elsewhere [than that of linguistics] … we are interested in making an epistemological study of the fundamental concepts of linguistics (sign, meaning, subject, etc.) before we use linguistics to constitute that which does not yet exist: a theoretically rigorous discourse on the *text*.' Kristeva, 1970a, p. 138.

17 Kristeva 1971a, pp. 20–1.

18 Kristeva, famously, presented the Russian linguist Mikhail Bakhtin in Barthes's graduate seminar in 1967, a name that until then had remained unknown to the French public. She presented her dissertation, 'Le Texte du roman', to a jury with Lucien Goldmann and Roland Barthes in it, but her important work in semiology was published in articles. She published her first texts on the 'sémanalyse' in *Tel Quel*, introducing notions such as intertextuality, dialogicity and polyphony. These notions became highly influential and important for the development of literary studies overall. Kristeva in *Sémeiotiké* first introduced the term intertextuality, which implies that all texts are produced in a textual universe where they are intertwined with each other. Kristeva 1969, p. 85. See also 1971d, pp. 139–69.

19 Kristeva 1970a, p. 124.

20 'Instead of searching for the negative in the dispersion of the signifier, or as imbedded in the construction of narrative strata, [one could regard] the discourse which is productive of the concept as a discourse incorporating the negative instead of as a discourse formation of the concept; in this way one could regard negativity – heterogeneity – to be a productivity traversing the subject.' Trans. by author. Kristeva 1971a, p. 22.

21 Kristeva 1970b, pp. 214–18. Discussion of an intervention by Catherine Backès-Clément on Lacan and Freud. It is interesting to note that, at this point, Melanie Klein is evoked by Backès-Clément but not by Kristeva herself.

22 Kristeva 1971c, pp. 135–41.

23 Kristeva 1971c, pp. 139: In French: 'la grande révolution culturelle prolétarienne chinoise'.

24 See the history of Forest, 1995, who discusses at length the involvement of the *Tel Quel* with an infamous Italian journalist, Maria-Antoinetta Macciocchi, whose account of Mao's China had been widely disputed as erroneous and propagandistic. Forest 1995, pp. 380–3.

25 Although there are of course no tendencies to totalitarian thinking in Kristeva's publications, there is little evidence of her distancing herself from veneration of the Cultural Revolution of the early 1970s. As late as 'Des Chinoises à Manhattan' (1977a) she is deploring the new China becoming more and more totalitarian, and effacing the traces of the Cultural Revolution. She is even deploring that no humanitarian organisation is looking into the effects of its effacement.

26 Kristeva 1983b, p. 53: In her memories Kristeva makes it clear that the political cannot be considered beyond the tools of psychoanalytic investigation; abjection having a privileged place in this analysis. This is also why she considers politics to be a modern religion: there is no difference between the

collective impulses finding an expression in religion and those finding an expression in politics.

27 'Our Maoism was an anti-organisation, and anti-partisan antidote, a pure utopia, which had nothing to do with the sects to the left (that were rightly suspicious of us), whether they were proletarian or not, they were all a fascinated and love-hating offspring of the P.C.' Kristeva 1983b, p. 51. Trans. by author.

28 Kristeva 1971c, p. 138.

29 Kristeva 1983b, p. 52. Trans. by author.

30 Kristeva 1972, p. 59.

31 See reviews on studies of Chinese poetry by Cheng Chi-Hsien and Michelle Loi. Kristeva 1972, pp. 69–71.

32 Kristeva 1973, p. 294.

33 Kristeva 1973, p. 296. Trans. by author.

34 Kristeva 1971a, pp. 2–34.

35 'The contradiction interior to social relation decenters the subject, articulates it as a site of passage, a non-place where oppositional tendencies are in conflict: needs, desire, drives the stases of which (the thetic moment, the representations) are linked to affective relations (parents, lovers) as well as class conflicts.' Kristeva 1973, p. 298. Trans. by author.

36 Kristeva 1973, p. 277. Such an idea of the self as enjoying its own splitting and falling apart is evocative of Barthes's notion of pleasure, in which pleasure is a pulsating movement between the coming together and falling apart of the self. The idea that transgression is related to an experience of going beyond the self is a model of enjoyment.

37 Kristeva 1973, p. 293.

38 This must be seen against the background of her interest in psychoanalysis. The third period, psychoanalysis and feminism, actually has its origin in 1969, when Lacan was thrown out of the École Normale. The *Tel Quel* group, however, protested by sitting in until the decision was reversed. From then on, psychoanalysis and Marxism become emancipatory projects to reconcile. As described in the history of the *Tel Quel* by Philippe Forest, 1995, pp. 442–63.

39 In 1970, Kristeva declared her independence of Lacan, countering a critique of Elisabeth Roudinesco. Roudinesco remarks that her tendency to obliterate representation altogether – even of 'a signifier for another signifier', which is the Lacanian definition of subjectivity – drives her into the position of a kind of Eastern mysticism in which subjectivity is negated altogether. See Kristeva 1970d; discussion with Roudinesco, pp. 134–40.

40 'In the symbolic order, the empty spaces are as significant as the full ones; it would appear, if one is to understand Freud today, that it is the gap of an empty space which constitutes the first step in all of his dialectical movement.' Lacan 1966, p. 392. Trans. by author.

41 As will be discussed in Chapter 3. Judith Butler has argued that the Lacanian distinction between the symbolic and the social is difficult to maintain; in its empty form the law cannot be but an ideality that in itself insists on the necessity of the social and historical reality of, for instance, the symbolic primacy of the father (2000, pp. 20–1). On similar grounds, Butler is critical also of Kristeva, who does not undermine the status of the symbolic with her concept of the semiotic; Kristeva does not give an account for how the paternal law generated bodies. See Butler 1990, p. 93. Butler's critique will be discussed further in chapters 2 and 4.

42 Kristeva, contrary to Lacan, introduces the social into the symbolic, defined as 'a social effect of the relation to the other established through the objective

constraints of biological (including sexual) differences and concrete, historical family structures'. Kristeva 1984, p. 29.

43 In *The Sense and Non-sense of Revolt*, Kristeva discusses the Oedipus complex, which is the foundational model of the symbolic in Lacanian theory; what has not been discussed, she argues, is the Freudian premise that Oedipus is destined to failure, not success, and it is the structural model of Oedipus that is not definitive in the psychosexual development of the individual. Psychoanalysis indicates an intricate triangulation between sexuality, thought and language, in which the symbolic insistence of the law of the Father is but one component. This is why Kristeva herself insists on the corporeal aspect of all symbolic identification, for instance through language, and the relation to the other, the object. See Kristeva 2000a, pp. 71–84.

44 Kristeva 1984, p. 24.

45 Kristeva 1984, p. 26.

46 '[T]he denoted object [the object of transference, drives, desire, etc.] does not disappear, it proliferates in mimetic, fictional, connoted object.' Kristeva 1984, p. 56.

47 According to Liddell and Scott.

48 Plato, *Timaeus*, § 51.

49 Referred to by Kristeva herself: *Positions*, Paris: Editions de Minuit, 1972, p. 101. In his commentary, Derrida draws attention to the subversive potential of Plato's concept of the *chora*, in relation to the metaphysical ontology that Plato has formulated afterwards. According to Derrida, the *chora* represents the idea of a shapeless cosmos outside of the philosophical paradigm, a cosmos that cannot be spoken of but is the very receptacle of the philosophical question itself: 'Philosophy cannot speak philosophically of that which looks as its "mother", its "wet-nurse", its "réceptacle" or its "mould". As such, it only speaks about the father and the son, as if the father engendered him on his own.' Derrida 1987, p. 293. Trans. by author.

50 '[T]he mother's body is therefore what mediates the symbolic law organizing social relations and becomes the ordering principle of the semiotic *chora*.' Kristeva 1984, p. 27. Others who have commented on the *chora* are Irigaray and Judith Butler: according to Irigaray, this image of the maternal is outside of language. It is enacting the excluded in language, in the shape of a patrilinear fantasy. The problem with Irigaray, according to Butler, is that she is miming this excess, that her economy of signs in her texts is only taking after the excess written in the dualism of Plato, which is excluding woman. Irigaray makes this excess to a specific feminine economy: when our lips speak together. According to Judith Butler, *Timaeus* makes the masculine a soul without a body, the feminine a matter without a body. Man is the form to be penetrated; woman that without form who lets itself be penetrated, but who can never penetrate the man. The body of psychoanalysis, according to Butler, is formed through the taboos of sexuality. Our sexual bodies are formed through a founding set of prohibitions. Butler 1993, p. 54.

51 Freud 1900, p. 602.

52 Fraser 1992, pp. 188–9.

53 Fraser 1992, p. 189.

54 Rose 1996, p. 154.

55 Butler 1990, p. 88.

56 Kristeva 1984, p. 68.

57 Kristeva 1968a, p. 89.

58 Freud 1900, p. 339.

59 Lyotard 1971, pp. 259–60.

60 Lacan 2001, pp. 63–4: 'The question is which version of the text we are given, of which Freud says it is all in the elaboration of the dream, that is, in its rhetoric. In all these rhetoric elements, metaphor, allegory, metonymy, synecdoche, repetition and so on, Freud teaches us how to read the open or demonstrative, covered or persuasive, revengeful or seductive intentions out of which the subject modulates his oneiric discourse.'

61 Kristeva 1969, p. 27.

62 Kristeva 1984, pp. 59–60.

63 Adorno 1997, p. 137.

64 Adorno 1997, p. 144.

65 Adorno 1997, p. 140.

66 Jameson 1990, p. 147.

67 God, Zizek argues, is unconscious; he constitutes the fantasmatic knot tying the person together. The kernel of our subjectivity, then, is not a founding signifier but the lack of it, the Real in which the belief in the symbolic is erected. See for instance Zizek's foreword to *For They Know Not What They Do; Enjoyment as a Political Factor*, lxx–lxxii.

68 Barthes is describing this polarisation as intellectuality against pleasure, reason against sensation, cold abstraction against warm life. This polarisation leads the left to emphasise method, reason, commitment, at the detriment of a pleasure that has become close to immoral. Barthes 1975, pp. 22–3.

69 Barthes 1975, p. 21.

70 Kristeva 2000a, pp. 84–5.

71 Kristeva 1984, p. 17.

72 In Freud's 'Project for a scientific psychology' (1895), where psychic formations are discussed in conjunction with corporeal excitations, the body is an organism trying to relieve itself from tension. The pleasure principle having not yet been introduced, satisfaction is explained as a discharge of tension or displeasure. When a child is hungry, for instance, it soon learns to associate the relief from feelings of hunger with satisfaction. Memory traces are then activated through feelings of hunger, teaching the child how to seek satisfaction. Or, the memory traces can produce hallucinations, or hallucinatory fulfilments, for example in dreams, until 'the organism' learns to look for 'real' satisfaction. Later in life, it is the ego that performs 'reality testing' in order to achieve satisfaction. The search for satisfaction, then, is cast under the avoidance of displeasure and can only be served through it. But affects of all kinds, whether they are feelings of pain or displeasure or satisfaction or pleasure, threaten the reflective capacities of the mind: Freud's description of the ego is that of a protective shield against emotions or affects of any kind. Freud 1895, pp. 358–9. In 'Instincts and their vicissitudes' (1915c), Freud develops the economic model of the psyche and affirms the all-encompassing domination of the pleasure principle of the psyche in arguing that even sophisticated intellectual capabilities are affected through the instinctual tension between pleasure and displeasure that causes the organism to seek release; an 'instinct' is 'a concept on the frontier between the mental and the somatic, as the psychic representative of the stimuli originating from within the organism and reaching the mind, as a measure of the demand made upon the mind for work in consequence of its connection with the body'. Freud XIV, p. 122. Freud also tells us that the fate of instincts is to be reversed (transformation of love into hate), turned onto the self (for instance masochism), repressed or sublimated. Pleasure is, in this logic, associated with the preservation of the ego and related to narcissistic impulses of love, as well as with the satisfaction of needs, including the satisfaction of sexual instincts. The ego is therefore not simply one of physical needs, but auto-

erotic. Such an auto-erotic ego is also prone to the mechanisms of introjection and expulsion of objects of pleasure and displeasure.

73 Freud 1905, p. 182.
74 Kristeva 1984, p. 147.
75 Kristeva 1984, p. 149.
76 Kristeva 1984, p. 149.
77 Kristeva 2000c, p. 17.
78 Kristeva 1984, p. 75.
79 In Freud's *Totem and Taboo*, this moment is instituted through the son's murder of the father. The killing is a moment of transgression, which will later both prohibit and allow for that moment of transgression to reoccur; after the murder of the father, his symbolic power has become even bigger. But after that their drives will always be decapitated by the father, because they will be determined by guilt rather than desire. This institutes a limit of desire beyond which one finds *jouissance*, a possibility of transgression at play in every form of symbolisation. This is the defining moment in the writings of Freud, who does not make sexuality into the biological essence of man. What he does, rather, is to inscribe animality into culture. Kristeva 2000c, p. 15.
80 Kristeva 2000b, p. 90.
81 Kristeva 2000b, p. 90.
82 Kristeva 1984, p. 80.
83 Kristeva 1982, p. 65.
84 Ziarek shows that Kristeva reveals the factors when society regresses to libidinal impulses like projection and introjection, and the imaginary becomes social institutions. Fanon does the same thing. 'Symptomatic of the deflection of the abject into the social realm, the racist and misogynist fantasies display the "drive economy" always already rationalized and mediated by the social judgement' (Ziarek 2001, p. 123). Kristeva's argument is, in brief, that xenophobia or fear of the other springs out of the unwillingness or incapacity to recognise the mechanisms of projection and introjection that motivates our fear. An affirmation of the idea that the other is as frail and faulty as ourselves would, instead, offer us a bond of solidarity.

CHAPTER 2

1 van der Poel 1992, p. 50.
2 This has been described by Philippe Forest, who also makes it clear that the most violent attacks actually came from those academics challenged by the *Tel Quel*. Most importantly, however, the theoretical movement was not accepted at institutions such as the École Normale, which meant that it threatened the strictly ordered hierarchy of French intellectual life. Forest 1995, p. 299–302. Patrick Ffrench, also, has observed the terroristic streak in the method of theorisation of the *Tel Quel* group and has partly structured his understanding of *Tel Quel* theory around it. Ffrench has observed that the terroristic attitude of the group is both a question of position, that of being on the outside of political discourse, and a question of affirming the 'terror' of theory as a threatening and subversive tool. It is to a large extent the terroristic attitude that places the group at odds with the Marxist ideology. Ffrench 1995, p. 124–5.
3 This pun is taken from Forest, who talks about the 'théoricisme terroriste' of *Tel Quel*, quoting the accusations of the academic and cultural establishment. Forest 1995, p. 299.
4 In her talk from 1983 on 'Psychoanalysis and the Polis.'

5 Kristeva 1982, p. 137.
6 Kristeva 1989, p. 235.
7 Kristeva 1986a, p. 203.
8 Kristeva 1986a, p. 203.
9 Kristeva 1986a, p. 201.
10 Kristeva 1986a, p. 205. Kristeva's ambivalent relation to homosexuality will be discussed further on.
11 As argued in the essay 'Le Vréel', 'The True-Real', from 1979. Kristeva only mentions terrorism and terror as aspects of the true-real at the beginning of the essay; one can only infer that she is hinting to an argument that would constitute a follow-up to the discussion in 'Women's Time'. The link to terrorism is significant, however, since it allows for the construction of an argument on the relation between terrorism and the symbolic authority lacking in 'Women's Time'. Basing her argument on Freud's *Moses and Monotheism*, Kristeva also indicates the seminal place of the text for her understanding of a dissenting or terroristic politics.
12 Kristeva 1986b, p. 224.
13 Kristeva 1986b, p. 223.
14 Habermas 1987, p. 284.
15 Habermas 1987, p. 226.
16 Habermas 1987, p. 226.
17 Habermas 1987, p. 245.
18 Habermas 1987, p. 284.
19 This is quoted from Kristeva's discussion of Derrida's concept of *différance*, which is defined as the heterogeneous element in symbolic retention in Kristeva's text, and thereby as the counterpart to the semiotic. Kristeva 1984, p. 144.
20 Eagleton 1983, p. 190.
21 Leland 1992, p. 131.
22 Elliott 1992, pp. 229–30.
23 See Kristeva 1984, p. 105. Quoting Marx, Kristeva argues that the text is a realm of 'freedom' beyond the necessity of labour.
24 Coole 2000, p. 7.
25 Kristeva 1984, p. 109.
26 '[T]hese individuals who have felt the fear of death, of their absolute master, again submit to negation and distinctions, arrange themselves in the various spheres, and return to an apportioned and limited task, but thereby to their substantial reality.' Hegel, *Phenomenology of Spirit* § 593.
27 Hegel, *Phenomenology of Spirit* § 590.
28 See in particular Kristeva 1971a.
29 Freud 1915, p. 236.
30 Kristeva 1984, p. 111.
31 Kristeva 1984, p. 119.
32 Kristeva 1984, p. 122.
33 Kristeva 1984, pp. 138–9.
34 In The Politics of Negativity, Diana Coole has evoked this problem, and called for a reading of Kristeva's theory as a dialectic, where the interesting aspect of the radical power of the negativity at work is considered to be its positive and manifest aspects: 'the question of negativity's representation is not about Truth or an ability to reach the thing-in-itself, but concerns a dialectical circling through the very becoming of knowledge and subjectivity as they are practised'. Coole 2000 p. 215.

35 See for instance the discussion by Diana Coole, 2000, pp. 228–9, in which she rightly compares the semiotic project of Kristeva to the struggles of Nietzsche's will to power, affecting mind, body and matter.

36 Fraser 1992, p. 187.

37 Kristeva 1970a, pp. 137–8. This is also why Kristeva's project could be considered what Jay Bernstein has called a post-aesthetic; rather than enhancing and enforcing the autonomy of a work of art, Kristeva considers it as giving witness to conditions of alienation marking modernity, thereby enhancing its political relevance and impact. This means that she, rather than considering a work of art as a disclosure of truth in the metaphysical sense, examines the grief following the loss of such truth. Art, in turn, will necessarily leave its confinement within the realm of autonomy and show its place in a community where the intertwinement of politics and aesthetics is a reality to be faced.

38 Kristeva 1974b, p. 21 (1981, p. 167).

39 Ziarek 2001, p. 148.

40 See Butler 1990, p. 1–6: 'Paradoxically, "representation" [in political terms] will be shown to make sense only when the "subject" of women is nowhere presumed', p. 6.

41 Kristeva's only real major article on the question of feminism in *Tel Quel* appears in a special issue: 'Recherches féminines' [feminine studies], in which the introduction by Kristeva speaks about 'Un nouveau type d'intellectuel: le dissident', Kristeva 1977b, pp. 3–8.

42 Kristeva 1977b, p. 4.

43 Kristeva 1977b, p. 8.

44 Kristeva 1986b, p. 295.

45 Kristeva 1977b, p. 5.

46 Kristeva 1986a, p. 58.

47 'It brings into play notions such as the following: the necessity of speaking one's language (not necessarily equated with one's native tongue) in its irreducible singularity (Scarpetta); the crossing of all linguistic and national boundaries (Kristeva); the free circulation of ideas, discourses and individuals; the rejection of any utopian vision of any ideal society, or of any political reduction of reality; the refusal of the mutilation of the subjective by the collective (Scarpetta). In this respect, dissidence is less a set of social and political values than a cultural ethics.' Marx-Scouras 1996, p. 189.

48 Moi, 2002, p. 168.

49 Kristeva's rejection of contemporary feminism is thus repeated in her latest work on feminine genius, Kristeva 1999, pp. 11–12.

50 Kristeva 1999, pp. 65–9. It is symptomatic that Kristeva chooses to refer the term of natality to birth (*naissance*) and thus give it a more corporeal and embodied connotation than Arendt does herself.

51 Fraser 1997, p. 166.

52 Kristeva 1986b, p. 37. Interestingly in view of our final chapter on temporality, Kristeva talks about feminism as a specific temporality – the women who stay outside of the affairs of the world remain beyond time, in a realm of mysticism and passivity.

53 Kristeva 1977b, p. 6.

54 See the discussion on Butler below.

55 Elliott 1992, p. 230.

56 Doane and Hodges 1992, p. 62.

57 Doane and Hodges 1992, p. 77.

58 Freud 1931, p. 223 ff.

59 Kristeva 2000a, p. 105.

60 Allison Weir (1993) has rightly seen this connection: 'Identification with the Divided Mother: Kristeva's Ambivalence', pp. 79–91, argues that Kristeva is promoting a heterogeneous politics through bisexual forms of identification, through identification with paternal law and with the mother as well.

61 Kristeva 1989, p. 244. Although Kristeva's analysis of the object investment in Duras's women is focused on limited examples in Duras's writings, it is quite clear that these examples are picked out for their exemplarity.

62 See for instance Kristeva's discussion of these connections in 2000a p. 75. According to Judith Butler, the problem with Kristeva's acceptance of Lévi-Strauss is that it causes her to posit the nature of homosexuality as psychotic (1990, p. 84 ff.). One may however extend that critique and infer that it causes her to pathologise bonds between mother and daughter all in all, perverting the pansexual capacity of the child in accordance with a patriarchal norm.

63 Kristeva 1987a, p. 55.

64 Kristeva 1987a, p. 71.

65 Kristeva 1986b, p. 29.

66 Kristeva 1989, p. 28.

67 In contrast, one may, as Sarah Cooper has done, argue for a Kristevan queer ethics, since Kristeva does not subscribe to the notion of a stable sexual identity. Cooper 2000, p. 161.

68 Butler 1990, p. 88.

69 Ziarek in Oliver 1993a, pp. 72–3.

70 Ziarek in Oliver 1993a, p. 76.

71 His delusion, says Freud, goes so far as to force an 'overcoming of the instinct which compels every living thing to cling to life', i.e. of the libido. Freud 1915a, p. 246.

72 Kristeva 1989, p. 25.

73 Kristeva 2000c, pp. 225–57. It is true that Beauvoir, like Kristeva, situates the feminine between nature and culture, and argues for the time of natality and the principle of birth against Hegel's struggle to the death. In Beauvoir's conception, however, such a position is stifling rather than productive.

CHAPTER 3

1 Kristeva 1991, p. 192.

2 Kristeva 2000b, p. 99.

3 Kristeva 2000b, p. 101.

4 See 'Women's Time', Kristeva 1986a, p. 194. The sacrificial concept of universality will be discussed further in chapter 4.

5 This can be seen in the second part of *The Origins of Totalitarianism*, where Hannah Arendt sees the irony persisting between those from prosperous and secure nations idealistically arguing for 'inalienable' human rights and the rightless, who are the refugees and the stateless. Ever since the declaration of the Rights of Man, man is defined through the people and not the individual. The rightless are not only deprived of the protection of the law, they are driven to transgress it because of that deprivation. In her argument, Arendt points to the close connection between the function of recognition and universalist ideology. The rightless are also stateless, and deprived of community, Therefore they are deprived of the possibilities to act. In this, the rightless are no longer recognised as human, or as a beings of speech and action. Arendt 1973, pp. 296–7.

6 In this regard, argues Ziarek, Kristeva is continuing the work of Franz Fanon: 'Symptomatic of the deflection of the abject into the social realm, the racist and

misogynist fantasies display the "drive economy" always already rationalized and mediated by the social judgement.' Ziarek 2001, p. 123.

7 Kristeva 1993b, p. 67.
8 Zizek 2001, p. 70.
9 Kristeva 1993b, p. 52.
10 Kristeva 1993b, p. 42.
11 McAfee 2000, p. 19. McAfee considers Kristeva's politics of psychoanalysis to be inadequate since it is an individualism. But at the same time she equates Kristeva's interest in psychoanalysis with the personal (p. 104), whereas in my view Kristeva is rather interested in widening the scope of political issues, and in redefining the political from the point of view of a subjectivity that is irreducible to individuality or to the personal.
12 Kristeva 1991, p. 229.
13 Kristeva 1991, p. 182.
14 Cf. Jean Graybeal, Oliver 1993a, p. 32–40.
15 As has been pointed out by Jacqueline Rose. Rose, also, holds Kristeva to be concerned not only with questions of identity, but also rather with the whole dark and anxiety-provoking area that lies beyond the actual splitting of identities. Rose 1996, p. 150.
16 Rose 1996, p. 159–60. At the same time though she shows the maternal abyss in that lack of fixed identity: 'if we stop at the critique of identity – the celebration of a heterogeneity which it is too easy politically to rebuff – we avoid the more troubling area which consists of the psychic ambivalence of the drive'.
17 Kristeva 1991, p. 132.
18 Kristeva 1991, p. 228–9.
19 In the master–slave parable self-consciousness demands another consciousness, which the self is to define in a negative way in order to supersede pure existence. Self-consciousness cannot be reduced to an individual with mere life. To attain that, one would have to ascertain something attached to that self-consciousness which allows it to transcend that of merely having life. Hegel calls this having freedom. Self-consciousness is achieved in a struggle to the death in which one is exposed to death or annihilation, to an alterity which also proves oneself as having a value, and as having freedom: 'the individual who has not risked his life may well be recognized as a person, but he has not attained to the truth of this recognition as an independent self-consciousness'. *Phenomenology of Spirit*, § 187.
20 *Phenomenology of Spirit*, § 186. For spirit to be free, it has not to be self-will anymore. For instance, the master is prone to regard the slave as a thing, a relation detrimental to his own access to self-consciousness: he holds the slave in subjection. With Hegel, power becomes an existential issue. In order to gain your life, you have to be prepared to die. No such struggle is ever given to the master. Sheer mastery is never a moment for recognition. Consciousness can only develop as dependence. It cannot just think itself to be free: this is an illusion. Most importantly, however, we must overcome the stage of scepticism where we perceive the world as truly contradictory, as two forms of consciousness, lord and bondsman, as free and not free.
21 It is not enough to say that everyone has a right to vote, regardless of race and sex etc. Each person should be recognised for his own specific identity. This means that all those that have been left outside, hidden or forgotten, or treated as if they are part of a universal kind must be recognised as different and treated as such. A politics of recognition may, however, be formulated not as one but as two conflicting principles: the first, a politics of equality, aims to enhance the idea that everyone has a universal right to respect. This is argued

by Kant, and social contract theorists like Rousseau. That which gives us the right to respect, for instance reason, is the same for each and every one. A politics of differentiation, on the other hand, aims to enhance difference and claims recognition on the basis of that difference. There is no respect unless difference is recognised. Defining another axis in modern politics, Charles Taylor observes an ideology of authenticity developing in romanticism; Rousseau is also the origin of a new discourse of *value*. Rather than accepting that only some people be given value, he assumes everyone to be worthy. Rousseau, therefore, becomes the father of the basic notions underlying the work of philosophers closer to our understanding of recognition. With his master–slave model, Hegel pursues what Charles Taylor calls 'a politics of equal dignity' that seems to be incomparable with a politics of differentiation; this is the conflict of traditions that multicultural society find itself caught in. Taylor 1992, pp. 50–1.

22 In the end, Taylor's argument is striving to undo the attempts of the homogenising tendencies that may lie in the demand for recognition; as well as ethnocentricity. In placing recognition amidst the group rather than place it in universal constructions Taylor breaks a multicultural politics out of a universalist tradition of recognition. Taylor 1992, pp. 72–3.

23 Kristeva 1991, p. 2. Kristeva argues that modern democracies have failed to include the individual in its universalist ideals; the symptom of that failure is the erroneous belief of the modern individual that symbolic structures such as the nation makes him strong and unitary rather than split and heterogeneous.

24 Kristeva 1991, p. 185.

25 Kristeva 1991, p. 181.

26 Kristeva 1991, p. 187.

27 Kristeva 1991, p. 14.

28 In Kristeva's view this would support Karl Appiah's critique of Taylor's piece on identity politics. There are various problems with believing in authentic identities at all. The definition or the experience of the collective identities that we have formed are not very abling ones; they are disabling. Karl Appiah is quite critical of using the concept of recognition as a parameter of identity politics. It can serve only as a confirmation of a self-hatred that has become interiorised, on the basis of collective identity precisely. Rather than becoming an emancipatory tool, identity becomes a kind of straitjacket. He has highlighted the problem with using the concept of recognition for a threshold politics of multicultural differentiation. The idea that multicultural identities need certain kinds of education, certain rights, etc. is not just a question of right. It is also assuming and claiming an identity for the individual, which may be experienced as a violence, or as force, or at least as restraining and restrictive. Every concept of identity has a normative aspect to it.

29 Kristeva 1984, p. 128–9.

30 See Cornell in Cornell *et al.* 1992.

31 McAfee 2000, p. 161.

32 McAfee 2000, p. 162.

33 Kristeva 1984, p. 111.

34 Huntington 1998, p. xix.

35 Huntington 1998, p. 11.

36 Edelstein goes on to distinguish those projects that are discursively based and those that are irreducible to given discourses: 'Rhetorics and metanarratives of liberation or emancipation will be achieved. But liberatory practices, like ethics and like subject-formation, are ongoing, heterogeneous, recursive processes which can never reach an end.' See Marilyn Edelstein, 'Toward a Feminist Postmodern Poléthique. Kristeva on Ethics and Politics'. In Oliver 1993a, p. 202.

37 Young 1990, p. 145.
38 Young 1990, p. 148.
39 Young 1990, pp. 152–3.
40 Kristeva's mistake, according to Beardsworth, is her recourse to a Freudian traumatology that remains within a narcissistic logic of return to the same, where the subject lacks the means of breaking the cycle of repetition. Such a traumatised subject, in Beardsworth's account, is one of projection and intro- jection, which remains within a narcissistic framework and disallows for a true ethics of alterity. Beardsworth 2004a, pp. 202–6.
41 In the case of feminism, for instance, and the question of how one is to relate the subject of 'woman' to a political struggle, this opens for Mouffe's conclu- sion to the age-old debate between liberal feminists and those that adhere to a politics of difference and recognition: 'To ask if women should become iden- tical to men in order to be recognised as equal, or if they should assert their difference at the cost of equality, appears meaningless once essential identities are put into question.' Mouffe 1992b, p. 373.
42 In *Hegemony and Socialist Strategy*, Laclau and Mouffe argue that the dispersal of the subject is only one part of the analysis. The various formations in which the feminine is constructed as a subject position – law, family, cultural forms etc. – have in common that the feminine is subordinated under the masculine. The hegemonic struggle must then focus on the construction of femininity as a kind of 'unity' as a term of sexual difference. Laclau and Mouffe 2001, pp. 117–18.
43 Laclau 1996, p. 13.
44 Guberman 1996, pp. 24–5.
45 Kristeva 2000b, p. 103.
46 Kristeva 2000b, p. 103.
47 In this sense, Kristeva's politics becomes an ethics. This is also something she announces in 'Sujet dans la langue et pratique politique', 1974a. Since the political is about the communal, and literature is about the singular, she argues, the most pertinent issues on art are ethical rather than political. This is a posi- tion that she will later modify, leaving the question of the ethical behind or simply conflating it with the political; or construing a *poietique*, as suggested by Patricia Huntington (1998).
48 At the same time, however, it is subjected and acknowledged only in its natural state: 'In politics "woman" is the subject of experience – the denatured, defemi- nized subject – that measures the gap between an acknowledged part (that of sexual complementarity) and a having no part.' Politics, argues Rancière, always involves the question of subjection, although the true philosophical question of the political revolves around the freedom of the 'demos', the people. Given that a political subject can never escape the force of the sign, politics produces subjects that are empty of a given content, such as 'woman' or 'worker'. The production of such identities is never arbitrary; they are defined in what Rancière calls a natural order, which means that they hold a given function in social and economic domains. Such identities appear to hold no mystery: 'Anyone can tell *who* is meant.' But political subjectivation neces- sarily forces a misfit between the natural order in which it is supposed to be defined and the political order that fails to recognise it as a subjectivity. The modern political animal is therefore a 'literary' one, an empty form that will never really fit its natural or social description. Rancière 1998, p. 36. Politics begins, according to Rancière, when those that do not have a part seek to be a part, or when those that do not have a voice seek a voice.
49 Arendt 1998, p. 183.

50 Arendt 1998, p. 180.
51 Kristeva 1991, p. 192.
52 Arendt 1998, p. 242.
53 Arendt 1998, p. 242.
54 Arendt 1998, p. 52.
55 'Nothing is unconditioned; nothing carries the root of its own being in itself ... [Subject and object, man and matter] each is only *relatively* necessary; the one exists only for the other, and hence exists for itself only on the strength of a power outside itself; the one shares in the other only through that power's favour and grace.' Hegel 1998, p. 31.
56 Hegel 1998, p. 31.
57 Honneth 1995, p. 63.
58 As quoted through Honneth 1995, p. 38.
59 Honneth 1995, p. 38.
60 Honneth 1995, p. 107.
61 Honneth 1995, p. 173.
62 According to Freud's text on Narcissism and the text of the Project. The organism avoids displeasure, and in an analogous way the child learns how to avoid and dissolve threatening situations through screaming for help from the outside. Man's original helplessness, says Freud, constitutes 'the primal source of all *moral motives*'. Freud 1914, p. 318.
63 Kristeva takes the maternal love of the child as the new measure of politics, because it encompasses the recognition of another subject that cannot be reduced to an object of need or of eroticism: 'It is not impossible that in strengthening this bond, in becoming aware of its risks and its depth, women will transfer it from private intimacy or esthetics, to which tradition has confined it, and adapt their speech in the civic sphere to its measure. This would not be their least contribution to a politics that remains to be constructed, as a regime not of authority and domination but of harmonization of differences – which is precisely the goal of modern democracies.' Kristeva 2000b, p. 106.
64 Kristeva 1991, p. 182.
65 Kristeva 1987a, p. 274.
66 Huntington 1998, p. 98.
67 Huntington 1998, p. 99.
68 Guberman 1996, p. 38.
69 Guberman 1996, p. 17. Ewa Ziarek (2001), on the other hand, considers Kristeva's most important contribution be made in the domain of ethics, an ethics that can be lifted or transposed into the domain of the political.
70 See Kristeva 1989, pp. 13–15.
71 Kristeva 2000a, p. 68.
72 Kristeva 1987a, p. 25.
73 Kristeva 1987a p. 61. Sara Beardsworth has thoroughly examined the relation between Kristeva's conception of psychoanalysis and that of nihilism. Psychoanalysis, she argues, reveals the nihilism of modernity through semiotic articulations in the imaginary discourses of art and religion. Psychoanalysis, therefore, has a privileged position in Kristeva's work, according to Beardsworth, which cannot be equalled to that of the other discourses. Whereas art and religion are discourses restoring the possibility of meaning, psychoanalysis gives witness to their necessity in focusing on the suffering of a subject. Beardsworth 2004a, p. 116.
74 The theme of forgiveness was brought up already in *Black Sun* where it is presented as a precondition for sublimation through the transferential relation

of love: 'My unconscious is reinscribable beyond the gift that another presents me by not judging my actions.' Kristeva 1989, p. 205.

75 Forgiveness is counted as one of the thematics in which the crisis of modernity is being played out. The other thematics are time, the intimate and the image, which we will discuss in the following chapter, where the temporality of forgiveness will be brought up as well.

76 In the case of guilt, Kristeva refers also to Heidegger as a thinker who has shown *Dasein* through its very existence always to be indebted to something that it is not itself, being. Kristeva 2002a, p. 17.

77 The Western tradition of politics has excluded forgiveness and reduced it to religion, says Hannah Arendt, arguing that forgiveness is political in that it is never a consequence to an action that has been undertaken but constituting a radical break, productive as action in and out of itself. Arendt 1998, pp. 138–41.

78 Oliver 2003, p. 285.

79 Kristeva and Clément 2001, p. 24.

80 'Joying in the Truth of Self-division', Graybeal in Crownfield 1992, pp. 129–40.

81 Kristeva 1982, p. 89.

82 Kristeva 1982, p. 111.

83 Kristeva 2000a, pp. 12–13: the brothers killing the father in *Totem and Taboo* form social bonds through the renunciation of the feminine, and thereby also through the absorption of femininity in themselves. One may argue that art, in a similar manner, lives both against and with the foundational laws of society.

CHAPTER 4

1 Butler 1990, p. 93.

2 Butler 1990, p. 93. Butler compares Kristeva with Foucault in finding a theory of laws and prohibitions as productive not only of transgression but also of emancipatory movements.

3 Arendt 1998, p. 191. Action has a double face: on the one hand it helps produce relationships (incorporated through political institutions), while on the other it threatens to overstep the boundaries of those relationships.

4 Sallis 1996, p. 71. The *chora*, says Sallis, is that which makes an outside possible. It is a receptacle that functions as a paradigm. Coining the concept of the chorology, he attempts to find a term for Arendt's idea of a productivity both productive of boundaries and transgressing of those: this would constitute an alternative to the *arche* of the logos in which the notion of being is intertwined with the constitution of the order of the city. To consider the political as a productive means, rather than as connected with logos, would mean 'to think it as a displacement to the outside of being, just as, according to the chorology, sensible things come to the outside of being, even if sharing both name and looks with being', pp. 69–70.

5. Gatens 1996, p. 53. Other examples of a shared vocabularies are, as mentioned by Gatens, 'constitution', 'regime' and 'diet'. The first feminist thinker to evoke the gender problem inherent in the modern body politic was, famously, Carole Pateman, who has shown contract theory to have incorporated gender issues in the form of conjugal and thereby patriarchal rights. The original contract has been replaced in modern society by the systematic submission of women in other forms: a fraternal patriarchy, she calls it. Pateman 1988, p. 3.

6 Gatens 1996, p. 99.

7 Alison Weir has thoroughly investigated the topic of sacrificial identity in contemporary feminist theory; dedicating the last chapter to Kristeva in her

book *Sacrificial Logics* (1996), she rightly notes that the process of identification cannot be dissociated from experiences of pleasure. I would, however, disagree with Weir's interpretation that Kristeva argues for a pleasurable formation of self-identity in social interaction with others; pleasure, rather, must be considered in terms of a polymorphous experience of the body that remains an entity of radical alterity in relation to the self. Cf. Weir 1996, pp. 150–1.

8 Kristeva 2000b, p. 101.

9 Butler 1990, p. 89.

10 The interest in China marks the entrance of feminism in *Tel Quel* in 1974, even if the feminist legacy does not flourish until the special issue on feminism in 1977.

11 Kristeva 1986b, p. 86.

12 Kristeva 1986b, p. 151.

13 Kristeva 1986b, p.151.

14 Kristeva 1974c, pp. 26–9.

15 The critique of such naturalisation is in fact echoed in Butler's own work; in *Antigone's Claim* (2002), Butler argues for a politicisation of a family structure that has become normative through its naturalisation in psychoanalysis, among other practices.

16 Kristeva 1986b, p. 197.

17 Kristeva 1986b, p. 121.

18 Beauvoir has dedicated a chapter to the Marriage Law of 1950 in *La Longue Marche* (1957, p. 123–60). Beauvoir, like Kristeva, writes an apology and defence of the new China, aiming to show that its decision to do away with feudal structures has been beneficial to women above all, and that China has come further than Europe in promoting the cause of women.

19 Patrick Ffrench has argued that with psychoanalysis, Kristeva's politics becomes more of an ethics: the cure in Kristeva the psychoanalyst aims for the subject to become integrated by the law rather than subverted by it — literature becomes curative (cathartic) rather than subversive avant-garde. Ffrench 1995, p. 202. As we will see in this chapter, however, the concept of sublimation is not used in that sense, and although literature certainly is a compared to the psychoanalytic cure, it does not mean that its subversive value is lost.

20 Kristeva 2000a, p. 6.

21 In the 1940s a big debate took place in the psychoanalytic association in England around the question of the notion of fantasy. Ernest Jones welcomed the widening of the concept of fantasy to include unconscious fantasy — regarding it as important as Freud's widening of the concept of sexuality. King and Steiner 1991, p. 331. 'Hallucinatory wish-fulfilment' is a term that Freud used himself. Others called it 'inner reality', 'psychic representative on instincts' or 'instinctual derivatives'. King and Steiner 1991, p. 347.

22 Klein 1988a, p. 190.

23 Kristeva 2000c, p. 65. The use of the concepts of *savoir* and *connaissance* is Kristeva's own in this context, and has not been developed by Klein.

24 Freud 1895, pp. 317–21.

25 Kristeva 2000c, p. 104. Thus the internalised object is radically heterogeneous and is irreducible to the kind of dual relation characterising the imaginary as theorised by Lacan.

26 The formless is a word invented to designate that which thought cannot grasp and that escapes the desire of philosophy to define in shapes and 'coats': 'affirming that the universe resembles nothing and is only *formless* amounts to saying that the universe is something like a spider or spit' (Bataille 1985, p. 31). The concepts of the formless should be seen together with 'base materi-

alism', a materialism that is 'low' and studying waste material and dirt, as well as those parts of the body that may appear obscene and frightening: 'Base matter is external and foreign to ideal human aspirations and it refuses to allow itself to be reduced to the great ontological machines resulting from these aspirations' (Bataille 1985, p. 51).

27 Kristeva 1982, p. 2.

28 Kristeva 2000c, p. 125. Unlike the abject the superego can, however, also be an ally. This is based on the fact that the superego is an instance not only of destruction but also of reparation in Klein: it is, as Kristeva puts it, a source of love, albeit such a love will always remain ambivalent.

29 Kristeva 1982, p. 70–1.

30 Kristeva 1982, p. 10.

31 Kristeva 1982, p. 18.

32 Kristeva 1982, p. 41.

33 The cult of the abject can be seen in, for instance, the gut-wrenching images of Cindy Sherman staging non-descript intestines and filth in various colours on large-sized photos. Andreas Serrano's photos of corpses shot in the morgue are abjects at the border between human and inhuman. Kiki Smith is one of many women artists to work with corporeal waste products such as hair.

34 Here, Kristeva's analysis joins to a certain extent that of Sigfried Krakauer on German pre-war film, for example, or Klaus Theweleit's analysis of the songs of the SS Freikorps in *Male Fantasies*. Theweleit's book was originally published in Germany 1977–8. Its thesis is that the culture of Nazism, as opposed to other societies, does not repress what it cannot accept but kills it. Theweleit's analysis of its leading symbols reveals an ideology of purity that is nothing but a protection against all those substances of dirt that threaten to bury it. Theweleit's book is close to Kristeva's understanding of fascism as an abjectal symptom. What makes Kristeva's analysis original is that she underlines the fact that cultures are founded on a law that in turn will help produce abjection. She points to anti-Semitism as the privileged example of abjection, arguing that since Judaism appears as a strong incarnation of the law, abjection follows as a form of regressive repudiation of what that law has repressed: femininity, weakness, etc. Kristeva 1982, p. 180. Tina Chanter's work on abjection has helped clarify that the phenomenon of abjection is situated between the level of the subject and the level of community and culture. She calls for a reworking of the signification of abjection, enabling a move into the maternal region of signification that would not allow for a rejection of the other as the equivalent of abjection. 'Abjection, of Why Freud Introduces the Phallus: Identification, Castration Theory and the Logic of Fetishism', in Beardsworth and Mader 2004, pp. 48–66.

35 Céline defended the Vichy regime during the Second World War, living and working as an anti-Semite. After the war he was pursued as a traitor by the French government and fled to Denmark, where he lived until 1951. The French government condemned him on the grounds that he had been involved in hostile campaigns against France, particularly through a work called *Guignol's Band*. In Denmark, he was placed in custody, but not handed over to the French who sentenced him to death. In 1951 the French government changed the verdict, however, and he died in France in 1961.

36 Kristeva held her first seminar on Céline in 1976, where she made him a vehicle for her idea of a literature that is not only showing itself as revolt, but also working that revolt through the elaboration of style and syntax. cf. Forest 1995, p.p 550–3.

37 Kristeva 1982, p. 137.

38 Kristeva 1982, p. 207.
39 Guberman 1996, p.232.
40 Céline 1962 pp. 66–7. The self-hatred is produced precisely through the inca-
    pacity to identify with the nation: the narrator is called a rat since he does not
    want to go to war. a description which he happily and willingly complies with
41 Céline 1962, p. 173.
42 Interview quoted in Kristeva 1982, p. 178.
43 Céline 1962, p. 86.
44 One could mention August Strindberg, Tomas Bernhard, Elfriede Jelinek
    among Europeans with a strong anti-nationalist pathos.
45 Kristeva 1993b, p. 3.
46 Kristeva 1982, pp. 155–6.
47 Kristeva 1982, p. 185.
48 As argued in *Tales of Love*, unity of meaning can only be metaphorical.
    Metaphor, in turn, is always already constituted through several layers of signi-
    fication that make it a heterogeneous construction *per se*. Kristeva 1987a, p. 37.
49 Barthes is describing this polarisation as intellectuality against pleasure, reason
    against sensation, cold abstraction against cold life. This polarisation leads the
    left to emphasise method, reason, commitment, at the detriment of a pleasure
    that has become close to immoral. Barthes 1975, pp. 22–3.
50 Although such a laughter may be interpreted as a form of displacement of the
    abjective symptom. Kristeva 1982, p. 8.
51 In Zizek's reading, *The Idiots* performs a perverted fixation under the superego
    which does not so much liberate us from the constraints of bourgeois life as it
    shows the constraints of bourgeois life itself: the Idiots are in fact incapable of
    the kind of regression that they are attempting to perform, and therein lies the
    provocation of the film. Zizek 2002, pp. lxvi–lxvii.
52 Ziarek 2001, pp. 124–5. Kristeva shows that the ethics of psychoanalysis
    implies a politics: 'the changing emphasis in Kristeva's work raises a crucial
    question for an ethics of dissensus: namely, in what sense can an acknowledg-
    ment of the internal alterity and antagonism within the subject be a condition
    of responsibility in intersubjective relations'. Ziarek proposes that embodiment
    is a condition of ethical judgment. She therefore proposes a politics that is not
    agonistic in terms of its struggles in sexual and racial terms. That would take
    hold in an ethics of dissensus.
53 Ziarek 2001, p. 126.
54 Kristeva 1991, p. 136.
55 Kristeva 1991, pp. 145–6.
56 Kristeva 1991, p. 14.
57 The English translation of the passage to which we are referring has suppressed
    the French original's straightforward reference to idiocies and reads: 'The strange
    man, spasmodic and pantomimic, would be the inhabitant of a country without
    power, the sociological symptom of a political transition. If he claimed strangeness
    to the point of idiosyncrasy ('the older the institution the more the idioms; the
    worse the times become, the more the idioms multiply'), would it not also be
    because political institutions that are undergoing a crisis no longer assure the
    symbolic identity of the power and the persons?' Kristeva 1991, p. 140.

CHAPTER 5

1 Kristeva 2002a, p. 44. Kristeva compares such a *psukhe* to Arendt's life of the
   mind, in order to underline that interior activities such as fantasy, thought,
   affects, etc. are activities and not passive responses and perceptions.

2 Arendt 1998, p. 69. Arendt argues that intimacy is a modern concept, connoting a flight to interiority in an era when the inner world of the subject has lost its protection in the private realm. The social sphere has diluted both private and public, thus blurring a distinction which is crucial for Arendt's notion of the political.

3 Kristeva 2002a, p. 44. Cf. Kristeva 1989, p. 235, and the reading of Duras where the increasing distance between private and political is discussed as a 'malady of death'. The politics of the public sphere has withdrawn form the reality of life, whereas the private sphere has become hypertrophied as the only concern of modern man. At this point, Kristeva has no conception of a sphere of singularity that would cross both these domains and produce another form of sharing.

4 Kristeva 2002a, p. 11.

5 Kristeva 2002a, p. 33. Such a temporality is clearly described in *The Interpretation of Dreams*, where Freud shows the dream and the unconscious to be lacking any kind of temporal direction.

6 See Chapter 5 in my *The Antigone Complex*, Stanford: Stanford University Press (2005).

7 Kristeva 2002a, p. 154. In defining two leading metaphors in Heidegger's conception of being: repulsion and transcendence, Kristeva compares his work towards presenting being together with Nothingness in 'What is Metaphsyics?' with her own description of subjectivisation as abjection in *Powers of Horror*. Heidegger's language is throughout, she argues, loaded with negativity as libidinal impulses rather than as negation or nihilation proper. *Stimmung* is, she argues through Sartre, a form of shared commonality and co-existence through the incommunicable and the singular (2000a, p. 181).

8 Kristeva 2002a, p. 9. In *Black Sun*, melancholia is attributed as the anxiety or *Stimmung* productive of philosophical thought itself, as a form of anxiety in being itself. Kristeva 1989, p. 9.

9 The desire for One meaning and the delirium are two sides of the same, modern disease, to which the heterogeneity of psychoanalysis can respond. Kristeva 2002a, p. 21. In 'Psychoanalysis and the Polis' (Kristeva 1986a, p. 301–20), the political character of psychoanalytical interpretation is emphasised; involving both death-drive and sexuality, psychoanalysis shows that the desire for meaning is in itself motivated by heterogeneous drives and should never be reduced to unitary fixations.

10 Kristeva 2000a, p. 182. Kristeva's reading of Heidegger is mediated through Sartre. This is perhaps the reason why temporality in Heidegger is interpreted as a form of negativity, and made compatible with the unconscious. It is worth noting, however, that all reference to *Mit-Sein* as a historical destiny has been obliterated in Kristeva's discussion as has, indeed, all discussion of historicity.

11 Arendt 1998, p. 191.

12 Kristeva 2002a, p. 6.

13 Beardsworth's project has consisted of a reading of nihilism as seen from a psychoanalytic point of view: the nihilistic condition, she argues, is born out of a separation between the semiotic and the symbolic, instituting a loss of faith, of the law, of futurity, etc. Psychoanalysis does not only reveal the sufferings of the Western subject, or the loss of a paternal symbolic, it institutes a method of witnessing that is typical of the very symptomatology it is set to examine, the results of the separation between semiotic exspression and symbolic law: 'the more "narrowly" individual or subjective the object of analysis appears to be, the more it represents the wider cultural and societal conditions'. Beardsworth 2004, p. 57.

14 Jameson 2002, pp. 52–3. Jameson refers to Heidegger's reading of Descartes in order to move beyond traditional conceptions of the cogito.

15 Jameson 2002, p. 136.

16 Adorno 1999, pp. 193–4.

17 Adorno 1999, p. 204.

18 Adorno 1999, p. 366.

19 Kristeva 1989, p. 25.

20 Kristeva 1971a, pp. 20–1.

21 'Au lieu de chercher le négatif dans la dispersion du significant, ou dans une imbrication *non-close de strates narratives*, le discours producteur de concept incorpore le négatif au lieu *même* de la formation du concept; c'est dans la mesure ou il exhibe la négativité – l'hétérogénéité – le produisant à travers *le sujet*.' Kristeva 1971a, p. 22.

22 '[D]'une part, d'une analyse de la matérialité signifiante; d'autre part, d'une analyse de l'instance politique négligée par Freud, instance dont la stratégie pluriuelle, régie par la lutte des contraires, semble l'apparenter au manque à être du sujet dans son rapport au signifiant.' Kristeva 1970b, p. 215.

23 Laclau and Mouffe 2001, p. 115.

24 Ewa Ziarek's book on an ethics of dissensus has helped me make the observation of a link between the notion of dialectical negation in Kristeva and political antagonism in the work of Mouffe/Laclau. I would, however, like to argue against Ziarek that the emphasis in Kristeva's work does not lie in the creation of new, social imaginaries, since her writings remain uninterested in goal-oriented visions, including those of new collectivities. This is also what makes her notion of negativity original: it institutes a temporality of return and displacement unconcerned with the 'new' or with progress. It is also unconcerned with developments at the collective level. I would consider Laclau/Mouffes's notion of dislocation in a similar manner, as unconcerned with progress and as lacking visions of new collectivities. This is, however, also what makes it radical. Ziarek 2001, pp. 137–50.

25 This section was inspired by a collection by Swedish poet Katarina Frostenson: one summer day, in 1984, two black, plastic sacks were discovered at the edge of the city of Stockholm. They contained the remains of a woman, cut in pieces with the skill of a professional butcher. Everything was there, except her head. The case of Catrine da Costa, which was the name of the woman, took many years to be processed in the courts and kept building in the public imagination. A modern myth of incest, child abuse, satanic rites, prostitution, heroin addiction, necrophilia, decapitation, a missing head etc., everything surrounding the case was coloured by 1980s obsessions. More importantly, she became a symbolic figure in an important feminist debate. But it was surprising for most when Katarina Frostenson, a poet with a reputation for being elitist and unworldly, spun a collection, *Joner* from 1997, around her dead body. No one had expected Frostenson to engage in an actual debate. Frostenson is very much a poet's poet, working in a universe of intertextuality, fragmentation and rhythm, rather than with open reference and reflection. Her work is, put in terms of Kristeva's poetics, dominated by the semiotic. However, what is important in this context is that the weight of Frostenson's text cannot be detached from the emblematic importance of a beheaded woman that Frostenson was evoking, indicating the wide array of literary and philosophical questions that can be raised by the image of a severed female body. Intertwining an Orphic theme where the positions of Orpheus and Eurydice are reversed, Frostenson examines the question of representation through an actual

event and its treatment in the media, while invoking the complexities of the Orphic myth; its space and time are shown to be gendered.

26 Kristeva 1996, p. 3.
27 Kristeva 1996, p. 8.
28 Kristeva 1998c, pp. 37–9.
29 Kristeva 2002b, pp. 319–22.
30 Kristeva 1996, p. 10.
31 Kristeva 2000a, pp. 195–6.
32 Bronfen 1995.
33 Heidegger 1996, pp. 84–120.
34 As shown in the third chapter of my *The Antigone Complex; Ethics and the Invention of Feminine Desire*, Stanford: Stanford University Press, 2004.
35 Kristeva discusses the image and its relation to the so-called domain of the imaginary through Sartre: The imaginary is not just images without thinking; it is images with thinking. Freedom is in fact the capacity to imagine, which in this way gets close to psychoanalysis. There are two kinds of images: on the one hand it can function as a reification of the object, which is belying the transcendental capacity of consciousness that must always be related to nothingness. The painted object, however, has a nihilating function, and belongs to the imaginary domain of thought. It teaches us nothing about the object, but about our perception of it and our consciousness. Kristeva 2002a, pp. 169–73.
36 Kristeva 2000a, p. 178.
37 Kristeva 2000a, p. 127.
38 Kristeva 2000a, p. 180.
39 Kristeva 1996, p. 8.
40 Blanchot 1981, p. 99.
41 Freud 1913, p. 31. Any transgression of the taboo must be punished by other members of the community since it has a contaminating effect. Violence is thus inscribed in its foundation in various ways: in the transgression, in the punishment of transgression, but also in the contaminating effects of its very erection.
42 Kristeva 2002a, p. 233.

BIBLIOGRAPHY

Adorno, Theodor (1997) *Dialectic of Enlightenment*, trans. John Cumming, London: Verso.

—— (1999) *Negative Dialectics*, trans. E.B. Ashton, New York: Continuum.

—— (2002) *Aesthetic Theory* trans. Robert Hullot-Kentor, London: Continuum.

Arendt, Hannah (1973) *The Origins of Totalitarianism*, New York: Harvest.

—— (1998) *The Human Condition*, Chicago: University of Chicago Press.

Balibar, Etienne (1997) 'Ambiguous Universality', *Differences* 7(1).

Barthes, Roland (1975) *The Pleasure of the Text*, trans. Richard Miller, New York: Hill & Wang.

Bataille, Georges (1985) *Visions of Excess. Selected Writings, 1927–1939*, trans. Allan Stoekl, Minneapolis: University of Minnesota Press.

Beardsworth, Sara (2004a) *Julia Kristeva: Psychoanalysis and Modernity*, Albany: State University of New York Press.

—— (2004b) '*Kristeva's Idea of Sublimation*', in Beardsworth and Mader, pp. 122–37.

Beardsworth, Sara and Mader, Mary-Beth (2004) *Julia Kristeva's Ethical and Political Thought*, Spindel Conference 2003, Vol. XLVII, *Southern Journal of Philosophy*.

Benhabib, Seyla (1996a) *The Reluctant Modernism of Hannah Arendt*, Thousand Oaks: Sage Publications.

—— (1996b) *Democracy and Difference. Contesting the Boundaries of the Political*, Princeton: Princeton University Press.

Benhabib, Seyla and Cornell, Drucilla (eds) (1987) *Feminism and Critique: Essays on the Politics of Gender in Late Capitalist Society*, Cambridge: Polity Press.

Benhabib, Seyla, Butler, Judith, Cornell, Drucilla and Fraser, Nancy (1995) *Feminist Contentions: A Philosophical Exchange*, New York: Routledge.

Bernard-Donals, Michael (1994) *Bakhtin, Between Phenomenology and Marxism*, Oxford: Oxford University Press.

Bernstein, Jay (1992) *The Fate of Art. Aesthetic Alienation from Kant to Derrida and Adorno*, Cambridge: Polity Press.

Blanchot, Maurice (1981) *The Gaze of Orpheus*, trans. Lydia Davies, New York: Station Hill.

Braidotti, Rosi (1994) *Nomadic Subjects: Embodiment and Sexual Difference in Contemporary Feminist Theory*, New York: Columbia University Press.

Brandt, Joan (1997) *Geopoetics. The Politics of Mimesis in Poststructuralist French Poetry and Theory*, Stanford: Stanford University Press.

Brennan, Teresa (1993) *History after Lacan*, London: Routledge.

Bronfen, Elisabeth (1995) *Over Her Dead Body*, Manchester: Manchester University Press.

Butler, Judith (1990) *Gender Trouble*, London: Routledge.

—— (1993) *Bodies That Matter*, London: Routledge.

—— (2000) *The Psychic Life of Power*, Stanford: Stanford University Press.

—— (2002) *Antigone's Claim*, New York: Columbia University Press.

Butler, Judith and Scott, Joan (eds) (1992) *Feminists Theorize the Political*, London and New York: Routledge.

Céline, Ferdinand (1932) *Voyage au bout de la nuit*, ed. Henri Mondor, *Oeuvres I*, Paris: Gallimard.

Chanter, Tina (2004) 'Abjection, or Why Freud Introduces the Phallus: Identification, Castration Theory and the Logic of Fetischism', in Beardsworth and Mader, pp. 48–67.

Coole, Diana (2000) *The Politics of Negativity*, London: Routledge.

—— (1993) *Women in Political Theory*, London: Lynne Rienner.

Cooper, Sarah (2000) *Relating to Queer Theory. Rereading Sexual Self-Definition with Irigaray, Kristeva, Wittig and Cixious*, Oxford: Peter Lang.

Cornell, Drucilla, Rosenfeld, Michel and Carlson, David Gray (1992) *Deconstruction and the Possibility of Justice*, London: Routledge.

Crownfield, David R (1992) *Body/Text in Julia Kristeva*, Albany: State University of New York Press.

Dean, Jodi (ed.) (1997) *Feminism and the New Democracy: Revisiting the Political*, London: Sage.

—— (2000) *Cultural Studies and Political Theory*, New York: Columbia University Press.

de Beauvoir, Simone (1957) *La Longue Marche. essai sur la Chine*, Paris: Gallimard.

de Courtivron, Isabelle and Marks, Elaine (eds) (1980) *New French Feminisms*, Amherst: University of Massachusetts Press.

de Nooy, Juliana (1998) *Derrida, Kristeva, and the Dividing Line*, London: Garland Publishing.

Derrida, Jacques (1987) *Positions*, Paris: Éditions du Seuil.

Doane, Janice and Hodges, Devon (1992) *From Klein to Kristeva. Psychoanalytic Feminism and the Search for the 'Good Enough' Mother*, Ann Arbor: University of Michigan Press.

Eagleton, Terry (1983) *Literary Theory*, Minneapolis: University of Minnesota Press.

Elliott, Anthony (1992) *Social Theory and Psychoanalysis in Transition*, London: Blackwell.

Felman, Shoshana (1987) *Jacques Lacan and the Adventure of Insight*, New York: Johns Hopkins University Press.

Fletcher, J. and Benjamin, A. (1990) *Abjection, Melancholy and Love: The Work of Julia Kristeva*. New York: Routledge.

Ffrench, Patrick (1995) *The Time of Theory. A History of Tel Quel (1960–1983)*, Oxford: Clarendon Press.

Forest, Philippe (1995) *Histoire de Tel Quel 1960–1982*, Paris: Éditions du Seuil.

Foster, Hal (1996) *The Return of the Real*, Cambridge: MIT Press.

Foucault, Michael (1984) *The Use of Pleasure, The History of Sexuality 2*, London: Penguin.

Fraser, Nancy (1992) 'The Uses and Abuses of French Discourse Theories for Feminist Politics', in Fraser and Bartky, pp. 177–95.

—— (1997) *Justice Interruptus; Critical Reflections on the 'Postsocialist' Condition*, New York: Routledge.

Fraser, Nancy and Bartky, Sandra Lee (1992) *Revaluing French Feminism: Critical Essays on Difference, Agency and Culture*, Bloomington: Indiana University Press.

Freud, Sigmund (1895) 'Project for a Scientific Psychology', SE I, pp. 283–399, in *The Standard Edition*, London: The Hogarth Press, 1953.

—— (1900) *The Interpretation of Dreams*, SE IV–V.

—— (1905) *Three Essays on the Theory of Sexuality*, SE VII.

—— (1913) *Totem and Taboo*, SE XIII, pp. 1–165.

—— (1914) 'On Narcissism: An Introduction', SE XIV, pp. 73–105.

—— (1915a) 'Mourning and Melancholia', SE XIV, pp. 243–59.

—— (1915b) 'Repression', SE XIV, pp. 146–59.

—— (1915c) 'Instincts and their Vicissitudes', SE XIV, pp. 111-40

—— (1919) 'The Uncanny', SE XXII, pp. 368–407.

—— (1925a) 'Negation', SE XIX, pp. 235–9.

—— (1925b) 'Some Psychical Consequences of the Anatomical Difference between the Sexes', SE XIX, pp 248–61.

—— (1931) 'Female Sexuality', SE XXI.

—— (1939) *Moses and Monotheism*, SE XXIII.

Gatens, Moira (1996) *Imaginary Bodies*, London: Routledge.

Guberman, Ross Mitchell (1996) *Julia Kristeva Interviews*, New York: Columbia University Press.

Habermas, Jürgen (1987) *Knowledge and Human Interests*, trans. Jeremy J. Shapiro, Boston: Beacon Press.

Hegel, G.W.F. (1977) [1807] *Phenomenology of Spirit*, trans A.V. Miller, Oxford: Oxford University Press.

—— (1998) 'Love', in *The Hegel Reader*, ed. Stephen Houlgate, Oxford: Blackwells, pp. 31–3.

Heidegger, Martin (1996) *Hölderlin's Hymn 'The Ister'*, trans. W. McNeill and J. Davis, Bloomington: Indiana University Press.

Honig, Bonnie (2001) *Democracy and the Foreigner*, Princeton: Princeton University Press.

Honneth, Axel (1995) *The Struggle for Recognition*, Chicago: Chicago University Press.

Huntington, Patricia (1998) *Ecstatic Subjects, Utopia, and Recognition*, New York: State University of New York Press.

Husserl, E. (1995) *Cartesian Meditations*, trans. Dorion Cairns, London: Kluwer Academic Publishers.

Hutcheon, Linda (2002) *The Politics of Postmodernity*, London: Routledge.

Jameson, Fredric (1990) *Late Marxism. Adorno, or the Persistence of the Dialectic*, London: Verso.

—— (2002) *A Singular Modernity*, London: Verso.

Jones, Ann Rosalind (1984) 'Kristeva on Femininity: The Limits of a Semiotic Politics' in *Feminist Review* 18, November.

Kauppi, Niilo (1994) *The Making of an Avant-Garde: Tel Quel*, Berlin: Mouton du Gruyter.

Keltner, Stacy (2004) 'Sacrificial Promises in the Time of Obsession: Kristeva and the Sexual Contract', in Beardsworth and Mader, pp. 96–116.

Kemp, Sandra and Squires, Judith (1997) *Feminisms*, Oxford: Oxford University Press.

King, Pearl and Steiner, Riccardo (eds) (1991) *The Freud–Klein controversies 1941–45*, London: Tavistock/Routledge.

Klein, Melanie (1988a) *Love, Guilt and Reparation*, London: Virago.

—— (1988b) *Envy and Gratitude*, London: Virago.

Kristeva, Julia (1968a) 'La Sémiologie comme science critique', in *Théorie d'Ensemble*, with the Tel Quel Group, Paris: Seuil, pp. 80–93.

—— (1968b) 'Problèmes de la structuration du texte', in *Théorie d'Ensemble*, with the Tel Quel Group, Paris: Seuil, pp. 297–316.

—— (1969) *Sémeiotiké*, Paris: Èditions du Seuil.

—— (1970a) 'Literature, sémiotique, marxisme', discussion with Christine Glucksmann and Jean Peytard, in *La Nouvelle Critique* 38: 28–35.

—— (1970b) Discussion of an intervention by Catherine Backès-Clément on Lacan and Freud, *La Nouvelle Critique* 38: 214–18.

—— (1970c) 'Littérature et idéologies', in *La Nouvelle Critique*, Colloque de Cluny II, nr spécial 39 bis: 24–8, discussion on pp. 40–5, 79–85, 96–100.

—— (1970d) 'Idéologie du discours sur la littérature', in *La Nouvelle Critique* 39 bis: 122–7, Mitsou Ronat: 'Questions sur les idéologies qui président á, et naissent de, l'utilisation de théories linguistiques par la littérature', pp. 128–33, discussion on pp. 134–40.

—— (1970e) *Le Texte du roman*, Paris: Mouton.

—— (1971a) 'Matière, sens, dialectique', *Tel Quel* 44: 2–34.

—— (1971b) 'Comment parler à la litterature', *Tel Quel* 47: 27–49.

—— (1971c) 'POSITIONS DU MOUVEMENT DE JUIN 71' (with the Tel Quel group), *Tel Quel* 47: 135–41.

—— (1971d) 'L'Expansion de la sémiotique', in Julia Kristeva, Josette Rey-Debove and Donna Jean Umiker (eds) *Essais de Sémiotique*, Paris: Mouton, pp. 31–46.

—— (1972) Reviews of Cheng Chi-Hsien and Michelle Loi, *Tel Quel* 48–9: 59, 69–70.

—— (1973) 'Bataille: l'expérience et la pratique', in Philippe Sollers (ed.) *Bataille*, Actes des colloques d Cerisy-la salle, UGE. p. 267–301.

—— (1974a) 'Sujet dans le langue et pratique politique', from a colloqium in Milan on Psychanalyse et politique 1973, *Tel Quel* 58: 22–6.

—— (1974b) 'La femme, ce n'est jamais ça', *Tel Quel* 59: 19–30.

—— (1974c) 'Les Chinoises a "contre-courant"', *Tel Quel* 59: 26–9.

—— (1974d) 'Pratique signifante et mode de production', *Tel Quel* 60: 21–34.

—— (1975) 'D'une identité á l'autre', *Tel Quel* 62.

—— (1977a) 'Des Chinoises à Manhattan', *Tel Quel* 69: 11–16.

—— (1977b) 'Un nouveau type d'intellectuel: le dissident', *Tel Quel* 74, 'Recherches féminines', pp. 3–8.

—— (1977c) 'Hérétique de l'amour', *Tel Quel* 74, 'Recherches féminines', pp. 30–49.

—— (1980a) *Desire In Language*, Oxford: Blackwell.

—— (1980b) 'Oscillation between Power and Denial', in de Courtivron and Marks.

—— (1981) in A. Jardine, A. Kuhn, H.V. Wenzel and L.S. Robinson, *French Feminist Theory*, Chicago: University of Chicago Press.

—— (1982) *Powers of Horror*, trans. Leon S. Roudiez, New York: Columbia University Press.

Kristeva, Julia (1983a) *Histoires d'amour*, Paris: Éditions Denoël.

—— (1983b) 'L'Hyperbole de ma mémoire', in *L'Infini* 1: 39–55, 'My memory's hyperbole', trans. Athena Viscusi, in Domna C Stanton and Jeanine Parisier Plottel (eds) *The Female Autograph*, New York: Literary Forum, pp. 261–76.

—— (1984) *Revolution in Poetic Language*, trans. M. Waller, New York: Columbia University Press, *La Révolution du langage poétique*, Paris: Éditions du Seuil, 1974.

—— (1986a) *The Kristeva Reader*, ed. Toril Moi, London: Blackwell.

—— (1986b) *About Chinese Women*, trans. Anita Barrows, New York: Marion Boyars, *Des Chinoises*, Paris: Éditions des femmes, 1974.

—— (1987a) *Tales Of Love*, trans Leon S. Roudiez, New York: Columbia University Press.

—— (1987b) *In the Beginning Was Love*, New York: Columbia University Press, trans. A Goldhammer, *Au commencement était l'amour*, Paris: Hachette, 1985.

—— (1989) *Black Sun*, New York: Columbia University Press.

—— (1990) *Les Samouraïs*, Paris: Fayard.

—— (1991) *Strangers to Ourselves*, trans. Léon Roudiez, New York: Columbia University Press.

—— (1993a) *Les Nouvelles Maladies de l'âme*, Paris: Fayard.

—— (1993b) *Nations without Nationalism*, trans. Leon S. Roudiez, New York: Columbia University Press.

—— (1993c) 'The speaking subject is not innocent', in Barbara Johnson (ed.) *Freedom and Interpretation*, the Oxford Amnesty Lectures 1992, New York: Basic Books, pp. 147–74.

—— (1994) *Le Temps sensible*, Paris: Gallimard.

—— (1996) *Possessions*, trans. Barbara Brey, New York: Columbia University Press.

—— (1997) 'Psychoanalysis and the polis', in Kemp and Squires, pp. 228–31.

—— (1998a) *L'Avenir d'une révolte*, Paris: Calmann-Lévy.

—— (1998b) *Contre la depression nationale*, entretien avec Philippe Petit, Paris: Textuel.

—— (1998c) *Visions capitales*, Paris: Réunion des Musées Nationaux.

—— (1999) *Le Génie feminin I: Hannah Arendt*, Paris: Fayard.

—— (2000a) *The Sense and Non-sense of Revolt*, trans. Jeanine Herman, New York: Columbia University Press.

—— (2000b) *Crisis of the European Subject*, trans. Susan Fairfield, New York: The Other Press.

—— (2000c) *Le Génie féminin II,: Melanie Klein*, Paris: Fayard.

—— (2002a) *The Intimate Revolt*, trans. Jeanine Herman, New York: Columbia University Press.

—— (2002b) *Le Génie féminin III: Colette*, Paris: Fayard.

Kristeva, Julia and Clément, Catherine (2001) *The Feminine and the Sacred*, New York: Columbia University Press.

Lacan, Jacques (1966) *Écrits*, Paris: Éditions du Seuil.

—— (1988) *Freud's Papers on Technique 1953–1954*, seminar 1, trans. J. Forrester, London: Norton.

—— (2001) *Écrits: A Selection*, trans. Alan Sheridan, London: Routledge.

Laclau, Ernesto (1994) 'Why Do Empty Signifiers Matter to Politics', in J. Weeks (ed.) *The Lesser Evil and the Greater Good*, London: Rivers Oram Press.

—— (1996) *Emancipation(s)*, London: Verso.

Laclau, Ernesto and Mouffe, Chantal (1990) *New Reflections on the Revolution of Our Time*, London: Verso.

—— (2001 [1985]) *Hegemony and Socialist Strategy*, London: Verso.

Lechte, John (1990) *Julia Kristeva*, London: Routledge.

Leland, Dorothy (1992) 'Lacanian Psychoanalysis and French Feminism: Toward an Adequate Political Psychology', in Fraser and Bartky, Bloomington: Indiana University Press, pp. 113–36.

Liddell, Henry George and Scott, Robert (1996) *A Greek–English Lexicon*, Oxford: Oxford University Press.

Lyotard, Jean-Francois (1971) *Discours, figure*, Paris: Klincksieck.

—— (1988) *The Differend*, Minneapolis: University Of Minnesota Press.

McAfee, Noëlle (1993) 'Toward an Ethics of Respect', in Oliver 1993a, pp. 116–34.

—— (2000) *Habermas, Kristeva, and Citizenship*, Ithaca: Cornell University Press.

—— (2004) *Julia Kristeva*, London: Routledge.

Marx-Scouras, Danielle (1996) *The Cultural Politics of Tel Quel. Literature and the Left in the Wake of Engagement*, University Park: Pennsylvania State University Press.

Meyers, Diana T. (1992) *The Subversion of Women's Agency in Psychoanalytic Feminism: Chodorow, Flax, Kristeva*, in Fraser and Bartky, pp. 136–62.

Moi, Toril ((2002) *Sexual/Textual Politics*, second edn, London: Routledge.

Mouffe, Chantal (1992a) 'Hegemony and New Political Subjects', in Cary Nelson and Larry Grossberg (eds) *Marxism and the Interpretation of Culture*, Chicago: University of Chicago Press.

—— (1992b) Feminism, Citizenship and Radical Democratic Politics', in Butler and Scott, pp. 369–84.

—— (1993) *The Return of the Political*, London: Verso.

Nancy, Jean-Luc (1990) *The Inoperative Community*, trans. Peter Connor, Minneapolis, MN: University of Minnesota Press.

Oliver, K. (1990) 'Revolutionary Horror: Nietzsche and Kristeva on the Politics of Poetry', *Social Theory and Practice* 16(1): 305–20.

—— (ed.) (1993a) *Ethics, Politics and Difference in Julia Kristeva's Writing*, London: Routledge.

—— (1993b) *Reading Kristeva: Unravelling the Double Bind*, Bloomington: Indiana University Press.

—— (2003) 'Forgiveness and Subjectivity: Hegel, Derrida, Kristeva', *Philosophy Today* 47(3): 280–92.

Pateman, Carole (1988) *The Sexual Contract*, Cambridge: Polity Press.

Patton, Paul (2000) *Deleuze and the Political*, London: Routledge.

Plato, *Timaeus*, trans. R.G. Bury, London: William Heinemann, New York: Putnam's Sons.

Rancière, Jacques (1998) *Disagreement: Politics and Philosophy*, Minneapolis: University of Minnesota Press.

Riley, Denise (1983) *War in the Nursery*, London: Virago.

Ronat, Mitsou (1977) 'Questions sur les idéologies qui président à, et naissent de, l'utilisation de théories linguistiques par la littérature', *Littérature et ideologies, la nouvelle critique* 69: 128–33.

Rose, Jacqueline (1996 [1986]) 'Julia Kristeva – Take Two', in *Sexuality in the Field of Vision*, London: Verso, pp. 141–64.

Sallis, John (1996) 'A Politics of the Chora', in Reginald Lilly (ed.) *The Ancients and the Moderns*, Bloomington: Indiana University Press, pp. 59–71.

Silverman, Kaja (1988) *The Acoustic Mirror, the Female Voice in Psychoanalysis and Cinema*, Bloomington: Indiana University Press.

Smith, Anna (1996) *Readings of Exile and Estrangement*, London: Macmillan.

Smith, Anne-Marie (1998) *Julia Kristeva: Speaking the Unspeakable*, London: Pluto Press.

Sollers, Philippe (1968) 'Écriture et révolution', in the Tel Quel group, *Théorie ensemble*, Paris: Seuil.

Sjöholm, Cecilia (2002) 'Love. Recognition and the Political Subject: Kristeva and Honneth', in Birgit Christensen (ed.) *Knowledge, Power, Gender*, Zürich: Chronos.

—— (2003a) 'Terrorisme, teorisme, kjaerlighet – Kristevas intime revolt', *Agora* 1, Oslo: Aschehaug & Co.

—— (2003b) 'Kristeva and *The Idiots*', *Radical Philosophy* 122.

—— (2004) 'The Temporality of Intimacy; Kristeva's Return to the Political', in Beardsworth and Mader, pp. 73–88.

Squires, Judith (1999) *Gender and Political Theory*, Cambridge: Polity Press.

Stavrakakis, Yannis (1999) *Lacan and the Political*, London: Routledge.

Taylor, Charles (1992) *Multiculturalism and 'The Politics of Recognition'*, Princeton: Princeton University Press.

van der Poel, Ieme (1992) *Une révolution de la pensée. Maoïsme et feminisme à travers Tel Quel, les temps modernes et esprit*, Amsterdam: Rodopi.

Weir, Allison (1993) 'Identification with the Divided Mother: Kristeva's Ambivalence', *Ethics, Politics and Difference in Julia Kristeva's Writing*, London: Routledge, pp. 79–91.

—— (1996) *Sacrificial Logics, Feminist Theory and the Critique of Identity*, London: Routledge.

Young, Iris Marion (1990) *Justice and the Politics of Difference*, New Jersey: Princeton University Press.

Ziarek, Ewa (2001) *An Ethics of Dissensus. Postmodernity, Feminism, and the Politics of Radical Democracy*, Stanford: Stanford University Press.

—— (2004) '*Kristeva and Fanon: The Future of the Revolt or the Future of an Illusion?*' in Beardsworth and Mader, pp. 25–42.

Zizek, Slavoj (1992) *Tarrying with the Negative*, Durham: Duke University Press.

—— (1994) *The Metastases of Enjoyment*, London: Verso.

—— (2001) *On Belief*, London: Routledge.

—— (2002) *For They Know Not What They Do; Enjoyment As a Political Factor*, second edn, London: Verso.

INDEX

INDEX

INDEX

A library at your fingertips!

eBooks are electronic versions of printed books. You can store them on your PC/laptop or browse them online.

They have advantages for anyone needing rapid access to a wide variety of published, copyright information.

eBooks can help your research by enabling you to bookmark chapters, annotate text and use instant searches to find specific words or phrases. Several eBook files would fit on even a small laptop or PDA.

NEW: Save money by eSubscribing: cheap, online access to any eBook for as long as you need it.

Annual subscription packages

We now offer special low-cost bulk subscriptions to packages of eBooks in certain subject areas. These are available to libraries or to individuals.

For more information please contact webmaster.ebooks@tandf.co.uk

We're continually developing the eBook concept, so keep up to date by visiting the website.

www.eBookstore.tandf.co.uk